D0162078

FIFTY KEY THINKERS ON GLOBALIZATION

Fifty Key Thinkers on Globalization is an outstanding guide to often-encountered thinkers whose ideas have shaped, defined and influenced this new and rapidly growing field. The authors clearly and lucidly survey the life, work and impact of fifty of the most important theorists of globalization including:

- Manuel Castells
- Joseph Stiglitz
- David Held
- Jan Aart Scholte.

Each thinker's contribution to the field is evaluated and assessed, and each entry includes a helpful guide to further reading. Fully cross-referenced throughout, this remarkable reference guide is essential reading for students of politics and international relations, economics, sociology, history, anthropology and literary studies.

William D. Coleman is Professor of Political Science at the University of Waterloo and the Balsillie School of International Affairs in Canada. He has published widely in the areas of globalization studies and global public policy.

Alina Sajed is Assistant Professor of International Relations at the University of Hong Kong in Hong Kong, China.

ALSO AVAILABLE FROM ROUTLEDGE

Globalization: The Key Concepts
Annabelle Mooney and Betsy Evans
978-0-415-36860-5

Globalization: A Reader
Charles Lemert, Anthony Elliott, Daniel Chaffee and Eric Hsu
978-0-415-46478-9

FIFTY KEY THINKERS ON GLOBALIZATION

William D. Coleman
and Alina Sajed

Routledge
Taylor & Francis Group

LONDON AND NEW YORK

First published 2013
by Routledge
2 Park Square, Milton Park, Abingdon, Oxon OX14 4RN

Simultaneously published in the USA and Canada
by Routledge
711 Third Avenue, New York, NY 10017

Routledge is an imprint of the Taylor & Francis Group, an informa business

British Library Cataloguing in Publication Data
A catalogue record for this book is available from the British Library

Library of Congress Cataloging in Publication Data
Coleman, William D. (William Donald), 1950–
Fifty key thinkers on globalization / William Coleman, Alina Sajed.
p. cm. – (Routledge key guides)
1. Globalization. 2. Globalization–Social aspects. I. Sajed, Alina. II. Title.
JZ1318.C638 2013
303.48'20922–dc23
2012020753

ISBN: 978-0-415-55931-7 (hbk)
ISBN: 978-0-415-55932-4 (pbk)
ISBN: 978-0-203-08005-4 (ebk)

Typeset in Bembo
by Taylor & Francis Books

CONTENTS

ALPHABETICAL LIST
OF ENTRIES

ACKNOWLEDGEMENTS

The authors would like to acknowledge and thank Nancy Johnson for the highly professional, timely and insightful editorial assistance that she provided in preparing the final manuscript for this book. We also thank Professor Eric Helleiner for his comments on some entries in this book and for his enthusiastic support for the project. Alina Sajed wishes to thank Leslie Wee for his immense support over the past few years and for agreeing to follow her to the heart of globalization, which is Hong Kong.

INTRODUCTION

This book provides the reader with a 30-year span of debates over globalization and its history. As one of our key thinkers, Jan Aart Scholte, has observed, the word 'globalization' is a relatively late addition not only to the English language but to other languages as well. The term itself was only coined in the second half of the twentieth century. The word 'globe' as a denotation of a spherical representation of the Earth dates to the fifteenth century. The word 'global' entered the scene in the late seventeenth century but came to mean 'planetary-wide scale' only in the late nineteenth century. The words 'globalize' and 'globalism' emerged during the 1940s (see Scholte 2005: 50–51), while 'globalization' entered academic analysis of particular processes that potentially take place on a trans-planetary scale during the 1980s. The term 'globalization' was, at the same time, picked up by public intellectuals and then entered fully into public discourse in many parts of the world, particularly more wealthy countries, at the start of the 1990s. In reviewing the ensuing debates about globalization both in the academic and the broader public realms, we see gradual changes to meanings of the term but never consensus. And, of course, these various meanings themselves become a subject for study, particularly in humanities disciplines where the contours of public discourses are interpreted and assessed.

This book presents a study of thinkers in the academy, in society at large and in social movements who have commented at some length on what globalization(s) means as processes. In reading the works of the 50 thinkers in this book and of many others in preparation for selecting our entries, we concluded that the use of the word 'globalization' points to concerns, conclusions, questions and observations about significant changes in the contemporary world. What these changes involve remains a matter of debate to be sure. But there seems little doubt in the minds of globalization thinkers that profound challenges of unusual character and geographical extensity confront the world's varied peoples.

1

A changing world

The thinkers in this book point to significant events and changes that mark a profound shift in the world and engage with these by drawing upon the concept of globalization. Some thinkers see these changes as unique in human history, while others view them as an intensification of globalizing processes that have been occurring for centuries. Unique or new variations on old, the changes that have triggered their thinking about the connectedness of the world and their interest in the concept of globalization concern five interrelated domains: capitalism, technology, environmentalism, culture and identity, and governance.

Capitalism

Many globalization thinkers point to the collapse of the post-World War II economic order in the early 1970s as a key event triggering globalization. The US abandoned its role in that order, one which saw the US dollar currency serve as the regulator of the world's economy. In floating its currency on financial markets, the US responded to a growing crisis in its own economy. In doing so, its decision led to the floating of other currencies and gradually the end of capital controls by almost all the wealthier countries in the world. Some argue that this decision by the US led to a process of 'financialization' – that is, a period in which financial leverage overwhelmed capital or equity and financial markets came to dominate over the more traditional industrial and agricultural markets. Some globalization thinkers see these events as marking the beginning of the end of US hegemony over the world economy and a movement towards global financial markets.

Accompanying these changes in the world economy, many thinkers also point to the rise in importance of neoliberal theories and policies. The thinking behind these theories emphasizes the greater efficiency of markets when compared to the nation-state's provision of public goods, particularly related to the social welfare of its population. Complementing this thinking was an emphasis on individualism, a subtly masculinist view of the rugged individual fending for himself in the dynamic economic realm. As these ideas gained influence, they led to important policy changes by the US and the UK, in the first instance, and by many other governments later on. At the same time, these ideas were picked up by international financial institutions, themselves dominated by the US and its allies, particularly the International Monetary Fund (IMF) and the World Bank. The ideas were imposed upon poorer countries in the world that needed financial support to deal with their growing economic difficulties in the changing economic order.

These two changes, in turn, led to the rise of a less fettered capitalism in the wealthier countries belonging to the Organization for Economic Cooperation and Development (OECD). The IMF and the World Bank, in turn, promoted this form of capitalism in the so-called Third World where countries had been experimenting with socialism or border controls to expand their economies. As these countries were being impelled by these international institutions to open up their economies to an unbridled capitalism, the Iron Curtin suddenly collapsed. The world's largest economy, China, had already begun to embrace capitalism beginning in 1978. During the early 1990s, other formerly communist states in Eastern Europe and Russia ended their experiments with socialism and adopted capitalism as well. By the early 1990s, these rapid and comprehensive economic changes involving capitalism's reaching into virtually every part of the globe contributed to a sense of the world being one in ways never before experienced.

Technology

Almost simultaneously with the breakdown of the world economic order in the early 1970s, the world was on the verge of what many have called the information technology revolution. Synergetic development in three technological fields – micro-electronics, computing and telecommunications – culminated in the creation of the desktop computer. When networking technologies that were being developed independently in the 1960s were adapted for desktop computing, the key elements for the emergence of what is now called the internet were in place (Castells 1999: chapter 1). Quickly, restrictions on the use of the internet were lifted such that from the early 1980s, there have been continuous rounds of innovation that have permitted the linking together of persons, corporations and other technologies in more and more places.

A fourth component of the technological revolution – gene technology – also began to take shape during the 1970s. Rapid advances in microbiology and chemistry since the end of World War II had increased scientists' understanding of genes. With these advances, genetic engineering technology gained increased prominence: the capacity to act on genes, themselves nodes of information, led to important advances in medicine, controversial inventions in agriculture, and new understandings of what 'life' means, challenging longstanding religious beliefs.

There have been important synergies between the information technology revolution and capitalism: the global marketplaces that have emerged over the past 40 years depend heavily upon the transworld instaneity now possible with the new technologies and their being made widely available. Beyond these synergies, however, the kinds of linkages that became possible between individuals have ushered in profound social changes in varying degrees in more and more countries and societies in the world. These social changes, in turn, have tended to reinforce a sense of experiencing the world as one, which has come to be associated with global capitalism.

Environmentalism

Concern about the impact of human and technological development upon the environment also became a growing worldwide movement by the early 1970s. Those participating in what is often called environmentalism advocate the sustainable management of resources and stewardship of the plants, animals, oceans, lakes, atmospheres and other aspects of the 'natural' world. In 1972, the United Nations sponsored the Conference on the Human Environment in Stockholm, Sweden, which for the first time united the representatives of multiple governments in discussions relating to the state of the global environment. Since that time, the movement has spread to include followers in virtually every part of the world. It has led to increasing discussion of environmental protection not only by states, but also by non-governmental organizations, transnational corporations and social movements. Further world conferences occurred in 1987 and 1992, while nation-states have begun negotiating several agreements to cooperate in protecting the environment.

Crucial to understanding contemporary globalizing processes is again the sense of sharing a common destiny by sharing a common environment. These linkages foster globality, the idea of being together on the planet. However unique this globality might be, environmentalism, in fostering the concept of a unique natural world, reinforces changes in capitalism and technologies that link people together across the planet.

Culture and identity

While these economical, technological and environmental changes were taking place and as 'globalization' became part of public

4

discourses worldwide, questions arose about culture and identity. Were the changes experienced in the world going to level the cultural differences between societies? Would the new technologies coupled with capitalism create a form of materialism that will undermine cultural practices everywhere? Would the power of the wealthier countries, particularly that of the US after the fall of communism, lead to a single worldwide, consumer-based culture? Almost immediately, as these questions emerged, a counter-discourse developed about how economic and technological changes were, in fact, reinforcing differences between cultures.

These discourses pushed to a global scale debates over the role of women in human societies that had been gathering force since their emergence in the 1950s and 1960s out of the second wave of the women's movement. Simply raising the question about women's roles pointed to what Anna Lowenhaupt Tsing (2005) terms the 'frictions' that occur when supposedly universal ideas in one part of the world, in this case the roles of women in societies, are introduced into places in other parts of the world. What appears as 'universal' to some societies appears as 'localized' and 'from another place' to other societies. In the religious realms, some scholars noted a growth in fundamentalist interpretations and practices within Christianity, Hinduism, Islam, Judaism, Sikhism and other religions, which constitute assertions of difference in profound ways. What is important about these debates, conflicts and new identities surrounding the transformations of culture in a globalizing world is that they are again anchored in perceptions of the world as one.

Governance

By the beginning of the 1970s, the legal processes of decolonization had been largely completed. Accordingly, the United Nations hosted a much larger and more diverse set of states than it had at its founding in 1945, where the US and the UK were dominant players. By the 1960s there were already hints of challenges to transnational governance arrangements favouring wealthy countries from poorer countries. Notable among these was the United Nations Conference on Trade and Development (UNCTAD), held in 1964, which went on to be institutionalized in representing the poorer countries in discussions of the world economy. Its presence, in turn, led to a counter-reaction by the wealthy countries: the definition of a more formal role for what is now known as the OECD, the home of the dominant 'industrial powers'. The establishment of these opposing organizations presaged the growing efforts by the countries outside the OECD to have a role in governing global matters. By the early 1970s, the number of less wealthy countries endorsing the human rights covenants of the UN had also risen, with human rights becoming more globalized as a political and social ideal.

The early 1970s also saw the growing presence of indigenous peoples' organizations at the United Nations. With the UN being open to participation in its activities in limited ways by non-governmental organizations (NGOs), this period signals the establishment of conditions for 'global' governance. In this usage, the word 'global' means the trans-world dimensions of governance issues, on the one side, and the involvement of non-state actors such as NGOs, social movements and transnational corporations, on the other. Outside the UN, in 1974, the world's financial powers had set up a transnational organization to deal with some of the changes in risk arising from rapidly growing global financial markets. These endeavours foreshadowed new governing institutions that have become more globally extensive over time.

In summary, these discussions of the arrival of global capitalism, the rapid advances in communication and information technologies, the increasing acceptance of the concept of a world environment, the global scale of debates over cultural practices and accompanying new identities, and increasing involvement of poorer countries in governance have together fostered the growth of a planet-wide consciousness involving more places and more people than at any time in human history. In wrestling to understand these changes, many persons have focused on the concept of globalization as a conceptual way of comprehending them. How the concept is used, how it is understood, and how it structures discourses are remarkably variable. Most agree that over the past four decades there is not one globalization, but many globalizations. These processes sometimes complement, but just as often contradict, one another. What the thinkers in this book share is the belief that studying these processes carefully constitutes an important step towards a better understanding of the contemporary world.

Globalization thinkers

Our objective in writing this book is to increase understanding of globalization in all of its dimensions. One of the thinkers discussed in this book, John Tomlinson, points out that the complexity of globalizations includes:

[...] phenomena which social scientists have laboured to separate out into the categories into which we now, familiarly, break down human life: the economic, the political, the social, the interpersonal, the technological, the environmental, the cultural and so forth. Globalization arguably confounds such taxonomy.

(Tomlinson 1999: 13)

For us to realize our objective, therefore, we needed to consider thinkers who in their own right have tended to be interdisciplinary. They understand that if they do not see the multidimensional character of globalizations, they would be misrepresenting the phenomena. As Tomlinson (1999: 14) adds: 'lose the complexity and you have lost the phenomenon'.

Accordingly, our goal has not been to present a 'hall of fame' of globalization thinkers. Rather we have selected scholars, public intellectuals and activists whose works, when put into dialogue with each other in this book, will enrich readers' understanding of globalizations. Our work is limited and incomplete, however, because we have only chosen thinkers whose publications are available in the English language. Admittedly, many of our authors have published in other languages as well, with English being a second language. We want readers to come away from this book with a deeper understanding of the world in which we are living. We believe that the book will assist them to be more aware of the long history of globalizing processes and how the processes we experience today have roots in the past. We also aim to help readers understand better what is particularly distinctive and novel about contemporary dynamics of change. We hope that readers will have new thoughts about how they might be active in seeking social change, anchored on enriched thinking about globalizing processes.

Hundreds, if not thousands, of persons have written about globalization over the past three decades. It is inevitable that readers of this book will find some thinkers with whom they are familiar and others whom they do not know. They will wonder why still other thinkers are not included in the book. All authors of books in the Routledge Thinkers series face these reactions. They also need to address the intellectual challenge of not presenting an 'A to Z' of a given phenomenon. Rather, their task is to write an integrated book, involving a diverse set of thinkers, which when read together increases readers' knowledge about given phenomena. The choice of thinkers is targeted at ensuring that readers can realize this goal.

The majority of authors in this book have a base in academia. They have 'home disciplines', so to speak. In studying globalizations, however, they have reached beyond their disciplines; they are interdisciplinary in their approaches. Some of them are 'early' contributors to the discussion in that their writings were influential during the late 1980s and early to mid-1990s. Others engaged in research and entered the debate in reaction to the public controversies about globalization that emerged during the 1990s and to the so-called, but usually misnamed, anti-globalization movement. In fact, the more or less universal disappearance of the latter term points to new generations of globalization scholars. These scholars emphasize the multiplicity of globalizations and point to the possibilities of 'counter-hegemonic' globalizations.

In moving from one thinker to another, we have inserted references to other thinkers so that the reader can gain a full appreciation of the range of scholarship and public discussion in the field of study. At the end of each entry, we provide readers with a short bibliography should they want to explore a given author's writings on globalization in greater depth. All of the thinkers in this book have written books and articles about other topics; in fact, they may be better known for their expertise in those other areas. In this book, however, we point readers only to their writings on globalization. If we are successful in our goal of deepening understanding of globalizations, we hope that our work will foster further study of the increasing trans-planetary connections and their effects in the contemporary world.

Works cited

Castells, M. (1999) *The Rise of the Network Society*, 2nd edition, Oxford, UK: Blackwell.

Scholte, J. A. (2005) *Globalization: A Critical Introduction*, 2nd edition, London: Palgrave Macmillan.

Tomlinson, J. (1999) *Globalization and Culture*, Chicago, IL: University of Chicago Press.

Tsing, A. L. (2005) *Friction: An Ethnography of Global Connection*, Princeton, NJ: Princeton University Press.

FIFTY KEY THINKERS ON GLOBALIZATION

JANET ABU-LUGHOD (1928–)

Janet Abu-Lughod (née Lippman) completed her BA and MA degrees at the University of Chicago and her Ph.D. at the University of Massachusetts, US. Trained as a sociologist, she taught at Smith College, American University of Cairo, Northwestern University, and the New School for Social Research. She has published over 100 articles and 13 books dealing with urban sociology, the history and dynamics of the world system, and Middle Eastern cities, including an urban history of Cairo that is still considered one of the classic works on that city, *Cairo: 1001 Years of the City Victorious*.

Her contribution to the study of globalization is primarily through her work on the history of globalization and global cities. Most notable here is her highly influential book on the thirteenth century, *Before European Hegemony: The World System AD 1250–1350*. Scholars who have written about the history of globalization usually highlight processes that began in the sixteenth century and feature aggressive hegemony-seeking European actions over increasingly large parts of the world. Abu-Lughod argues that our understanding of this history is enriched if we take into consideration the nature of the world system in the thirteenth and fourteenth centuries, specifically between AD 1250 and 1350. This world system was as extensive as the early European one, but took a different form. Continuing her work on this theme, she also looks at 'global cities' and makes an argument that this phenomenon is not new in the contemporary period, but extends back in history through the era of developing European hegemony (see also **Amin**, **Arrighi**, **Braudel**, **Brenner**, **Taylor**).

Globalization

Abu-Lughod builds history into her conception of globalization by defining it as:

> [...] an ongoing process whereby larger and larger portions of the world become increasingly linked to one another – via material exchanges of resources, commodities, and currencies as well as through a widening of the geographic range over which populations move.

(Abu-Lughod 1999: 399)

She adds that this process involves more integration not only economically and politically, but also more contact on the symbolic and cultural levels. Accordingly, globalization can include:

> [...] an increased 'range' and 'depth' of awareness, as larger numbers of people in many regions of the globe know about one another and can be influenced, at least potentially, by ideas, values and practices that originate far beyond the localities in which they live.

(Abu-Lughod 1999: 399)

World systems vary over time, therefore, based on the range and depth of such interconnections.

She adds that the experience of globalization is not equally distributed across the world: 'effects are disproportionately caused by forces emanating from hegemonic powers (whether imperial, neo-colonial or class based) and hegemonic cultures' (Abu-Lughod 1999: 399). This variability is also seen in 'global cities' ('urban concentrations or nodes through which a disproportionate fraction of national and international interaction flows') (1999: 400). These are cities that contain the command centres for the global system. London and New York are command centres, for example, when it comes to global financial markets (see also **Sassen**). In rounding out her definition, Abu-Lughod cautions against assumptions often made that globalization brings increasing convergence in culture: 'what we are experiencing is rapid, incomplete and highly differentiated flows in global transmission. We have a globalizing but not necessarily homogeneous culture' (Abu-Lughod 1997: 135).

History of globalization

Abu-Lughod enriches our understanding of the history of globalization through her study of the 'world system' that had developed by AD 1250 and lasted about 100 years. She identifies three circuits of trade and communication that became systematically linked during this period: one from Western Europe built around Flanders, east-central France, and Genoa and Venice; a second in the Middle East, including Constantinople, Alexandria and Cairo, Baghdad and some coastal areas of East Africa; a third that contained China, South-East Asia and parts of India. Of these three circuits, the European one was the least developed. This world system was not entrenched in all parts of the world, but did contain a large portion of the world's population at that time.

The three geographic areas shared some similarities (Abu-Lughod 1989: 15–17). All contained important manifestations of capitalism, which permitted the development of a commercial network of production and exchange. States played an important role in minting, printing (China had gone to a paper money system by 1280) and guaranteeing currencies. They had mechanisms for pooling capital and distributing risk. In each area, wealthy merchants independent of the state played an important role. China had reached a high level of economic development and was the strongest area in the world system. The Chinese had invented paper and printing, iron and steel, and made important innovations in weaponry, shipbuilding and navigation techniques. They also had begun producing sophisticated artistic forms with silk and porcelain.

Within this world system, a large variety of cultural systems coexisted and cooperated, despite important differences. Christianity, Buddhism, Confucianism, Islam, Judaism and Zoroastrianism existed side by side, as did different economic systems ranging from 'near' private capitalism with some state support to 'near' state capitalism, assisted by private merchants (1989: 355). The latter differences were not congruent with geographic region or religious domain. For example, the state built boats for trade both in Venice and China, whereas elsewhere privately built vessels were commandeered when states felt the need (1989: 355).

Looking at later world systems, Abu-Lughod argues that these systems arise when connections increase and decline when connections diminish along older pathways. The connections in the thirteenth-century world system fell into disuse as a result of the bubonic plague. When they were resurrected in the sixteenth century by a world system in which Europe moved towards an increasingly hegemonic role (see **Braudel**), links across the Atlantic to the Americas were added, as well as to parts of Eastern Europe and Western Africa. Consistent with her definition of globalization, successive world systems became increasingly global as they came to include more and more of the world, while the depth of the economic and cultural relations rose as more people from various strata of societies were involved. Abu-Lughod predicts the rise of the US to hegemon as the last step in the development of the European-led world system (see also **Arrighi, Braudel, Cox, Helleiner**). She sees the world shifting away from European and American hegemony towards a return to a system balancing multiple centres, as occurred in the thirteenth-century system (1989: 371) (see also **Amin, Arrighi, Braudel**).

Global cities

Abu-Lughod's research on global cities adds more layers to our understanding of the history of globalization. She looks at the role of cities as nodes in world systems in supporting global expansion. She challenges arguments by scholars such as **Sassen** who suggest that 'global cities' have emerged only in the contemporary phase of globalization, and points to cities in earlier world systems that were already playing these roles in early phases of globalization. That said, Sassen stresses the importance of global services firms in creating global cities, an emphasis not found in Abu-Lughod's work.

Abu-Lughod defines 'global cities' as 'urban concentrations or nodes through which a disproportionate fraction of national and international interactions flow' (Abu-Lughod 1999: 2–3). What distinguishes global cities from other cities integrated within world systems is their degree of economic, political and cultural dominance. Global cities contain the control or 'command centres' of the global system and thus are linked strongly to one another. Their role is different from other large cities whose function is to help mediate between the global system and more regional and local economies. In the UK, for example, London plays a role consistent with that of a global city, while Birmingham and Manchester function more as centres of the British economy (for a different point of view, see **Taylor**).

Defined in this way, Abu-Lughod argues that in earlier world systems, there were cities that fulfilled the global city role (1999: 401). She supports this argument through a historical study of three US cities: New York, Chicago and Los Angeles. She demonstrates that New York became a key node in the global economy in the latter half of the nineteenth century, followed successively by Chicago and Los Angeles. She also shows that the nature of these roles changed over time as the global economy expanded and deepened across the world. For example, although New York began as a weak node compared to London, it expanded its influence as financial markets globalized. As world systems have changed and become more global, some cities lost this role (e.g. Amsterdam, Genoa, Venice and Constantinople), while others grew into the role (Hong Kong, Singapore, Beijing, Tokyo and Mumbai).

Major globalization writings

Abu-Lughod, J. (1989) *Before European Hegemony: The World System AD 1250–1350*, New York, NY: Oxford University Press.

——(1990) 'Restructuring the premodern world system', *Review*, vol 13, no 2, pp. 273–286.

——(1997) 'Going beyond global babble', in A. King (ed.) *Cultural Globalization and the World System*, Minneapolis, MN: University of Minnesota Press.

——(1999) *New York, Chicago, Los Angeles: America's Global Cities*, Minneapolis, MN: University of Minnesota Press.

See also: **Amin, Arrighi, Braudel, Cox, Helleiner, Sassen, Taylor**.

SAMIR AMIN (1931–)

Samir Amin is an Egypt-born political scientist who is best known for his neo-Marxist writings on development theory and for his advocacy for the conscious self-reliance of developing countries. He has dedicated a major part of his work to studying the relationships between developed and underdeveloped countries. For him, the differences between state institutions in Northern and Southern countries can be found in the very basis of capitalism and globalization.

He gained a Ph.D. degree in political economy in Paris (1957) as well as degrees from the Institut de Statistiques and the Institut d'Études Politiques. He has held the position of full professor in France since 1966 and was the director of the United Nations African Institute for Economic Development and Planning (in Dakar) between 1970 and 1980. Since 1980 he has directed the African Office of the Third World Forum, an international non-governmental organization for research and debate. He is currently the president of the World Forum for Alternatives, an international network of research centres and militant intellectuals from the South and the North. He has written more than 30 books, mainly in French and Arabic.

Capitalism, imperialism and production

Amin argues that capitalism is invariably globalizing through its increasing expansion in various regions of the world and through its increasing commodification of various human activities. This global expansion of capitalism takes place through imperialism. The contemporary period, especially after 1980, has deepened globalization in unprecedented ways. Amin rejects the view held by some Marxist scholars that imperialism is a stage of capitalism. He also does not accept the position of mainstream economics scholars who speak about systems with 'market laws' that generate 'optimal equilibria' when left to themselves. In his view, capitalism is 'by its very nature a regime whose successive states of disequilibrium are produced by social and political conflicts beyond the market' (Amin 2003: 2). Therefore, references to 'deregulated markets' are misleading because these markets are steered by powers based on monopolies held by dominant groups outside the market. He stresses that imperialism is a permanent feature of the global expansion of capitalism. The combination of capitalism and imperialism invariably produces a polarization of wealth and power between a dominant core set of countries and those on the periphery.

In successive phases of the history of imperialism and globalization, the core countries enjoy certain 'monopolies' that secure their dominance. He identifies three phases of imperialist support of capitalism: a mercantilist one from 1500 to 1800; a 'classical' imperialist era from 1800 to the start of World War II; and the present era, which begins in 1945, but intensifies after 1980. Globalization intensified in the second phase with the European imperial powers securing the opening up of China and the Ottoman Empire, repressing the Sepoy mutiny in India, and carving up the African continent (2003: 7). As globalization has continued into the present day, the gaps between centres or dominant countries and peripheries have constantly widened.

In the third and current phase of capitalist imperialism, this widening gap results from the dominant powers' possession of five 'monopolies' (Amin 1997: 4–5; 2003: 63–64):

1 technological monopoly (only large and wealthy states can afford the huge expenditures needed);
2 financial control of worldwide financial markets;
3 monopolistic access to the world's natural resources;
4 media and communication monopolies;
5 monopoly over weapons of mass destruction.

In the second phase of imperialist capitalism, the space of (industrial) production coincided with the national space of political and social management. The nation-state thus shaped the structure of the international system (Amin 1997: 32). In the contemporary period, the relationship between the national and the global is reversed: 'whereas national power used to determine the global presence, it is now the reverse that happens. Transnational corporations, whatever their nationality, therefore have a common interest in the management of the world market' (Amin 2003: 71). The transnational corporations of today have common interests in running the global capitalist system, despite the competitive relationships between them (Amin 2006: 17). These interests are addressed and supported by states through enforcing the five monopolies noted above.

Contemporary imperialism and globalization

Between 1945 and 1980, the competitive conditions changed gradually to a point where corporations needed to succeed in markets of 500 to 600 million consumers (Amin 2003: 71). Accordingly, corporate battles took place in markets operating increasingly on a wider global scale, leading capitalists to push for deeper globalization. While these changes were becoming more necessary over the 1945 to 1980 period, Amin argues that this period was a unique one in that imperialism had less influence than in the periods before World War II and after 1980 (see also **Arrighi**, **Cox**). Due to the strengthening of the welfare state in the Western countries and the social protections provided by the communist state of the Soviet bloc societies, or by the national state in the 'Third World of Bandung', large-scale regional and social transfers took place, and high levels of growth and modernization of productive forces followed. The results included:

[...] the highest economic growth rates of modern times; huge social advances, in the core countries of the system and 'actually existing socialism', as well as in the great majority of countries in the liberated periphery; a flowering of new, proud and modern national identities.

(Amin 2006: 116)

Amin also comments positively on the role of the newly founded United Nations in preserving the peace during these years.

Gradually, over the same period, however, a new system of rule for the world capitalist system emerged around the five monopolies noted above. Unlike the situation of competing imperialist powers and empires that characterized the nineteenth and early twentieth centuries, there emerged a *collective* imperialism to oversee the deepening of globalization (see also **Hardt and Negri**). Amin terms this system the 'Triad': 'the United States plus its Canadian external province, Europe west of the Polish frontier, and Japan – to which we should add Australia and New Zealand' (Amin 2006: 9). The Triad developed a system of global governance to fit the needs of the transnational corporations and the world economy built around two pillars: economic and military. And holding up these pillars was the US as the world hegemon (see also **Cox**). In moving to this new system, the Triad has gradually pushed aside the United Nations in favour of the Group of 7 (G7: France, Germany, Italy, Japan, the UK, the US and Canada) and later the Group of 8 (G8: with the addition of Russia).

On the economic side, the World Trade Organization (WTO) was created largely by the Triad in order to increase the comparative advantages of transnational capitalists. Industrial and intellectual property rights were to perpetuate the monopolies of transnational corporations. The WTO was set up to 'create uniform rules for the management of both internal markets and the world market, to eliminate any distinction between them, in the name of an extreme vision of free trade that has no precedent in history' (Amin 2003: 96). Amin sees the role of the WTO to be analogous to the 'colonial ministries' of the nineteenth century: 'to prevent colonies from becoming competitors, by denying them the right to legislate and regulate in connection with the activities of metropolitan capital in their own countries' (2003: 96). The World Bank and the International Monetary Fund (IMF) play supporting roles in this system of global economic management.

On the military side, the Triad has pushed the North Atlantic Treaty Organization (NATO) to overturn international law and the

UN, particularly the General Assembly, to function as the disciplining institution on behalf of the 'international community'. Central to this discipline is the hegemon, the US, and its military. Since the end of World War II, the US has put in place a global military strategy, divided the world into regions and set up military commands to take responsibility for each. The goal, according to Amin, is to make the US the worldwide master of last resort, with NATO being its cover as it pursued its sovereign national interests (Amin 2006: 10).

Amin comments on the frequent use of war by the US since the collapse of the Soviet bloc as a means of exerting its hegemony. Convenient enemies are chosen, the odious behaviour of their leaders is exploited (while ignoring such behaviour elsewhere in the same region), and then war is declared on the given state, usually with NATO's help. When the war is finished, the US usually leaves behind one or more military bases to help establish 'stability'. The members of the Triad work with or defend the US in these 'adventures' because they share common interests in overseeing the world market and in securing the success of transnational corporations.

Alternative globalization

Amin also discusses potential alternatives to the neoliberal globalization dominated by the Triad, which manages the imperial capitalist system. He argues that any new, more democratic arrangements will still function on a global scale. He invokes the term 'polycentrism' to refer to the change (see also **Arrighi, Bello, Scholte**). By this term, he means that there will no longer be imperial powers exploiting peripheral societies. Instead, the world order would be decentred, with different regional arrangements in play, perhaps building on institutions such as the European Union, Mercosur, the Association of South-East Asian Nations (ASEAN) and so on. And with the emergence of a polycentric world, we would see the end of military imperialism, of global financial markets dominated by a small number of states and corporations, and of the military disciplining role of the US and NATO. The five monopolies would be replaced by arrangements that democratize each of these areas of dominance. Negotiations between the various regions of the world would be necessary to achieve the reduction of inequalities between people.

Throughout his writings on alternative globalization, Amin calls for a revitalization and a renaissance of the United Nations: 'The UN should be fully restored to its major responsibility of ensuring the security of peoples (and states), safeguarding the peace, prohibiting aggression on any pretext whatever (such as those mendaciously invoked on the occasion of the Iraq war)' (Amin 2006: 131). He would prefer to see the General Assembly given greater importance and to have a reformed Security Council being responsive and accountable to the Assembly.

He underlines the importance of international law and would like to see the establishment of a system of universal courts to uphold that law. International business law would become a responsibility of the UN, while the WTO, IMF and World Bank would be dismantled. He would like to see a reinvigoration of the United Nations Commission on Trade and Development (UNCTAD) (see also **Bello**) and of the International Labour Organization (ILO). Further discussion will be necessary on the sustainable and democratic management of the world's natural resources, including water, 'a common good of humanity'. Finally, he calls for fuller institutionalization of international justice. In summary, he writes: 'The alternative to worldwide apartheid is a pluri-centric globalization that can ensure different economic and political relations among regions and countries, less unequal and therefore less unfavourable to those which have suffered the most destructive effects of globalization' (2006: 155).

Major globalization writings (in English)

Amin, S. (1997) *Capitalism in the Age of Globalization: The Management of Contemporary Society*, London: Zed Books.

——(2003) *Obsolescent Capitalism: Contemporary Politics and Global Disorder*, trans. P. Camiller, London: Zed Books.

——(2006) *Beyond US Hegemony? Assessing the Prospects for a Multipolar World*, trans. P. Camiller, London: Zed Books.

Further reading

Johnson, C. (2004) *The Sorrows of Empire*, New York, NY: Henry Holt and Co.

See also: **Arrighi, Bello, Cox, Hardt and Negri, Helleiner, Scholte.**

ARJUN APPADURAI (1949–)

Arjun Appadurai was born and educated in Bombay (now Mumbai) before moving to the US. He completed his Ph.D. in 1976 at the University of Chicago, US. He has held academic positions at the University of Chicago, Yale, The New School and New York University. He is currently the Goddard Professor of Media, Culture and

Communication at the New York University's Steinhardt School of Culture, Education and Human Development.

Appadurai is one of the founding editors of *Public Culture*, a well-established interdisciplinary academic journal, known for its ground-breaking ethnographies and analyses of the cultural politics of globalization. Aside from his prolific scholarly career, Appadurai has been involved in the activities of various non-profit organizations, which aim to advance knowledge of the impact of global cultural processes upon urban spaces (such as Mumbai), and to help 'globaliz[e] the study of globalization' (www.appadurai.com/projects.htm).

In his research, Appadurai has engaged with a wide spectrum of issues and themes related to globalization, making him one of the most recognized and sophisticated contemporary thinkers on globalization. In his early work, *The Social Life of Things*, he reflected on the social and political ramifications of mass consumption and on how 'commoditization as a worldwide historical process' (Appadurai 1986: 17) is largely responsible for the production of a 'global middle class' (Appadurai 2009: 45). His interest in the 'circulation of commodities' allowed him to move on to a larger area of research, which focuses on 'circulation as a major fact of social life in globalization' (2009: 45). In *Modernity at Large*, arguably his best-known and most celebrated work on globalization, Appadurai engages the consequences of the interaction between media and migration, and its contribution to altering the social role of imagination in an age of global flows (Appadurai 1996: 3). His preoccupation with the impact of globalization upon academic research crystallized in a series of articles and projects, which reflect on the politics of research and on the dissemination of knowledge in an age of globalization. This research also involves an awareness of the need for a more sophisticated conceptualization of global flows to capture the complexity and layering of the various global processes (Appadurai 2000a, 2000b, 2002, 2003, 2006b, 2009). Most recently, Appadurai's research has focused on the link between current practices of sovereignty and ethnic violence under the pressure of global flows (Appadurai 2006a).

The globalization of imagination as a social practice

In *Modernity at Large*, Appadurai brings together his earlier reflections on the cultural politics of globalization to investigate the confluence of mass media and migration flows, and their impact upon the work of imagination. He conceives of these two elements not merely as new social practices with global reach, but also as political ones insofar as they contribute to the reconfiguration of the nation-state (Appadurai 1996: 10). The consumption of mass media is not seen simply as a passive social practice through which a compliant recipient accepts and internalizes the information conveyed to her. Rather, Appadurai presents it as a complex and complicated form of exercising agency and subjectivity by projecting one's desires and aspirations within a global context. Creating the linkage between mass media and migration flows permits Appadurai to reflect upon how contemporary 'diasporic public spheres' become possible in an age of globalization.

Crucial to his conceptualization of diasporic public spheres is the notion of 'deterritorialization' understood by Appadurai as movements of people, ideas and images 'that transcend specific territorial boundaries and identities' (1996: 49; see also **Scholte, Hannerz**). Such movements create disjunctures between nation and territory, between mobile social and political identities and the political logic of territoriality. Appadurai suggests that the role of imagination is central to the production of a 'postnational political world' (1996: 22). He is deeply influenced here by Benedict Anderson's work on the role of imagination and print media in the development of nationalism. Following Anderson's logic, he proposes that imagination can also contribute to the transcendence of the national frame and to the emergence of a post-national political logic.

In order to capture the 'flow' characteristics of cultural practices, Appadurai introduces the notion of *scape* as a suffix, such as ethnoscapes, mediascapes, technoscapes, financescapes and ideoscapes (1996: 33). *Scape* denotes fluidity, irregularity, but also the *imagined* character of contemporary flows and therefore the role of imagination as a social practice that constitutes contemporary subjectivities. Thus, by bringing diasporic communities – whether of migrants, exiles or refugees – into the discussion of globalization, Appadurai is able to illustrate how, for example, *ethnoscape* is a more apposite term for the current shifting ground of ethnicity. This term captures better the intersection between mobility and motion, the reconfiguration of ethnic and political identities that ensues (*ideoscapes*), and the role of electronic media (*mediascapes*; see also **Castells, Chow, Hannerz, Tomlinson**). Such intersections allow displaced individuals and groups to imagine themselves as part of larger de-territorialized communities.

It is noteworthy that Appadurai does not see the global as necessarily distinct and separate from the local (see also **Hannerz, Robertson, Sassen, Tomlinson**). To put it differently, imagination is constitutive not only of 'diasporic public spheres' – that is, of displaced and de-territorialized communities. Imagination also reconfigures the social and political space of the locale, since even societies as 'localized' as India have become 'inflected – even afflicted – by cosmopolitan scripts' that drive the desires and actions of its various social and political classes (1996: 63). What he calls 'the production of locality' is caught in 'the growing disjuncture between territory, subjectivity, and collective social movement' (1996: 189). Appadurai implies that the constitution of locality and of the neighbourhood has always been at odds with the project of the nation-state (1996: 191), since the former's particularity belies the latter's desire for homogeneous national space. The current conjuncture between electronic media and mobility has placed the uneasy relationship between locale and nation-state under further strain.

Grassroots globalization and transnational forms of activism

Appadurai continues his investigation of the role of imagination in globalization in a series of articles published in *Public Culture*, which discuss the emergence of what he calls a 'grassroots globalization'. Disenfranchised groups and the activist networks that support their struggles initiate this type of globalization 'from below' (see also **Escobar**, **Mignolo**, **Santos**). In one of these articles, he observes that the conceptualization of global processes (or what he calls 'the knowledge of globalization') trails behind contemporary global flows (Appadurai 2000a: 4). This temporal lag impacts negatively upon our 'research imagination' by limiting our intellectual perspectives to parochial and self-contained 'First World' horizons. Thus, a link must be made between the emancipatory potential of imagination in our contemporary world, which has informed people's desire to migrate, to mobilize and to congregate politically across national borders, and our impoverished research imagination, which does not yet have the adequate vocabulary to capture these rising transnational 'social forms' (2000a: 6). Researchers are yet to produce work that advances our knowledge of the links between the globalization driven from above and that from below (see also **Falk**). Such research would contribute to the creation of 'new forms of pedagogy' whose potential effect would be the empowerment by knowledge and perspective of various counter-globalization networks (see also **Santos**) (2000a: 10–11).

Following through with his preoccupation for new forms of pedagogy and research, Appadurai turns to a long-term exploration of grassroots movements that adeptly combine local activism with transnational networking (Appadurai 2002: 23). He situates his research within the larger debates surrounding the connection between global flows and the production of 'world-cities'. In such circumstances, global flows reconfigure urban geographies in ways that de-territorialize them from the political geography of the nation-state (see **Abu-Lughod**, **Sassen**, **Spivak**, **Taylor**). But Appadurai's focus lies on what he calls 'governmentality from below', which emerges from the struggles of the poor living in the slums of Mumbai who employ, for their own benefit, data-gathering techniques – usually the monopoly of public officials – such as surveys and censuses (2002: 35–36). Such data collection has emancipatory effects, opening the door to a new politics that Appadurai calls 'deep democracy'. He illustrates that such mobilizations, aside from having a solid local base, also link themselves to other similar projects across borders. Such linkages point to the transnational contours of a grassroots globalization that aims to counter the logics of the globalization from above and to empower those who are its victims and who suffer the consequences of its excesses (see **Escobar, Falk, Santos**).

Research and the globalization of knowledge

As discussed in the previous section, Appadurai expresses concern for the social exclusion of marginalized groups, which follows from an epistemological exclusion (see also **Mignolo, Santos**). The latter emerges from the lack of analyses on current globalization processes, which might empower those marginalized and offer alternatives to help them counter some of its negative consequences (2000a). To put it differently, those involved in transnational struggles against inequality and marginalization need to have a larger perspective both of the processes that disempower them and of the various strategies that might be able to alleviate their marginality. In one of his articles, Appadurai engages in an analysis of research as a *right* (Appadurai 2006b). What he understands by the latter 'is the capacity to systematically increase the horizons of one's current knowledge, in relation to some task, goal or aspiration' (2006b: 176). This definition of research as *right* allows for a broader perception of research as a skill to be acquired that is necessary in making informed decisions about one's future. Appadurai suggests that the skill of research contributes today to the empowerment of the top 20 per cent of the world's population, or 'the global elite' as he calls it (2006b: 168). At the same time, the bottom 50 per cent of the globe's population is deprived of the necessary knowledge skills that would allow them to exercise informed agency about their future and thus gain 'strategic knowledge' about the world in which they live (2006b: 168). He thus advocates for the 'democratisation of the right to research' and of knowledge. Such a democratization would enable various marginalized groups around the world to gain access to *full* citizenship rights.

New practices of sovereignty

Like other prominent scholars, Appadurai claims that globalization processes pose a new challenge to the relationship between nation and state, and have brought about a crisis for the sovereignty of the nation-state (Appadurai 1996; 2000a: 4; 2003; 2006a) (see **Harvey, Rosenau, Ruggie, Sassen**). This crisis of sovereignty implies, as mentioned earlier, a disjuncture between nation and state in an age where nation has become partly diasporic. New practices of nationalism and nation-building are being carried by flows of refugees, migrants, exiles, tourists, guest workers and other mobile subjects, thus challenging in profound ways the assumed conjunction between territorial sovereignty and nation (Appadurai 1996: 160–161). Unlike **Ong**, Appadurai perceives the onset of a post-national era, one which prompts us to rethink political categories and identities. The emergence of 'postnational social formations' (1996: 167) is evident in the struggles of both transnational groups (such as Kurds, Tamils and Sikhs) and diasporic communities whose loyalties and political mobilizations are either non-national or post-national (such as North Africans in France, Haitians in Miami and Moluccans in Holland) (Appadurai 1996: 165; 2003; see also **Hannerz**). As Appadurai aptly remarks, 'territory as the ground of loyalty and national affect [...] is increasingly divorced from territory as the site of sovereignty and state control of civil society' (Appadurai 2003: 340). This de-territorialization of national communities also entails practices of re-territorialization through which non-national spaces insert themselves within the cartography of nation-states, such as refugee camps, slums for 'illegal' migrants, detention centres for asylum seekers, free trade zones, and others. Also unlike **Ong**, he does not see such spaces as instances of the flexibility and adaptability of the nation-state under globalization, but as inroads by various 'postnational social formations' into the space of the nation-state.

Ethnic violence in an age of globalization

The disjuncture between nation and state under the pressure of global flows, coupled with what Appadurai perceives to be the inherent dangerous nature of the nation-state, has contributed to the rise of ethnic violence in the last two decades. Since the very idea of the nation-state entails a desired perfect congruence between the ethnic homogeneity of the nation and the integrity of national territory, the reality of 'incompleteness' in an era of global flows gives rise to various violent pathologies. As Appadurai notes, globalization exacerbates 'the anxiety of incompleteness' of the nation-state and triggers a global rage against national minorities (Appadurai 2006a: 8, 82). By investigating the dynamics of the ethnic violence that plagued India (against Muslim communities), Eastern Europe and Rwanda, he exposes 'the link between minorities *within* the modern nation-state and the marginalization *of* the nation-state by the forces of globalization' (2006a: 33). The global flows of migrants, media and ideas unsettle the assumed 'naturalness' of the majority group's identity and claims (2006a: 83). Thus, globalization intensifies the anxieties and insecurities of 'predatory identities' – those identities that draw their legitimacy from the vilification and destruction of a 'minor' identity perceived to be noxious and dangerous to the body of the nation (2006a: 51–52).

Appadurai introduces a novel conceptual framework for understanding the dynamics of political violence in an age of globalization by distinguishing between what he calls 'cellular' and 'vertebrate' forms of political organization. The former is characterized by horizontal transnational linkages and decentralization, and is perfectly attuned to the flexible logics of global capitalism. 'Terrorist networks' are thus perceived to be just such emerging forms of cellular organization, which challenge the centralized and vertical structures of the nation-state: the prime exemplar of a vertebrate organization. Therefore, in an age of terrorism, the radicalization of a minority of contemporary Muslims needs to be situated within a framework of 'global minority politics' (2006a: 111). Its cellular structure and mode of operation gestures towards the imagined contours of a transnational Muslim community (*ummah*), and contests the legitimacy of vertebrate political structures by indicating the growing disjuncture between nation and territory.

Major globalization writings

Appadurai, A. (1986) (ed.) *The Social Life of Things: Commodities in Cultural Perspective*, Cambridge, UK: Cambridge University Press.

——(1996) *Modernity at Large: Cultural Dimensions of Globalization*, Minneapolis, MN: University of Minnesota Press.

——(2000a) 'Grassroots globalization and the research imagination', *Public Culture*, vol 12, no 1, pp. 1–19.

——(2000b) 'Spectral housing and urban cleansing: notes on millennial Mumbai', *Public Culture*, vol 12, no 3, pp. 627–651.

——(2002) 'Deep democracy: urban governmentality and the horizon of politics', *Public Culture*, vol 14, no 1, pp. 21–47.

——(2003) 'Sovereignty without territoriality: notes for a postnational geography', in S.M. Low and D. Lawrence-Zúñiga (eds) *The Anthropology of Space and Place: Locating Culture*, Malden, MA: Blackwell.

——(2006a) *Fear of Small Numbers: An Essay on the Geography of Anger*, Durham, NC: Duke University Press.

——(2006b) 'The right to research', *Globalisation, Societies and Education*, vol 4, no 2, pp. 167–177.

——(2009) 'Arjun Appadurai: the shifting ground from which we speak', in J. Kenway and J. Fahey (eds) *Globalizing the Research Imagination*, London and New York, NY: Routledge.

Further reading

Appadurai, A. (ed.) (2001) *Globalization*, Durham, NC: Duke University Press.

See also: **Abu-Lughod, Castells, Chow, Escobar, Falk, Hannerz, Harvey, Mignolo, Ong, Robertson, Rosenau, Ruggie, Santos, Sassen, Scholte, Spivak, Taylor.**

GIOVANNI ARRIGHI (1937–2009)

Giovani Arrighi was born in Milan in 1937 and received his D.Phil. in economics from the Universitá Bocconi in 1960. Arrighi began his career teaching at the University College of Rhodesia (now Zimbabwe) and later at the University College of Dar es Salaam in Tanzania. During this period he developed arguments about how the labour supply and labour resistance affected the development of colonialism and national liberation movements. It was there that he met Immanuel Wallerstein, later a collaborator on a number of research projects. In 1979 Arrighi joined Wallerstein as a professor of sociology at the Fernand Braudel Center for the Study of Economies, Historical Systems and Civilizations at SUNY Binghamton. It was during this time that the Fernand Braudel Center became known as the main locus for world-systems analysis, attracting scholars from all over the world. He moved to Johns Hopkins University in 1998 to anchor the Sociology Department's comparative historical group. He served as director of the Institute for Global Studies in Culture, Power and History from 1999 to 2002, and as department chair from 2003 to 2006.

His most famous work is a trilogy on the origins and transformations of global capitalism, the first volume of which, *The Long Twentieth Century: Money, Power, and the Origins of Our Times* (1994), reinterpreted the evolution of capitalism. The book quickly became a classic in the field and was published in at least ten languages. Arrighi completed a second edition of it which was published posthumously in 2010. He published the second volume, *Chaos and Governance in the Modern World System*, with his colleague and partner Beverly Silver in 1999, and the third, *Adam Smith in Beijing: Lineages of the Twenty-first Century*, in 2007. He died peacefully at home of cancer on 18 June 2009.

Arrighi argued that the phenomena that have been labelled 'globalization' in the contemporary period are best understood as a stage of the centuries-long development of capitalism, including its increasing geographical scope and the political organization of territory that accompanies this expansion (see also **Bello, Braudel, Brenner, Cox, Harvey**). Arrighi suggests that the current world order under US hegemony shifted into a 'financial expansion' in the early 1970s, foreshadowing a crisis likely to end the period of US hegemony and to result in a new organization of territory and capitalism. What other scholars have termed 'globalization' are for Arrighi the changes in the organization of territory and capitalism taking place during this crisis period.

Changes in world orders and globalization

In order to understand Arrighi's thinking about globalization, we need to explore briefly his theory about the dynamics of capitalism.

The 'modern inter-state system' has featured 'the constant opposition of the capitalist and territorialist logics of power and the recurrent resolution of their contradictions through the reorganization of world political-economic space by the leading capitalist state of the epoch' (Arrighi 1994: 36). In a given stage of development, capitalism is thus identified with a particular hegemonic dominant state which also restructures the territorial organization of space. At the same time, particular forms of non-territorial business organizations seek to encompass more and more of the world in processes of investment (accumulation) while further pushing the development of capitalism. Eventually, the contradictions between territorial organization and capitalist accumulation become so powerful that accumulation shifts from focusing on goods and services to financial assets, a process termed a *financial expansion*. Arrighi argues that such financial expansions have recurred since the fourteenth century under various hegemons (Venice and Genoa, the Netherlands, Great Britain, the US), ultimately leading to terminal crises where a given order collapses and is fundamentally reorganized under a different hegemonic power.

Influenced by Gramsci (see also **Amin, Cox**), Arrighi defines hegemonic leadership as the capacity of a dominant state to present itself, and be perceived, as the bearer of a general interest (Arrighi and Silver 1999: 26). When transferred to the leadership of the *international system*, hegemony means that a dominant state, by virtue of its achievements, becomes the leader other states seek to emulate, thereby drawing them to follow along on its own path of capitalist development (1999: 27). The dominant power thus leads the *system of states* in a desired direction and is perceived as acting in the general interest of all states. 'Leadership in this sense inflates the power of the dominant state' and is thus 'the defining characteristic of the world hegemonies' (1999: 27).

Under a given hegemon, capitalist expansion increases the volume and dynamic density of the world system, eventually leading to competition among the given units (states) that are beyond the regulatory capacity of the institutions set up by the hegemon. In these circumstances, a hegemonic crisis arises marked by the intensification of interstate and inter-enterprise competition, growing numbers of social conflicts and the emergence of new configurations of power. Such crises are heralded by the diversion of investment into financial instruments which provide short-lived stability before the onset of 'systemic chaos': the disintegration of the institutions and organizational arrangements put in place by the dominant power. Arrighi invokes **Rosenau**'s concept of *turbulence* in describing this situation.

The development of the world system does not follow a single path over the centuries as some Marxist scholars, such as Wallerstein, argue. Rather, it is seen to have followed several distinctive paths laid down by specific complexes of governmental and business organizations:

> Under Dutch leadership, the emergent system of European states was formally instituted by the Treaties of Westphalia. Under British leadership, the Eurocentric system of sovereign states moved to dominion globally. And under US leadership, the system lost its Eurocentricity to further gain in reach and penetration.
>
> (Arrighi and Silver 1999: 22)

Arrighi and colleagues summarize this historical view of globalization as follows:

> [the] globalization of the world system has thus occurred through a series of breaks in established patterns of governance, accumulation, and social cohesion, in the course of which an established hegemonic order decayed, while a new order emerged interstitially and, over time, became hegemonic.
>
> (Arrighi and Silver 1999: 271)

The UK, the US and contemporary globalization

In order to better understand Arrighi's interpretation of contemporary globalization, it is useful to review briefly his summary of the transition from British to American hegemony and then the dominant features of US rule. Arrighi borrows the term 'free trade imperialism' to describe the world system of rule under the hegemony of the UK (Arrighi 1994: 52–53) during the nineteenth and twentieth centuries. The British world system differentiated itself from the old Westphalia rule under Dutch domination by adding new states to the Westphalia system. In this expanded inter-state system, only the UK was simultaneously involved in the politics of all regions of the world and it was uniquely powerful in holding a commanding position in most of them (1994: 53). It tightened the coordination, furthermore, with follower states through the Concert of Europe. As European imperial rule disintegrated in the colonial empires of the Americas, it expanded rapidly in other parts of the world. By 1914, the European states held 85 per cent of the world's surface, with the UK holding by far the largest share (1994: 53). The economics employed in governing these imperial holdings reflected the practice and ideology of free trade. As the UK recycled 'imperial tribute' from its far-flung empire, London became ever more dominant as a world financial centre.

Arrighi stresses the uniqueness of British hegemonic rule, which involved a new world order that was as much a 'world empire' as a 'world economy':

> The most important and novel feature of the world empire *sui generis* was the extensive use by its ruling groups of a quasi-monopolistic control over universally accepted means of payments ('world money') to ensure compliance to their commands, not just within their widely scattered domains, but by the sovereigns and subjects of other political domains as well.
>
> (Arrighi 1994: 58)

Drawing on this economic power, the UK was able to rule effectively over a much larger political-economic space, a globally extensive one, than any previous world hegemon had done.

The crisis leading to the demise of British hegemony began in the early twentieth century and culminated in World War II. Already during this period, the US was gradually moving more and more into a hegemonic role as it oversaw the creation of a new world order. The differences between the British and the new American order are many. Arrighi and Silver (1999) emphasize three main ones. First, the American economy was far larger in size relative to the world economy than was the British one and in that respect more self-sufficient. Through its empire, Britain was far more directly integrated within the world system than the US, which initially at least operated through 'soft power'. Second, the territorial configuration of the US differed from the UK. The US had so large an area and population, such abundant and balanced resources, and such strategic placement in having direct access to the world's two major oceans that it could have a much more direct influence on the world than Britain could through a dispersed and increasingly costly empire. The different approach of the US to governance was embodied in the creation of the United Nations, originally under Roosevelt's vision of bringing the New Deal to the world at large (Arrighi 2007: 152). Third, Britain had never been a leader in the industrialization of war, whereas the US had already become a leader in this regard during the latter part of the British era and soared to world military domination, relying on its technological innovation capacities by the end of World War II.

As a hegemon, the US put much less stress on free trade and more emphasis on free enterprise. It sought more regulation of world money through the Federal Reserve Board and the establishment of the International Monetary Fund. Through these tools, the US wielded effective control over world liquidity through the 1950s and 1960s (Arrighi 1994: 72). These features also created room for a significant and ever growing proportion of world trade to be 'internalized' within, and managed by, large vertically integrated transnational corporations (1994: 72). Arrighi stresses the differences between these corporations and the small number of joint stock companies during the British epoch, such as the British East India Company, as well as Britain's reliance on small- and medium-sized enterprises engaged in trade. Not only is the number of transnational corporations much larger than that of states, but they are also independent of states, not tools of states. In fact, Arrighi stresses that their growth and number have had the unintended result of disempowering Western states, rather than business organizations empowering states as in the British era (Arrighi 1999: 127–128). Arrighi concludes: 'the scale, scope, and effectiveness of US governance of the world, as well as the concentration of military, financial, and intellectual means deployed for the purpose, far exceeded the ends and means of nineteenth century British hegemony' (Arrighi 1994: 75).

Contemporary globalization and crisis

We have shown thus far that Arrighi understands globalization to have intensified over the course of several centuries, through fundamental shifts in the organization of territory and of capitalist accumulation and the contradictions engendered by these shifts. The beginning of a shift from one world order to another is 'signalled' by a 'financial expansion', with one of these beginning in the early 1970s, thereby pointing to the beginning of the end of US hegemony (Arrighi and Silver 1999: 273). For Arrighi, therefore, many of the phenomena collected under the concept of globalization by scholars such as those in this book are indications of this systemic change.

In analysing 'globalization' through these lenses, Arrighi points to several phenomena that are both distinctive about the crisis and indicative of a possible new world order to come. First, there has developed a bifurcation of military and economic capabilities. The present crisis has seen the further concentration of global military forces in the hands of the US, while global financial resources have shifted to new centres endowed with a decisive competitive edge for investment and growth (Arrighi 1999: 277–278). In particular, partially as a result of US military adventurism in Iraq and Afghanistan, there has been increasing movement towards the re-centring of the global economy in

East Asia, and within East Asia, in China (Arrighi 2007: 178). Arrighi often cites Adam Smith to support his argument that the global economy was dominated to a significant extent by China before the Industrial Revolution. Second, during the same period, the proliferation of transnational business organizations and communities has further accelerated, undermining US hegemony still more. This factor will 'continue to shape ongoing systemic change through a general, though by no means universal, disempowerment of states' (Arrighi 1999: 278).

In looking ahead, Arrighi speculates that this 'globalization' (i.e. hegemonic crisis) phase is unlikely to lead to a single state becoming a hegemon. Rather there might be a world of multiple centres of power existing in a somewhat balanced way (1999: 131) (see also **Amin, Bello, Santos**). Avoiding disastrous conflict will depend upon two conditions. First, the main centres of Western civilization prove able to adjust to less exalted status. Second, the main centres of a re-emerging China-centred civilization can 'collectively rise up to the task of providing system-level solutions to the system-level problems left behind by Western hegemony' (Arrighi and Silver 1999: 286).

Major globalization writings

Arrighi, G. (1994) *The Long Twentieth Century: Money, Power, and the Origins of Our Times*, London and New York, NY: Verso.
——(1999) 'Globalization and historical macrosociology', in J. Abu-Lughod (ed.) *Sociology for the Twenty-first Century: Continuities and Cutting Edges*, Chicago, IL: University of Chicago Press.
——(2005) 'Globalization in world-systems perspective', in R. P. Appelbaum and W. I. Robinson (eds) *Critical Globalization Studies*, London: Routledge.
——(2007) *Adam Smith in Beijing: Lineages of the Twenty-first Century*, London and New York, NY: Verso.
Arrighi, G. and Silver, B. J. (1999) *Chaos and Governance in the Modern World System*, Minneapolis, MN: University of Minnesota Press.

Further reading

Wallerstein, I. (1984). *The Politics of the World Economy: The States, the Movements, and the Civilizations*, Cambridge, UK: Cambridge University Press.

See also: **Amin, Bello, Braudel, Brenner, Cox, Harvey, Rosenau, Santos**.

ZYGMUNT BAUMAN (1925–)

Zygmunt Bauman is an East European critical theorist and sociologist. He grew up in Poznan, Poland, and moved as a youth to Russia with his family to escape the Nazi invasion. He fought in the Polish army during World War II and rose to the level of major, only to be discharged in the anti-Semitic wave of 1953. Bauman chose to work in the social sciences in the European tradition, where sociology is aligned with continental philosophy. In 1968, he was dismissed from the University of Warsaw and was persecuted in a subsequent anti-Semitic wave. Together with his family, Bauman left Poland for a position at Leeds University in the UK, where he developed a strong reputation as a sociologist and philosopher. In his recent work, he has devoted considerable attention to globalization as part of his larger focus on changes in modernity.

Globalization and the emergence of new forms of stratification

Bauman's references to globalization almost always underline the negativity of the processes involved. In discussing globalization, he pays particular attention to the new forms of stratification that it introduces. In this respect, globalization is a sub-theme for him, a set of observations about what in his earlier work he termed postmodernity and, in later writings, 'liquid modernity'.

Bauman argues that the compression of time and space is characteristic of globalization but the experience of the effects of this compression is highly uneven. This unevenness divides an elite population from the rest of the world's peoples, creating very different living conditions among the two groups. Whereas the elite group enjoys all the mobilities that come with globalization, the socially deprived group lives in increasingly degrading conditions. Whereas the elite group has access to the 'global' – that is, all parts of the world – the majority group becomes increasingly fixed in their 'locality' (see also **Castells**). Accompanying these divisions is the progressive spatial segregation, separation and exclusion of the elite from other populations in localities.

Of all the technical components of mobility, the most crucial is that of the transmission of information. Information travels more and more independently of its bodily carriers and also of its objects. In the end, with the advance of the internet, the very notion of information travelling disappears as it becomes instantaneously available across the world. This development undermines longstanding understandings of what 'community' means to the point that intra-community communication no longer has any advantage over inter-communal communication. For Bauman, this development has moral implications. For elites who are able to 'run away' from localities, it means that they can also run away from the consequences of their actions. The exercise of power becomes dislocated from its obligations. Environmental disasters in Bhopal, Alaska and the Gulf of Mexico all illustrate how difficult it becomes to talk about accountability or moral responsibility for the members of the global elite responsible for such disasters.

In short, Bauman argues that globalization permits the holders of power to become extra-territorial; they can no longer be held to account for their actions in specific places. And as power becomes de-territorialized, particular localities become ever more structured and zoned to isolate the power holders from the powerless. Within localities, the spaces occupied by the global elite are off limits for all others; their living spaces become what Bauman refers to as 'interdictory spaces', inaccessible to anyone not 'issued with an entry permit' (Bauman 1998: 20). If the new special 'exterritoriality' for elites ensures their freedom, the confining 'interterritoriality' for the rest of the population appears ever more like a prison. And in the process, public spaces in localities shrink in favour of private consumer spaces exemplified by shopping malls.

Bauman captures these differences by contrasting the ideal types of 'tourists' and 'vagabonds'. The 'tourists' are the members of the global elite. He begins to articulate the differences between the two types by commenting on a city such as Washington, DC. Those who live in the north-west can leave the city at any time, all the while living separately and securely from the 'vagabonds' in the other three-quarters of the city, who do not have the ability to leave. Whereas the tourists can travel to wherever their hearts desire, vagabonds only move when they are thrown out of a site or put in jail. Tourists have the privilege to move without papers; vagabonds are not allowed to stay without papers. The world of the vagabonds, the 'locally tied', is one where they are barred from moving, where they must bear passively whatever change or crisis or calamity is visited upon the locality in which they live (see also **Hardt and Negri**).

The tourists live in time; space does not matter for them because spanning any distance can be instantaneous for them. Vagabonds live in space, which ties down time and keeps it beyond their control. They are surrounded by the walls of immigration controls, residence laws, and demands for identification cards and 'papers'. Where the tourists travel in business–class luxury, the vagabonds are hidden in the holds of ships, in the backs of trucks or in trails in the wilderness. If spotted, they are arrested, jailed and deported. In Bauman's words:

> Mobility and its absence designate the new, late-modern or postmodern polarization of social conditions. The top of the new hierarchy is exterritorial; its lower ranges are marked by varying degrees of space constraints, while the bottom ones are, for all practical purposes, *glebae adscripti*.[1]
>
> (Bauman 1998: 105).

Consistent with this analysis of social and economic polarization, Bauman comments on the end of the nation-state as it has existed under modernity. Capital is sufficiently mobile that it is permanently a step ahead of any nation-state that might try to contain or redirect it. Contemporary capitalism is so globalized that it is beyond the realm of traditionally understood deliberate, purposeful and potentially rational policy-making (see also **Harvey**). The order created by the modern nation-states is being replaced by a 'new world disorder'. No one seems to be in control. Bauman writes:

> The deepest meaning conveyed by the idea of globalization is that of the indeterminate, unruly and self propelled character of world affairs; the absence of a centre, of a controlling desk, of a board of directors, of a managerial office.
>
> (Bauman 1998: 59)

He adds that all three tripods of the sovereignty of states have been broken: military, economic and cultural. The state is being overtaken by a process of world re-stratification in the course of which a new social-cultural hierarchy on a trans-planetary scale is being created (see also **Beck, Hardt and Negri**).

Liquid modernity

For Bauman, globalization clearly brings changes to modernity. Gradually, he has moved away from the term 'postmodernity' and settled upon the notion of liquidity or fluidity to characterize these changes. He speaks of 'liquid modernity' or the 'society of fluid modernity'. He chooses the notion of liquidity because he sees the changes arising from globalization unlocking the bonds which have restricted individual choices available in collective actions. Whether workers belonging to trade unions, business persons to local chambers of commerce, believers to churches, synagogues and temples, even citizens to nation-states, these bonds weaken under globalization. State-built and serviced social welfare policies which were designed based on notions of social solidarity are being progressively dismantled. Notions of belonging to organizations and to communities are being replaced, in Bauman's view, by self-directed individuals. In describing these changes as 'individualization', Bauman is stressing the melting away of collective action, the solidity of membership and the support of community in favour of the autonomous individual (see also **Harvey**). He writes: 'it is now left to individuals to seek, find and practise individual solutions to socially produced troubles' (Bauman 2007: 14). In these circumstances, the identity of individuals is no longer a given; it becomes a project, a task, something that persons must 'work upon' and create for themselves (see also **Castells**). With individualization comes the gradual corrosion and slow disintegration of citizenship itself.

This notion of liquidity grows out of Bauman's analysis of mobility and of its consequences for social segregation between elites and the 'vagabonds'. In his later writing, he extends the analysis of 'liquid modernity' by writing about 'liquid love', 'liquid fear', 'liquid times' and 'liquid life'. Liquidity thus becomes a crucial characteristic of modernity as a consequence of globalization.

Note

1 *Glebae adscripti* (persons attached to the soil) was a term applied to a class of Roman slaves attached in perpetuity to, and transferred with, the land they cultivated. Colliers and salt workers in Scotland were in a similar position until 1775.

Major globalization writings

Bauman, Z. (1997) *Postmodernity and its Discontents*, New York, NY: New York University Press.

——(1998) *Globalization: The Human Consequences*, New York, NY: Columbia University Press.

——(2000) *Liquid Modernity*, Cambridge, UK: Polity Press.

——(2003) *Liquid Love: On the Frailty of Human Bonds*, Cambridge, UK: Polity Press.

——(2005) *Liquid Life*, Cambridge, UK: Polity Press.

——(2006) *Liquid Fear*, Cambridge, UK: Polity Press.

——(2007) *Liquid Times: Living in an Age of Uncertainty*, Cambridge, UK: Polity Press.

See also: **Beck, Castells, Hardt and Negri, Harvey**.

ULRICH BECK (1944–)

Ulrich Beck was born in 1944 in the town of Stolp in the region of Pomerania that is now part of Poland. He began his university studies in 1966 at Freiberg University and then switched to Ludwig Maximilians University (LMU) in Munich to study sociology, philosophy, psychology and political science. He finished his doctoral studies in 1972 in sociology and his *Habilitation* in 1979 at the same university. That year, he was called to a chair in sociology at the University of Münster. He began editing the journal *Soziale Welt* in 1980. Since 1992, he has held a chair as professor of sociology at LMU in Munich. In 1997, he took up an appointment in sociology at the London School of Economics and Political Science. In 1999, he succeeded in obtaining funding from the German Science Foundation to lead a special research area on reflexive modernization. He has received many awards, including honorary doctorates from universities in Italy and Spain.

Beck introduced the concept of globalization into his work earlier than many scholars, using it as a descriptor to help him analyse the nature of a fundamental break in modernity. It surfaced in his now classic work *Risk Society*, originally published in German in 1986. The meaning of the term did not change as his work expanded in the subsequent two decades, but its consequences were elaborated upon significantly as Beck's thinking developed. In all instances, the processes of globalization are properties associated with a central concept in his work: that of risk.

Risk society and globalization

In *Risk Society* (1992), Beck defines risk as a 'systematic way of dealing with hazards and insecurities induced and introduced by modernization itself' (1992: 21). This definition links to his understanding of the fundamental changes taking place in modernity. The risks of concern are themselves the products of modernity; they are signs of modernity turning on itself and threatening its very existence. He characterizes this new phase, therefore, as 'reflexive modernization'. The fundamental changes at issue here are responsible, in his view, for a 'break' in modernity and, thus, the onset of a 'new modernity' (see also **Dirlik**). As his work proceeds, he uses various terms to describe this break, most commonly 'second modernity'. What is new is that risks arising out of the development of industrial societies no longer affect localities or particularly modern sites such as factories or coal mines. Rather, these newer risks cannot be contained within the territorial borders of nation-states; they speak to hazards that are 'supra-national', 'non class-specific' (a claim that would result in considerable criticism) and global.

These new 'modernization risks' possess an inherent tendency towards globalization; Beck speaks of a 'universalization of hazards'. At the time of writing *Risk Society*, Beck focused to a significant extent on the hazards that became evident from the nuclear accident at Chernobyl in present-day Ukraine. As a scholar living in Germany, he personally experienced the silent drifting of radiation across Western Europe and the profound debates in the country over nuclear waste and proliferation that were spawned by the accident. He also speaks of toxic chemicals from industrial plants and their pollution of the air (acid rain), lakes, rivers and oceans, and the soil. All of these kinds of hazards create risks arising out of the logic of industrialization and, thus, modernity itself. So globalization in his early writings on risk referred to risks of a transnational dimension that could not be contained within the territorial borders characteristic of modernity, particularly those of nation-states.

World risk society

In his book *What Is Globalization?* (2000), Beck discusses globalization in combination with another concept, that of 'world society'. He uses this latter term to refer to those social relationships that are not integrated within or determined by nation-states. By this definition, world society is not new – such social relationships have existed for several centuries. What is unprecedented, however, is the number and importance of these social relationships (see **Scholte**). And he attributes these changes to globalization. So globalization refers to processes that criss-cross the world, while being generated by trans-national actors such as corporations, social movements and new information and communication technologies. What is particular about world society under globalization, he adds, is that it is not reversible; nation-state-based modernity has been superseded. This irreversibility, in turn, means that we are in a new or 'second' modernity. He adds that what is also new about this world society is not only the placelessness of community, labour, capital and industrial hazards, but also the consciousness or awareness of the opening up of world or global horizons (for a different view of place, see **Bauman**, **Brenner**, **Escobar**, **Mignolo**, **Taylor**).

Accordingly, during the 1990s, Beck speaks more of 'world risk society' than of 'risk society', as defined in his writings of the 1980s. His addition of the adjective 'world' here is important because it reflects his growing awareness and analysis of risks that threaten the planet. He argues that we have entered a world of uncontrollable risk and of potential catastrophes. These risks are 'debounded', respecting neither state boundaries nor particular temporalities, nor are they clearly tied to one actor or source. These risks fall into three categories: financial, ecological and terrorism. Financial and ecological risks fit the model of modernity's self-endangerment or reflexivity, growing out of industrial capitalism. While ecological risks come from 'outside' or changes in the 'environment', financial ones come from 'inside', the very functioning of markets. In these respects, financial risks are more immediately apparent and individualized than ecological ones. If the catastrophic characteristics of these two categories of risk are 'unin-tentional', those arising from terrorism are 'intentional'. Contrary to financial and ecological risks which point to the limitations of nation-states, terrorist risks require the reinforcement of these same states. In fact, states define the identities of terrorists, and the de-territorialized, de-nationalized and flexible constructions of images that follow legitimize global uses of force as 'self-defence' (see also **Hardt and Negri**). In short, the globalization of market structures, of industrial processes harmful to the environment, and of human connections made possible by transportation, information and communication technologies all point to the 'de-bounding of risks'.

Throughout his writings, Beck demonstrates a passionate commitment to thinking about how world society might confront the ever more dangerous situations created by reflexive modernity. Gradually, the concept of cosmopolitanism and associated terms – the adjective 'cosmopolitan' and the process 'cosmopolitanization' – arrive at a central place in his thinking. Beck observes that cosmopolitanism arises from ancient Greece. Philosophers spoke of a dual citizenship, a citizen of the *cosmos* or world and a citizen of the *polis* – that is, of the city and the state. He references Kant, as well, where he wrote about war and moving towards a perpetual peace. For Kant, cosmopolitanism involved the extension of hospitality to strangers or foreigners; all persons had a right not to be treated with hostility, but hospitality. Universal hospitality then becomes the condition for cooperative relations and just conduct.

Beck adds, however, that the increased interdependence of actors across nation-state borders that is forced by the encounter with catastrophic economic, ecological and terrorism risks gives rise to a 'cosmopolitan moment' and an 'unintended and lived cosmopolitanism'. In this respect, he speaks of 'cosmopolitanization', a process where people are thrown together and unwittingly pressured to cooperate if they are to survive. We might say, then, that the unintended and lived cosmopolitanism of the twenty-first century is an effect of globalizing processes in each of the economic, political, cultural, social and environmental realms, particularly those associated with catastrophic risks.

Cosmopolitanism

Since the late 1990s, Beck has written extensively on cosmopolitanism, including books entitled *Cosmopolitan Europe* (with Edgar Grande, 2007) and *The Cosmopolitan Vision* (2006). His thinking here can be illustrated with two examples: his categorization of states in the second modernity and his critique of what he describes as 'methodological nationalism' in the social sciences.

In looking at the situation of second modernity, on the one side, and the challenges faced by states in confronting that situation, on the other, Beck constructs a typology of possible responses to this situation. He sees states responding differently to two opportunities, engaging with or withdrawing from the global interdependencies created by globalization and sharing or hoarding sovereignty. He terms those states that seek to withdraw from global engagements and to hoard sovereignty as 'ethnic': they focus on articulating an ethnic nationalist ideology while closing borders to economic, political and cultural global processes. Iran is an example of a state adopting this approach. A second form of state engages with global processes, all the while holding on tightly to sovereignty and refusing cooperative relations with other states. He describes this form as a 'neoliberal state'. Although he does not cite an example, one might point to some states in the Global South as they took form after the application of International Monetary Fund Structural Adjustment Programmes. Examples might include Tunisia or South Africa, or even Chile under Pinochet. He next identifies two forms of state that are 'transnational' – that is, they are willing to project sovereignty beyond their borders. The transnational surveillance state does so unilaterally, relying upon military strength and economic blackmail. Beck cites the US under the George W. Bush presidency as one example; contemporary Russia might be another. In contrast, the *cosmopolitan* state is one that seeks to engage with global dangers through sharing sovereignty and cooperating in multilateral agreements to solve problems. It replaces the notion of a national homeland with that of a dual homeland, which involves being open to and tolerant of different nationalities both within its borders and across borders. Such a state develops a commitment to the planet as a whole.

A second example of his thinking about cosmopolitanism is his critique of contemporary social sciences when it comes to their being able to understand second modernity and contribute to addressing the immense challenges it poses. He describes the contemporary situation as one of 'methodological nationalism' (see also **Scholte**, **Taylor**); social scientists equate societies with nation-state societies, and see states and their governments not only as the primary focus of analysis but also the fundamental categories of political and social organization. In short, the unquestioning of the boundaries, categories, notions of order and related state-based concepts prevents the social sciences from getting at the heart of the dynamics of the second modernity and of globalization.

Beck suggests that methodological nationalism needs to be replaced by 'methodological cosmopolitanism'. In such an approach, 'politics within borders' would be replaced by the 'politics of boundaries', an exclusive focus on nation-state regimes by the meta-games of 'global domestic politics', more focus on actors and strategies mobilizing across borders, a closer examination of transnational law and trans-legal domination, exchanging the ideal of national homogeneity for that of cultural diversity, and so on. Such an approach would certainly lead to the employment of new concepts of analysis such as 'network society' (**Castells**), 'denationalization' and 'global cities' (**Abu-Lughod, Sassen, Taylor**) and Beck's own notion of transnational cosmopolitan states.

Major globalization writings

Beck, U. (1992) *Risk Society: Towards a New Modernity*, trans. M. Ritter, London: Sage Publications.

——(1999) *World Risk Society*, Cambridge, UK: Polity Press.

——(2000) *What Is Globalization?*, trans. P. Camiller, Cambridge, UK: Polity Press.

——(2005) *Power in the Global Age: A New Global Political Economy*, trans. K. Cross, London: Polity Press.

——(2006) *The Cosmopolitan Vision*, Cambridge, UK: Polity Press.

——(2009) *World at Risk*, Cambridge, UK: Polity Press.

See also: **Abu-Lughod, Bauman, Brenner, Castells, Dirlik, Escobar, Hardt and Negri, Mignolo, Sassen, Scholte, Taylor**.

WALDEN F. BELLO (1945–)

Walden F. Bello was born in Manila, the Philippines, in 1945. In 1972, when Ferdinand Marcos took power, he was studying for a Ph.D. in sociology at Princeton University. He plunged into political activism and did not return to academia for another 20 years. Over those two decades, he became a key figure in the international movement to restore democracy in the Philippines, coordinating the Anti-Martial Law Coalition and establishing the Philippines Human Rights Lobby in Washington. In 1995, he co-founded Focus on the Global South (Focus), of which he later became the executive director. Focus seeks to build grassroots capacity to propose alternative policies that could address regional issues of development and capital flows in East and South-East Asia. When the Asian financial crisis struck two years later, Focus played a major role in advocating a different way forward. Bello is a strong environmentalist; he has also campaigned for years for the withdrawal of US military bases from the Philippines, Okinawa (Japan) and South Korea. He was a representative in the 14th Congress of the Republic of the Philippines and a professor of sociology at the University of the Philippines Diliman.

Bello concentrates his thinking on economic globalization, with a particular emphasis on corporate-led changes that took shape beginning in the 1970s and culminated in the creation of the World Trade Organization (WTO) in 1995. This 'corporate globalization' is enforced by the US drawing on its global military capacity and by the encoding of provisions into global law, which erect almost unassailable obstacles to economic autonomy for many poorer countries.

History of globalization

Bello understands globalization to include the processes by which pre-capitalist economic forms of activity are replaced by capitalist ones on an increasingly global scale. In this sense, he identifies the period of European imperialism in the second half of the nineteenth century up to 1914 as the first wave of globalization. During this period, land, labour and wealth became integrated within capitalist relations across the world to a degree not seen before (Bello 2002, 2003). In response to the deleterious effects of these changes, searches for new forms of community emerged in the forms of socialism, communism, social democracy and national liberation. In addition, of course, there were responses in the forms of counter-revolutions, racism and fascism.

Similar to **Amin, Arrighi, Cox** and **Harvey**, Bello distinguishes the period between 1945 and 1980 (the 'long boom') from what he calls the second phase of globalization. In the immediate post-war period, capitalism was still advancing globally but was shaped in important ways by the actions of states. In addition, the then recently created United Nations offered a global forum where newly decolonized states and other poorer countries could meet and develop policies for containing and shaping capitalist development. Bello singles out for special mention the thinking and leadership of the Argentinian economist Raul Prebisch (Bello 2001: 2–3). Prebisch's thinking about the worsening terms of trade between industrialized and non-industrialized countries was an inspiration for many organizations representing the interests of the latter group during the 1960s and 1970s. In particular, it was central to the establishment of the UN Conference on Trade and Development (UNCTAD) in 1964, and Prebisch served as its first secretary-general. The global reform strategy advanced by UNCTAD gained important influence in the economic agencies of the UN Secretariat, including the Economic and Social Council (ECOSOC) and the United Nations Development Programme (UNDP) (2001: 3).

Bello suggests that the 'long boom' came to an end during the 1970s as a crisis in capitalism arising from overproduction, over-capacity and overinvestment set in. UN estimates show that annual rates of growth of global gross domestic product (GDP) were 5.4 per cent in the 1960s, 4.1 per cent in the 1970s, 3 per cent in the 1980s and 2.3 per cent in the 1990s (Bello 2006: 1348). Bello argues that the dominant capitalist countries responded to this crisis by instigating a new phase of globalization buttressed by policies to reduce the power of states to intervene in economic matters (neoliberalism) and to open up new investment opportunities in financial products (financialization) (see also **Arrighi, Harvey, Helleiner**). These steps place limits on poorer countries' development, while opening up new accumulation options for transnational corporations, including finance, based in so-called advanced industrial countries. In many of his writings, Bello suggests that the dominant capitalist countries, led by the US, sought to bypass the UN by using the two Bretton Woods institutions: the International Monetary Fund (IMF) and the World Bank (WB) and by setting up new organizations of their own, most notably the Group of 7 (G7). Working with these institutions, the US led a new wave of economic globalization based on weakening state capacity in poorer countries, while creating new paths for investment by foreign transnational corporations (Bello 2002: 59).

In analysing the paths of this wave of economic globalization, Bello singles out for particular study the actions of the IMF and the WB in setting up Structural Adjustment Programmes (SAPs) in poorer countries during the 1980s and 1990s and the powers of the WTO, which began operations in 1995. The SAPs were imposed upon poorer countries which were facing major debt programmes. In exchange for loans, receiving governments were to reduce government spending drastically, liberalize imports, concentrate on expanding exports, remove restrictions on foreign investment, privatize state enterprises and deregulate other areas of state activity, devalue the currency to make exports more competitive, and cut or constrain wages to reduce labour costs and increase labour mobility. The results of these policies were effectively to end the state-assisted approach to development in play during the 'long boom' era, while sidelining the UN by working through the IMF and the WB. Consequently, transnational corporations could 'globalize' their activities more easily in poorer countries.

The creation of the WTO extended these constraints to poor countries that had escaped the SAPs, while formalizing global legal restraints on all such poorer states when it came to economic autonomy. In fact, Bello terms the WTO an 'Antidevelopment Agency' (Bello 2005: 141). The Trade-Related Investment Measures (TRIMS) agreement, when coupled with agreements to end import quotas, meant that these countries had 'signed away their right to use trade policy as a means of industrialization' (2005: 141), an approach to development that the US, the UK and other wealthier countries had used during the nineteenth and early twentieth centuries. Signing the Trade-Related Aspects of Intellectual Property Rights (TRIPS) agreement strengthened the monopoly of knowledge-intensive transnational corporations in key economic sectors during the late twentieth century. The WTO Agreement on Agriculture permitted the wealthier states to continue their subsidization of agricultural production while further opening up poorer states' markets for imports from the wealthy countries. In short, Bello writes, 'the WTO was established to dismantle trade barriers to commodities produced by TNCs [transnational corporations] while protecting the monopolistic production practices in northern agriculture and high-tech industry' (2005: 153).

De-globalization

Scholars critical of contemporary globalization processes fall generally into two groups when they think about how to address the problems arising from corporate neoliberal globalization: search for an alternative globalization or work towards unravelling capitalist-dominated global institutions in favour of nation-states and social movements active in transnational, national and local settings. Bello falls into the second group. He has been an active member of the World Social Forum (WSF) since its very beginning and he sees the collection of organizations, movements and peoples under this umbrella as constituting a 'global community' (Bello 2003: 70) that will look for alternatives to capitalist, corporate globalization as developed after 1980 (see also **Santos**).

He argues that some of those participating in this global community share two conceptions. First, they agree that the logic of the market should be subordinated to the values of security, equity and social solidarity (2003: 69). Second, he identifies a need for the 'deglobalization' of the national economy and the construction of a pluralist system for global economic governance (some participants in the WSF would prefer to work towards an alternative globalization rather than towards de-globalization, such as **Santos**). De-globalization requires the reorientation of economies away from an emphasis on production for export (that was emphasized in the SAPs and the thinking behind the WTO) to production for the local market. Bello is not interested in 'reforming' the 'TNC-driven WTO' or the IMF and the World Bank, but on decommissioning them or radically reducing their powers (Bello 2002: 116–117).

Accompanying such changes, he would like to see a revitalization of UNCTAD, multilateral environmental agreements, the International Labour Organization and regional economic groupings. He emphasizes that changes must focus on 'devolving the greater part of production, trade and economic decision-making to the regional, national and community level' (2002: 118). It is in a context that is 'more fluid, less structured, more pluralistic, with multiple checks and balances' that the world's peoples will be able to 'carve out the space to develop, based on their values, their rhythms and their strategies of choice' (Bello 2003: 69).

Major globalization writings

Bello, W. F. (2001) *The Future in the Balance: Essays on Globalization and Resistance*, Oakland, CA: Food First Books.

——(2002) *Deglobalization: Ideas for a New World Economy*, London: Zed Books.

——(2003) 'Global capitalism versus global community', *Race & Class*, vol 44, no 4, pp. 63–76.

——(2005) *Dilemmas of Domination: The Unmaking of the American Empire*, New York, NY: Metropolitan Books/H. Holt.

——(2006) 'The capitalist conjuncture: over-accumulation, financial crises, and the retreat from globalisation', *Third World Quarterly*, vol 27, no 8, pp. 1345–1367.

——(2008) 'A very capitalist disaster: Naomi Klein's take on the neoliberal saga', *Review of International Political Economy*, vol 15, no 5, pp. 881–891.

See also: **Amin**, **Arrighi**, **Cox**, **Harvey**, **Helleiner**, **Santos**.

FERNAND BRAUDEL (1902–1985)

Fernand Braudel was born in 1902 near Verdun, France. He studied history at the University of Paris, La Sorbonne, and took his degree in 1923. In 1932, Braudel encountered Lucien Febvre (1878–1956) for the first time, a professor of history at Collège de France. Three years earlier, Lucien Febvre and Marc Bloch had founded a journal called *Annals of Economic and Social History* (*Annales d'histoire économique et sociale*), which aimed to depart from traditional political and military history to explore economic and social history, and to focus on long-term perspectives. Eventually, Braudel was to succeed Febvre as the leader of the *Annales* school of history. He enrolled in the French army in 1939 and was captured by German forces following France's surrender in June 1940. He spent some time in Mainz, and was then shipped to a prisoner of war camp on the Baltic coast. During this captivity he wrote *La Méditerranée et le monde méditerranéen à l'époque de Philippe II*, the book that would become his first masterwork and his doctoral thesis, which he defended in 1949. His scholarship focused on three main projects, each representing several decades of intense study: *The Mediterranean* (1923–1949, then 1949–1966), *Civilization and Capitalism* (1955–1979) and the unfinished *Identity of France* (1970–1985). He had considerable success in making the *Annales* school the most important engine of historical research in France and in much of the world after 1950. He died on 28 November 1985.

Braudel's contribution to globalization studies is twofold. First, he developed an interdisciplinary methodology for thinking about historical change from a perspective that takes the world as a context for investigation. This thinking, in turn, has influenced the understanding of globalization of many scholars, including authors in this book (see **Amin, Arrighi, Cox, Harvey, Helleiner**). Second, although he died in 1985, a time when the contemporary period of globalization was beginning to accelerate, he also contributed significantly to our understanding of the history of globalization.

Studying global history

Braudel begins to build his theory of the history of capitalism, and with it a history of globalization, by focusing on the economy. He distinguishes between *the economy of the world* and a *world economy*. The first refers to the economy of the world as a whole. In contrast, a 'world economy' is the economy of only one part of the globe, one that forms an economic whole, a world to itself (Braudel 1977: 81; 1992, v3: 24). It generally includes a very large area in a specific part of the world, has defined boundaries and thus constitutes a geographic space. These boundaries also give it a cultural identity. Invariably, a world economy has a centre, usually a city, which is home to an already dominant form of capitalism. Accordingly, a world economy has hierarchies: a narrow dominant core built around an exceptional city, a fairly developed middle zone and very wide peripheral areas, subordinated to the centre. He suggests that at the end of the Middle Ages (if not before), the globe was already divided into more or less centralized and more or less coherent world economies (Europe, China, India, Insulinde (South-East Asia) and the world of Islam) (see also **Abu-Lughod**).

Complementing this understanding of the division of space, Braudel speaks of different time divisions: events, conjunctures, and the *longue durée*, or long term. Citing the example of the European world economy from the fourteenth to the eighteenth century, Braudel notes that over this *longue durée*, economic activity had several common features despite considerable upheaval: dependency upon a demographically fragile population, the primacy of water and ships for transport, merchants as primary actors, a prominent role for precious metals as currency (gold, silver, copper) and a disproportionate dependence upon one or two trade routes. It is by examining the long term, he argues, that the dominant features of a given period become more apparent.

During this long term, there were conjunctures such as cycles in the economy, and many events such as wars, technological innovations in sea transportation, weapons and currencies of exchange, and changes in leadership from one major city to others (such as from Venice to Antwerp, Amsterdam or London). By breaking up time into these three components (events, conjunctures and long term), Braudel suggests that we can better understand the key stages in the development of capitalism and the gradual expansion of economic activity to a global scale.

Braudel also stresses that one can only understand the economy by situating it with respect to other 'ensembles': politics, culture and social hierarchy (Braudel 1977: 64–65). He adds that the modern state did not create capitalism; rather, it inherited it. Sometimes the modern state favours capitalism, other times it inhibits its development. Capitalism only triumphs when 'it is the state'. Different eras in the development of capitalism feature different social groups. The first part of the period that began in the late eighteenth century saw the emergence of a *haute finance* (high finance) class as well as an organized industrial working class. During the contemporary period, we have seen this high finance class become fully global and the emergence of a counter-social phenomenon, transnational civil society networks increasingly functioning on a global scale.

Braudel also notes that cultures or civilizations order space just as much as economies do. 'Culture is the oldest character in human history: economies succeed each other, political institutions crumble, societies, replace each other, but civilization continues along its way' (Braudel 1992, v3: 65). Accordingly, within a world economy, the cultural and economic maps may differ considerably. For a long time, Venice and Genoa looked to Florence in cultural matters, and England and its capital, London, drew cultural sustenance from Paris and France. A civilization, then, is a cultural area, a locus, where there is a wide range of cultural characteristics that are grouped in regular ways, that recur frequently and that are ubiquitous. He adds that civilizations are dynamic: they export some of their cultural features while borrowing frequently from others. He includes technologies in these imports and exports, which contribute, in turn, to dynamic changes, both economic and cultural.

History of globalization

In his historical writing, Braudel begins by studying the changes in the European world economy from the fourteenth to the middle of the eighteenth century. He argues that the changes that occurred were not from feudalism to capitalism as observers such as Karl Marx had suggested. Rather, they were shifts in the centre of gravity of the European world economy. Braudel's conception of capitalism differed from that of Marx and other thinkers influenced by Marx (see also

Helleiner). His core idea was that the economy needs to be seen as a three-tiered structure: material life, market life and capitalism. In other words, 'capitalism' is not the same as 'markets'; indeed, for Braudel, capitalism was the 'anti-market' – by which he meant the world of oligopolies, giant corporations and rigged markets (often because of private economic actors' preferential treatment by the state) at the zenith of the economic hierarchy. With this unusual definition of 'capitalism', Braudel argues that capitalism has been around for a very long time, since the late thirteenth century (see also **Abu-Lughod**). Globalizing processes speak to capitalism becoming gradually a more important and influential part of the economy.

Although the dominant city in the European world economy shifted from Venice and Genoa to Antwerp, then to Amsterdam, and finally to London between the fourteenth and eighteenth centuries (see also **Arrighi**), the intrinsic features of capitalism did not change. Rather, the scale at which capitalism operated became ever more worldwide (Braudel 1977: 67). In addition, over the same period, the numbers of people living a 'material life' (subsistence living) began to decline as the 'market economy' and increasingly 'capitalism' affected more and more people, thus increasing standards of living. In this respect, Braudel is arguing that the extensity of the European world economy was reaching a global scale and the intensity of capitalist activity was penetrating ever deeper into European society and its increasingly global peripheries. He writes: 'the European world-economy gradually becomes more global, and multiplied its links with other still-autonomous world economies: India, Insulinde, and China' (1977: 83–84) (Insulinde corresponds roughly with the area of the world called South-East Asia today).

With the arrival of London as the centre of the European world economy in the eighteenth century, Braudel argues that a new 'era', and thus a new *longue durée*, began. Unlike its predecessors, London was not a city-state but the capital of the British Isles, a position that gave it the 'irresistible power of the *national market*' (1977: 95). England's and later Britain's economic and political dominance marked the end of an era of city-oriented world economies. This more extensive national base permitted Britain to project its power globally in ways not possible during the past. Second, Braudel points to more aggressive imperialism: 'For the first time the European economy – extending all over the world and shoving aside other economies – aspired to control the economy of the entire world and to be its embodiment all over the globe' (1977: 104). The British imperialism of the late eighteenth, nineteenth and early twentieth centuries propelled the world violently towards unity (Braudel 1980: 213). Britain, in turn, was to be replaced by the US in the 1920s, which built its world dominance on a much larger and continent-wide national economy, a point emphasized by **Arrighi**, whose work was highly influenced by that of Braudel.

In contemplating this new period, which brought intensifying globalization, Braudel draws our attention to how it is distinct from the previous era. Not only does the Industrial Revolution occur, but also the 'scientific revolution' and a 'biological revolution' ('an unprecedented flood of human beings such as this planet has never seen before') (1980: 213). 'From the beginning of the 18th century', he adds, 'we seem to have been transported to a new planet.' With changes in technology, economics and demography, there is a huge 'diffusion' of revolutions instigated by European and later American dominations. But, he claims, these 'diffusions' are proceeding independently of the West. These upheavals 'vary with each civilization, and each one, without wishing it, finds itself placed in a unique position, because of realities which have existed for a long time, and which are highly resistant, being part of its very structure' (1980: 216). This point is consistent with his position that cultural areas or civilizations continue even in the face of economic, political and societal change. In short, these global processes unleashed in the eighteenth century accentuate differences across the world as much as they bring similarities (see also **Brenner, Falk, Robertson, Tomlinson**).

Major globalization writings

Braudel, F. (1972) *The Mediterranean and the Mediterranean World in the Age of Philip II*, 3 vols, London: Collins.

——(1977) *Afterthoughts on Material Civilization and Capitalism*, Baltimore, MD: Johns Hopkins University Press.

——(1980) *On History*, Chicago, IL: University of Chicago Press.

——(1992) *Civilization and Capitalism: 15th–18th Century*, 3 vols, Berkeley, CA: University of California Press.

See also: **Abu-Lughod, Amin, Arrighi, Brenner, Cox, Falk, Harvey, Helleiner, Robertson, Tomlinson**.

NEIL BRENNER

Neil Brenner is Professor of Sociology and Metropolitan Studies and an affiliated faculty member of the American Studies Program at New York University. He holds a Ph.D. in political science from the University of Chicago (1999); an MA in geography from University of California, Los Angeles (UCLA) (1996); and a BA in philosophy, *summa cum laude*, from Yale College (1991). His writing and teaching focus on critical urban and regional studies, comparative geopolitical economy and socio-spatial theory. Major research foci include the development of critical urban theory; processes of urban and regional restructuring; the generalization of capitalist urbanization; processes of state spatial restructuring, neoliberalization and 'globalization'; and urban governance restructuring.

Globalization processes

Like other critical political economy scholars, globalization for Brenner is intimately linked with capitalism. Drawing on the thinking of David **Harvey**, Brenner sees capitalism as 'impelled to eliminate all geographical barriers to the "accumulation process" by seeking out cheaper raw materials, fresh and less costly sources of labour power, new markets and new investment opportunities' (Brenner 1999a: 42; 2004: 33). Accordingly, capitalism is always driven to do more things in less time (temporal acceleration) and to take root in more and more parts of the world (spatial expansion). In order to accomplish these things, capitalism requires certain material conditions: relatively fixed and immobile territorial infrastructures, long-distance communication capabilities, and states capable of regulating these processes (1999a: 43).

Brenner suggests that globalization processes occur when there are crises in capitalism. The crises arise from problems with the movement of commodities, capital and people through expanding geographical spaces at an accelerating pace. This expansion and acceleration requires new forms of socio-territorial infrastructure that will permit the needed reworking of established patterns of development in the world thus far (Brenner 2004: 35). Other critical political economy scholars such as **Abu-Lughod**, **Amin** and **Arrighi** tend to date the start of globalization at a time much earlier than the nineteenth century when the extension of capitalism reached a large part of the world. In contrast, Brenner argues that globalization processes begin with the shift from mercantile to industrial capitalism in the nineteenth century. This transition led to a need for large-scale territorial infrastructures for production, exchange, distribution, communication and transportation. A second globalization period begins in the early 1970s, a common starting point for critical political economy scholars.

What distinguishes the first wave of globalization that unfolded during the late nineteenth and early twentieth centuries from the second wave is the degree of centrality of the state. In this first period, the state became ever more central to the promotion, regulation and enhancing of industrial capitalism. Through military support, the promotion of innovations in transportation and communication, the securing of colonial spaces, and other activities, states provided the 'territorialized scaffolding' for accelerating capitalist geographical expansion. The state linked together subnational and supranational scales of activity. In this respect, Brenner writes, 'globalization and nationalization proceeded in tandem as mutually constitutive processes of socio-spatial restructuring' (Brenner 1999a: 45). It is in the same period that we see the development of a state-centric epistemology that has largely dominated the social sciences ever since. The state is viewed as the 'container of society', while the 'international system' is mapped in ways that distinguish 'domestic' and 'foreign' policy based on borders separating the 'inside' from the 'outside' (1999a: 45) (see also **Beck**, **Scholte**).

Beginning during the 1970s, the new phase of globalization moves away from this state-centrism as institutions and structures at other scales assume prominent roles in regulating and supporting capitalist expansion. Territorial borders become increasingly porous when it comes to flows of international capital; the capacity of states to control monetary policies declines; de-industrialization begins to accelerate in many of the wealthier countries; and regional and local scales of organization come to play more central roles. Super-regional blocs such as the European Union (EU), the North American Free Trade Agreement (NAFTA) and the Association of South-East Asian States (ASEAN) grow in importance, while new geographies of global urbanization drain influence from the state (Brenner 1999b: 432). It is these changes involving movement away from a singular focus on the state to other scalar structures that distinguish the new wave of globalization that emerged during this period.

De-territorialization, re-territorialization

In detailing his understanding of contemporary globalization, Brenner begins by critiquing two prominent theoretical positions. The first of these presents globalization as processes leading to the creation of a global space that mirrors state-based structures at the national scale. This theory, thus, speaks about the stretching of institutions to the global scale and points to global culture, global society, global polity, global civil society or global economy. He cites **Robertson**'s work as an example and his development of concepts such as *global field* and *global unicity*. Another example of work that would fall into this category is **Giddens**' portrayal of globalization as the extension of the institutions of modernity to a global scale. In contrast, the second theoretical position is built around the concept of 'de-territorialization'. Proponents argue that new geographies of networks and flows are supplanting the state-based geographies of the previous two centuries; the state is being hollowed out or is declining in relevance. **Castells'** development of the concept of 'spaces of flows', **Scholte'**s conception of 'supra-territoriality', **Held'**s notion of 'extensity' or **Tomlinson'**s discussion of de-territorialization and culture are all examples of this second theoretical position. In Brenner's view, they underestimate states' staying power and the central role they continue to play.

According to Brenner, the problem with the first approach is its use of an understanding of scale that remains rooted in state-centric territorial thinking. In contrast, the second approach suggests a significant weakening of the state and its regulatory capacity in the face of trans-border flows of goods, capital and people. Brenner counters these positions by arguing that current globalization has radically reconfigured the scalar organization of territorialization processes under capitalism. In particular, the national scale associated with the activities of nation-states, so central to the first phase of globalization, cedes importance to new forms of territorial organization at both subnational and supra-national levels. In this respect, he argues that globalization involves interlinked processes of de-territorialization and re-territorialization. In more concrete terms, the intensification of capitalism's operations on a global scale weakens the territorial base of the previous globalization in the nation-states (de-territorialization). At the same time, for this global expansion of capitalism to occur, there is a need for new fixed geographical infrastructures at different scalar levels that support the global circulation of capital, money, commodities and people (re-territorialization).

Characteristic, then, of contemporary globalization is the growth in importance of cities as containers of the important parts of the infra-structure needed for the capitalist global expansion (see also **Sassen, Taylor**). In the process of assuming this infrastructural role, the urban form itself is transformed. 'Through their role in articulating local, regional, national and global economies, cities have today become massive, polycentric urban regions' (Brenner 1999a: 437). In this changed role, the global economic power of cities has become increasingly autonomous from the territorial structures of inter-state relations. Cities are no longer subnational components of self-enclosed nation-state-based capitalist expansion. Rather, in the more recent phase of globalization, they become important nodes in global urban networks and, in these respects, the motors of the new global economy (1999a: 437).

In contrast, with the second 'de-territorializaton' hypothesis, Brenner argues that the rise in importance of global cities since the 1970s does not come at the expense of the nation-state. Brenner argues that the nation-state retains importance; it does not wane, as is implied by the theorization of globalization as a 'space of flows'. Nor are we speaking about a stretching of nation-state space to a global scale. Rather, the nation-state is joined by a range of subnational and supranational configurations in supporting the global expansion of capitalism: 'from global city regions, industrial districts, and regional state institutions to multinational economic blocks, supranational regulatory institutions, and regimes of global governance' (Brenner 2004: 45). Brenner describes the new situation as a 'polymorphic, multiscalar institutional mosaic composed of multiple, partially overlapping institutional forms and regulatory configurations that are neither congruent, contiguous, nor coextensive with one another' (2004: 46).

Neoliberalization

Brenner defines neoliberalization as processes of regulatory change that prioritize market-based, market-oriented or market disciplinary responses to regulatory problems. These processes also intensify commodification of all realms of social life; they mobilize speculative financial instruments to open up new arenas for capitalist profit-making (Brenner *et al.* 2010a: 329–330). Consistent with his understanding of globalization, Brenner adds that these policies are not simply designed by multilateral institutions and then implemented at national and subnational scales. Rather, the varying models are polymorphic policy designs growing out of 'transnational, national, and newly developed subnational (urban conglomeration) frameworks' (Brenner *et al.* 2010b: 196). Once applied at one scale, they may be tried at another scale and then purposely recirculated back into their previous scalar networks.

Accordingly, Brenner and his colleagues, Jamie Peck and Nik Theodore, argue against a view of neoliberalization as a relatively homogeneous set of regulatory tools that is being implemented everywhere in the world in roughly the same way (see **Harvey**). They claim that neoliberalization is highly variegated, taking a wide range of forms in pursuit of different objectives in varying locations across the world. The market-oriented regulatory forms and policies differ widely from one setting to another. Consequently, the regulatory frameworks develop unevenly across settings (see also **Tsing**).

The 'worldwide landscapes of neoliberalization are *constitutively* and *systemically* uneven' (Brenner *et al.* 2010b: 195). Like globalization, neoliberalization is not 'a single, unified phenomenon, but a "syndrome" of related activities implemented across otherwise diverse sites, territories and scales' (Brenner *et al.* 2010a: 330).

Brenner emphasizes as well that neoliberalization is path dependent: regulations are drawn up to reshape particular institutions and rule systems in given places. Insofar as they 'necessarily collide with diverse regulatory landscapes inherited from earlier rounds of landscape formation (including Fordism, national developmentalism, and state socialism), their forms of articulation and institutionalization are quite heterogeneous' (Brenner *et al.* 2010a: 330). It follows from this point that the forms of neoliberalization may become increasingly differentiated over time across the world, being built on different infrastructures in pursuit of varying policy outcomes. As each form is designed to reshape the regulatory processes for marketization, and as further reforms have been made successively to these initial designs for over 40 years now, the institutionalization of neoliberalization will look different from one global city, or city-region, or nation-state or multi-state region to another. They may contradict one another and be discontinuous from one setting to another.

In summary, Brenner's arguments about the nature of globalization and of neoliberalization differ strongly from views of these processes that emphasize growing similarities in economic, political, social and cultural ways of living across the world. If anything, with the relativization of the role of the nation-state and its accompanying tools of nationality, the diversity and contradictions across the world have intensified considerably over the past 40 years. Like **Taylor**, Brenner sees a much more important role being played by city-regions linked in networks no longer constrained by nation-states. Visions of world governance or an integrated global economy or a global society are not part of contemporary globalization, based on his analysis.

Major globalization writings

Brenner, N. (1999a) 'Beyond state-centrism? Space, territoriality, and geographical scale in globalization studies', *Theory and Society*, vol 28, no 1, pp. 39–78.

——(1999b) 'Globalisation as reterritorialisation: the re-scaling of urban governance in the European Union', *Urban Studies*, vol 15, no 3, pp. 431–451.

——(2004) *New State Spaces: Urban Governance and the Rescaling of Statehood*, Oxford, UK: Oxford University Press.

Brenner, N., Peck, J. and Theodore, N. (2010a) 'After neoliberalization?', *Globalizations*, vol 7, no 3, pp. 327–345.

——(2010b) 'Variegated neoliberalization: geographies, modalities, pathways', *Global Networks*, vol 10, no 2, pp. 182–222.

See also: **Abu-Lughod, Amin, Arrighi, Beck, Castells, Giddens, Harvey, Held, Robertson, Scholte, Taylor, Tomlinson, Tsing.**

MANUEL CASTELLS (1942–)

Manuel Castells was born in the small town of La Mancha, Spain, in 1942. He spent the critical years of his adolescence in Barcelona and still considers himself a Catalan. Completing secondary school at the age of 16, he studied for both a *Licenciatura* in law and a *Licenciatura* in economics at the University of Barcelona. At this time, he became involved with an anarchist group opposing the Franco regime, leading to his being sought by police. He escaped to France, where he finished his degree at the Sorbonne in Paris. He developed an interest in sociology, particularly as it examined the working class. He was referred to Alain Touraine who encouraged him to enter the École des Hautes Études en Sciences Sociales. He studied urban social movements in France under Touraine's supervision, and then took up an appointment in the Department of Sociology at the University of California at Berkeley. There he launched a new research programme focused on technology, economy and society. This programme was to culminate in the publication of his monumental trilogy *The Information Age: Economy, Society, and Culture*, which he completed while fighting cancer. After a return to good health in the late 1990s, he revised and published second editions of the series.

It is only in the second editions of his trilogy and his publications after 2000 that one finds explicit use of the word 'globalization'. The significance of his work, however, arises from providing a wide-ranging, empirically grounded and in-depth analysis of the changes in economy, society, the state and culture that came with the arrival of what he has come to call the electronic informational-communication paradigm. In this respect, his work is crucial to understanding contemporary globalization processes.

Industrialism and informationalism

Castells argues that the world is undergoing a fundamental shift in its 'mode of development' – that is, in the technological arrangements through which labour works on matter to generate a product. The previous mode of development is industrialism, which grew out of new technologies for generating energy, particularly electricity. Beginning in the 1970s, a new technological paradigm, termed initially 'informationalism' and later 'electronic informational-communication', gradually brought change to the world, based on information communication technologies (ICTs), including genetic engineering. These technologies are distinctive from those in the past in their self-expanding processing and communicating capacity in terms of volume, complexity and speed. In addition, they are able to recombine on the basis of digitization and recurrent communication. Finally, they are remarkably flexible as they operate through interactive digitized networks.

The information communication revolution – built around technologies such as the personal computer, the computer chip and the internet – has gradually come to reshape and change virtually every aspect of social living for select groups of people in the world. Similar to the electrical power of the Industrial Revolution, the ICTs of the informational revolution reshape and create new possibilities for all existing technologies. In this respect, then, Castells speaks of a change in the technological paradigm, observing, however, that informationalism does not replace industrialism; rather, it subsumes and presupposes it.

The network society

In seeking to understand resulting changes in societies across the world, Castells distinguishes between two structural forms: horizontal networks and vertical hierarchical organizations. Both forms have existed from the very beginning of human societies. When it came to getting things done efficiently in societies, however, vertical hierarchical organizations culminating in the nation-state were superior to networks. Castells notes that prior to the information technology revolution, industrial societies, whether capitalist or statist, were predominately structured around vertical organizations, whether these were factories, educational institutions, religious organizations or political ones, with totalitarian systems being the most extreme examples.

Networks, he argues, have now become the more efficient structural form due to their flexibility, their scalability and their survivability. He writes:

> Thus what is specific to our world is the extension and augmentation of the body and mind in networks of interaction powered by microelectronics-based, software operated, communication technologies. These technologies are increasingly diffused throughout the entire realm of human activity by growing miniaturization. They are converging with new genetic engineering technologies able to reprogram the communication networks of living matter. It is on this basis that a new social structure is expanding as the foundation of contemporary life: the network society.
>
> (Castells 2004: 7)

The network structural form becomes increasingly predominant in the economy, as evidenced by global financial markets and the emergence of the 'network enterprise' and global business networks. It also gains more importance in the realm of culture. Cultural expressions of all kinds are fundamentally changed and reshaped as networks permit the formation of an electronic hypertext that enables television, radio, print media, film, video, art and the internet to be integrated and networked within an increasingly global system. Corresponding to this growth of official transnational networks is the networking of social movements, often characterized as the emergence of a global civil society.

This understanding of changes in social structure is important because it provides a sociological basis for globalization. As Castells (2004: 22) notes: 'Digital networks are global, as they know no boundaries in their capacity to reconfigure themselves. So a social structure whose infrastructure is based on digital networks is by definition global. Thus the network society is a global society.' This form of social structure creates profound distinctions among individuals based on a new logic, that of inclusion/exclusion. Those who are included in the networks become the privileged and the power holders; those excluded from them comprise the less wealthy and the less autonomous. Those who function within the dominant networks are said to be part of the 'space of flows' and their situation contrasts with the excluded, who live in 'spaces of places' (for an alternative view, see **Brenner, Dirlik, Escobar**).

Capitalism

Basic social structures arise from the interaction between modes of development and modes of production. By the mid-twentieth century, the industrialism mode of development had combined with two distinct modes of production, a capitalist one and a 'statist' one. Castells uses the latter term to characterize the mode of production that emerged in the Russian Empire after the Bolshevik Revolution and that was to be reproduced in many other societies, including those in Eastern Europe, Cuba and China (after its 1949 revolution). What is characteristic of the contemporary period is the end of the 'statist' mode of production almost everywhere, which has opened the way for the capitalist mode to become fully globalized – that is, active in virtually every part of the world.

The capitalism of today combines with the informational mode of development to create a new technico-economic system that Castells (2000a) terms 'informational capitalism'. Led by the most powerful capitalist states, the new capitalism accelerates production on a global scale, leading, in turn, to changes in the role of the state. States shift their attention away from social protection to promoting competitiveness in the global economy (see also **Cerny**). Informational capitalism thus differs from industrial capitalism in two ways. First, it is global in shaping social relationships across the entire planet. With the end of the statist mode of production, informational capitalism deepens its penetration of countries, cultures and ways of life. As Castells notes (2000b: 369): 'In spite of a highly diversified social and cultural landscape, for the first time in history the whole planet is organized around a largely common set of economic rules.' Second, informational capitalism is structured around a network of financial flows. Although finance capital has always been crucial in capitalism, never has it been as dominant as it is in the early twenty-first century (see also **Amin, Arrighi, Cox, Helleiner**). Financial markets, whether in New York, London, Tokyo, Shanghai, Paris, Frankfurt, Mumbai or Zürich, work as a unit in real time. Accordingly, domestic financial crises are unlikely to remain domestic for very long, as the East Asian crisis of the late 1990s and the US sub-prime mortgage crisis of the first decade of the twenty-first century have illustrated. Castells concludes:

> There is not, sociologically and economically, such a thing as a global capitalist class. But there is an integrated, global capital network, whose movements and variable logic ultimately determine economies and influence societies. Thus, above a diversity of human-flesh capitalists and capitalist groups there is a faceless collective capitalist, made up of financial flows operated by electronic networks.
>
> (Castells 2000a: 505)

Social division of labour

Whereas the Fordist organization of mass production was the dominant form in industrial capitalism, it is being supplanted by a new organizational form under informational capitalism. The usual business practice shifts towards one of alliances, partnerships and collaborations that are specific to a given product, process, time and space. For example, if we look at how an automobile is manufactured today, we see that it is being produced by a network, not a factory. The product emerges out of separate contributions from different plants of the firm around the world, plus the networks of supplier firms providing parts and business services, such as design and advertising. These collaborations are based on sharing capital and labour, and, most fundamentally, information and knowledge in order to win market share (Castells 2004: 27–28).

This social structure, in turn, changes the division of labour. In contrast to the classical industrial enterprise where production and labour were concentrated in the same physical site, labour is disaggregated at a variety of sites across the world, on the one side, while capital is aggregated on a global scale, on the other. In the process, labour loses its collective 'class' identity and large integrated labour unions decline, if not disappear altogether. Castells writes:

> Labor is disaggregated in its performance, fragmented in its organization, diversified in its existence, divided in its collective action. Networks converge toward a meta-network of capital that integrates capitalist interests at the global level and across sectors and realms of activity: not without conflict but under the same overarching logic.
>
> (Castells 2000a: 507)

In this world, there is a global tendency to increased social inequality both within societies and between societies (see also **Bauman**). Those who are included in the networks as capitalists and as self-programmable workers become wealthier, while those doing generic labour and who are excluded from networks become more impoverished. As social exclusion from the network society becomes more palpable and pauperizing, the poor are drawn into the increasingly global criminal economy focused on drugs, sex workers, arms and money laundering: the 'black holes of informational capitalism'.

Culture and identity

Castells also traces linkages between the network society and culture and identity. Changes in the technological paradigm and the transformation of capitalism have led to powerful expressions of collective identity where communities respond to these changes through assertions of cultural singularity. In the prologue to his trilogy, he writes:

> In a world of global flows of wealth, power and images, the search for identity, collective or individual, ascribed or constructed, becomes the fundamental source of social meaning [...] People increasingly organize their meaning not around what they do, but on the basis of what they are or believe they are [...] *Our*

> *societies are increasingly structured around a bipolar opposition between the Net and the Self.*
>
> (Castells 2000a: 3)

Castells distinguishes between three kinds of identity-building. *Legitimizing* identities are cultivated by the dominant institutions of society and rationalize their domination over social actors. Whether they are built around the imagined nationalities erected by states or other identities connected to churches, unions, interest associations or political parties, these identities generate a *civil society* through which domination functions. In contrast, *resistance* identities are built by actors who are stigmatized or devalued by the dominant institutions of a society. In response, they build 'trenches of resistance' based on principles that challenge the mainstream societal institutions and practices (see also **Sen**). This type of identity-building leads to the formation of *communes* or *communities* through which dominant institutions are challenged. Castells provides detailed analysis of such resistance through discussions of religious fundamentalism, ethnic nationalism, local community-building and social movements that challenge the global order. When it comes to these latter movements, he focuses, in particular, on the environmental, feminist and gay and lesbian liberation movements.

Last, but not least, he postulates *project* identities, where social actors build a new identity that redefines their position in society; in the process, these actors come to seek the wholesale transformation of the social order. Communities become *subjects* – that is, collective social actors through which individuals gain a holistic understanding of their situation and their experiences. He sees these project identities as growing out of resistance identities rather than the more traditional legitimizing identities.

For Castells, therefore, the world is not moving towards a single global culture, but the reverse. The response to the increasing social inequality and processes of exclusion arising from the network society is the formation of cultural communes that build walls around themselves not only against the dominant societal order but also against other communes. Thus, feminist and sexual liberation movements stand adamantly opposed to religious fundamentalists, global criminal gangs, armed xenophobic patriots or global terrorist networks. And these battles take place not only on the ground but also in cyberspace, where these communes make full use of digital technologies and the internet to build collective identities.

At the end of his trilogy, Castells does not identify a way forward. He observes that whenever an intellectual has tried to answer the question

'What is to be done?', it has ended in a human catastrophe. He believes that the information communication revolution has unleashed unprecedented capacity of the human mind. He sees the potential of the network society to build protocols of communication between different cultures not in the pursuit of shared values but of communication itself. Such communication protocols, in turn, might lead to allaying ancestral fears of the other and thus a sharing of a diverse world. He is sanguine in these thoughts, however, because he understands better than most the obstacles that lie in the way of such communication.

Major globalization writings

Castells, M. (2000a) *The Rise of the Network Society*, 2nd edition, Oxford, UK: Blackwell.

——(2000b) *The End of Millennium*, 2nd edition, Oxford, UK: Blackwell.

——(2001) *The Internet Galaxy: Reflections on the Internet, Business and Society*, Oxford, UK: Oxford University Press.

——(2003) *The Power of Identity*, 2nd edition, Oxford, UK: Blackwell.

——(2004) 'Informationalism, networks, and the network society: a theoretical blueprint', in M. Castells (ed.) *The Network Society: A Cross-cultural Perspective*, Cheltenham, UK: Edward Elgar.

Further reading

Castells, M. and Ince, M. (2003) *Conversations with Manuel Castells*, Cambridge, UK: Polity Press.

See also: **Amin, Arrighi, Bauman, Brenner, Cerny, Cox, Dirlik, Escobar, Helleiner, Sen**.

PHILIP G. CERNY (1946–)

Philip G. Cerny is Professor Emeritus of Politics and Global Affairs at the University of Manchester, UK, and Rutgers University, US. He studied at Kenyon College in Ohio and the Institut d'Études Politiques in Paris, and holds a Ph.D. from the University of Manchester. He also taught at the Universities of York and Leeds, UK, and held visiting positions at Harvard University, Dartmouth College and New York University. His initial research focus was French politics, but he gradually expanded his research into the field of international relations, most notably global political economy. Here he developed considerable expertise in the area of global finance. His interest in globalization began during the early 1990s, when he observed important changes in the role of the state. Over time, he has explored the governance issues arising from globalization more broadly.

Globalization

In defining globalization, Cerny warns against simplistic views that postulate about movement towards a borderless world or the decline of the state. Drawing on his expertise in global political economy, he observes the growing expansion and multi-layering of markets in ways that transform the *international* economy into a *global* one. The international economy is seen to be made up of holistic national economies interacting on the basis of *national* competitive advantages (Cerny 2010: 32). In the global economy, competitive advantages can be manipulated in ways that are not so dependent upon the nation-state but more open to a wide range of pressures. Economic actors come to see globalization as a set of opportunities at diverse scales from local craft-style industries to global finance with its highly integrated financial markets. What is significant about economic globalization, then, is that there is a profusion of market activities at various scales in company with a much bigger global playing field. None of these new markets is necessarily coterminous with the territorial boundaries of the nation-state.

Socially, globalization encompasses a breaking down of the often rather weak cultural identities nurtured and shaped by nation-states. Cerny argues that the isomorphism between state boundaries and identities has been a short-lived phenomenon confined to the past 150 years and characteristic of some but far from all nation-states. With globalization, the world is returning to a former situation of cross-cutting multiple identities and loyalties. Ethnic groups, religious communities and ever-expanding diaspora groups such as the overseas Chinese construct new and strong identities. These are associated with collectivities that form at scales above or below nation-state boundaries. At the same time, Cerny sees the development of an embryonic transnational class structure, particularly for the wealthy and the powerful (see also **Amin, Ong**).

Finally, political globalization takes the form of fundamental shifts in the organizational goals and institutional processes found in nation-states themselves. In the early 1990s, Cerny coined the term 'competition state' to capture these types of changes. Economic globalization, particularly the emergence of fully global markets, especially in finance, meant that states had less and less capacity to control, stabilize and regulate the national economy. In losing these capacities, states had more difficulty in supplying public goods, particularly productive and distributive ones. Without these capacities, it was more difficult for states to maintain and support the various social and educational policies that were central to the social welfare state.

The decline of these capacities, however, does not mean that the state is withering away. To the contrary, the state becomes more active by pursuing increased marketization of activities, including social ones, in order to make economic activities located within the national territory more 'competitive' in international arenas and markets. Thus, the competition state concerns itself with human capital (having a workforce with the skills, education and training needed for global competition), infrastructure, a critical mass of research and development activities, basic public services to support a good quality of life for those professionals who might be globally mobile, and a policy environment favourable to global investment (Cerny 1995, 1997) (see also **Ong**).

According to Cerny, these changes in the role of the state arising from economic and political globalization contribute to an erosion of democracy. Liberal democracy had been constructed upon the assumption that the underlying society to be governed was a 'national society' and that the democratic state was the expression of that society (Cerny 1999). To the extent to which the state is forced to shift away from providing social welfare goods for that society, the exercise of these new roles undermines that 'national society'. When these changes are complemented by the social and cultural changes that come from the information and communication technologies of the contemporary era, the sense of a national identity and a commitment to social solidarity so central to democracy are also undermined. In Cerny's view, there is little likelihood that liberal democracy can transfer easily to the new global order (see **Scholte**). In short, globalization is not kind to democracy (for a more optimistic outlook, see **Held**).

Global politics and policy

With this understanding of complex globalizing processes and of their implications for longstanding conceptions of the role of the state in hand, Cerny expanded his research to focus on what he terms the 'pluralization of world politics'. In doing so, he makes the important point that globalization also constitutes a *discourse*. As such, it alters the ideas and perceptions that people have of the world around them, including some of the very categories we have just been discussing, such as the state. Consequently, 'the very idea of globalization leads people to seek out and try to adopt both intellectual and real-world strategies and tactics that, in turn, may restructure the game itself around a different government rationality' (Cerny 2010: 27). He terms this new rationality *raison du monde*, one that contrasts with the dominant *raison d'état* of the previous 150 years. The latter gave meaning to the building and expanding of the role of the state. In contrast, *raison du monde* propels states, along with other actors, to promote globalization and global competition.

With a rationality focused on the world as a whole, states are joined by new non-state actors in political processes operating on a global scale. Cerny suggests the concept of pluralism as a starting point for understanding such processes. Pluralism had been a theory most widely used by political scientists in the analysis of political outcomes in the US: organized groups representing 'interests' seek to gain influence and power by bargaining, competing with other groups, and building coalitions among themselves and state actors. In this political environment, outcomes are not predetermined – there are multiple equilibria. Which equilibrium emerges will depend upon the results of the bargaining, competing and coalition-building by the various groups. Moreover, the power dynamics vary from one issue area to another as a result of the constellations and capacities of the groups involved.

Cerny's central hypothesis, then, is that global political processes are best understood as ones of 'transnational neopluralism'. The actors most likely to be successful at influencing and shaping policy outcomes will be those who (a) perceive and define their goals, interests and values in international, transnational and trans-local contexts; (b) are able to build cross-border networks, coalitions and power bases among a range of potential allies and adversaries; and (c) are able to coordinate and organize their strategic action on a range of international, transnational, and trans-local scales in such a way as to pursue transnational policy agendas (2010: 106). Cerny emphasizes, therefore, that globalization grows out of complexity and creates further complexity by opening up widening numbers of international and transnational policy spaces, where a form of pluralist politics takes hold: 'World politics is consequently being transformed into a polycentric or multinucleated global political system, operating within an increasingly continuous geographical space and/or set of overlapping spaces' (2010: 98).

Characteristic of the new form of world politics, the determinants of political power are no longer vertical and channelled exclusively through states. Rather, the organization of power is increasingly horizontally stratified according to issue area. It is structured through economic and social linkages across borders, and thus less amenable to control and centralization by states. Concepts such as 'denationalization of the state' (**Sassen**) or 'polycentrism' (**Scholte**) also seek to capture these kinds of changes. In this environment, notions of 'publicness' or the division of public versus private in state-led politics are undermined. Entering into the discourse are concepts such as private authority or the privatization of governance. 'New architectures' are required to recreate public spheres through more complex network structures operating on a global scale.

In seeking to develop theoretical concepts that might help with understanding global policy-making, Cerny returns to domestic policy analysis and selects the notion of 'iron triangles'. Political scientists developed this concept initially for explaining policy outcomes in the US political system, but it has been adapted and used in policy analysis of many other Organization for Economic Cooperation and Development (OECD) countries as well. Growing out of the concept were other ones such as issue networks, policy networks and policy communities. What analysts of public policy had observed was that relatively narrow communities of actors, some in government and some outside government in civil society, came together in regularized patterns, often sharing common professional backgrounds, to develop and put into effect public policies. A common type of 'iron triangle' in US politics might be comprised by politicians serving on narrowly focused congressional committees, public servants with expertise in the area working in the executive branch, and well-organized interest groups with their own particular knowledge and expertise in the field.

Cerny suggests the notion of *flexible pentangles* for understanding and studying contemporary global policy processes. The first three categories of actors in these arrangements are those from the older concept: domestically based politicians, bureaucratic officials and organized interest groups. These actors, however, no longer confine their activities to the domestic policy scene. Since most areas of national policy-making are now shaped by international, transnational and trans-local dynamics, these actors belong to networks that operate on a wider, usually global, scale. Joining these actors are organizations and their representatives from the *transnational public sector*. Examples would be officials working for institutions such as the World Health Organization (WHO), the World Bank, various United Nations organizations such as the United Nations Children's Fund (UNICEF), and so on. The fifth side of the pentangles draws actors from what Cerny terms the *international private sector*, which includes transnational corporations, transnational social movements and issue networks constituted on a global scale through digital technologies.

Cerny concludes that globalizing the policy process:

[...] involves the continual and growing interaction of both old and new elements of the political opportunity structure, giving political entrepreneurs considerable scope to shape that evolution. It strengthens the hand of transnationally linked interests and actors and shifts the balance of agenda setting, policy bargaining, and policy outcomes toward globalizing coalitions and protocoalitions.

(Cerny 2010: 127)

Major globalization writings

Cerny, P. (1990) *The Changing Architecture of Politics: Structure, Agency, and the Future of the State*, London: Sage.

——(1993) (ed.) *Finance and World Politics: Markets, Regimes and States in the Post-hegemonic Era*, Aldershot, UK: Edward Elgar.

——(1995) 'Globalization and the changing logic of collective action', *International Organization*, vol 49, no 4, pp. 595–625.

——(1997) 'Paradoxes of the competition state: the dynamics of political globalization', *Government and Opposition*, vol 32, no 2, pp. 251–274.

——(1999) 'Globalization and the erosion of democracy', *European Journal of Political Research*, vol 36, no 1, pp. 1–29.

——(2010) *Rethinking World Politics: A Theory of Transnational Neopluralism*, New York, NY: Oxford University Press.

Cerny, P., Menz, G. and Soederberg, S. (2005) 'Different roads to globalization: neoliberalism, the competition state, and politics in a more open world', in S. Soederberg, G. Menz and P. Cerny (eds) *Internalizing Globalization: The Rise of Neoliberalism and the Decline of National Varieties of Capitalism*, New York, NY: Palgrave Macmillan.

See also: **Amin, Held, Ong, Sassen, Scholte.**

DIPESH CHAKRABARTY

An India-born Bengali historian, Dipesh Chakrabarty completed part of his education in India before embarking on a Ph.D. in history at the Australian National University. After completing his doctoral degree in 1984, he held various teaching and research positions in Australia, the US, Europe and India. He is currently the Lawrence A. Kimpton Distinguished Service Professor, Department of History and Department of South Asian Languages and Civilizations, at the University of Chicago, US.

An expert in modern South Asian history, Chakrabarty has been a longstanding member of the Subaltern Studies group. The group's preoccupation has been the investigation of postcolonial modernity in South Asia (and beyond) from the perspectives of the subalterns – those marginalized and oppressed groups whose voices are not included in national historiographies. This preoccupation is reflected in Chakrabarty's first book, *Rethinking Working Class History*, published in 1989. Here he exposes the Eurocentric limits of Marxist theories of the working class by examining them through the prism of Bengali modernity, which did not comprise a liberal heritage or a structure of bourgeois hegemony. His relentless examination of such limits has produced insightful reconsiderations of the discipline of history and of the confines of its Eurocentric parameters (Chakrabarty 2000a, 2000b, 2002, 2006a); of the globalization of knowledge and its impact upon democratic practices in post-colonial societies (2003, 2005, 2006b); and of humanism and the concept of the human in an age of globalization (2009a, 2009b). Currently, he is developing a project that reflects on the debates surrounding climate change and on how they affect our understanding of global history (2009a).

The limits of global modernity and its postcolonial encounters

Chakrabarty's interest in global modernity informs two of his most important books, *Provincializing Europe* (2000a) and *Habitations of Modernity* (2002), as well as a series of other publications. He understands global modernity to entail the worldwide dissemination of European categories such as the nation-state, citizenship, civil society and democracy (see also **Beck**, **Dirlik**, **Giddens**, **Mignolo**). We might say, then, that these categories have themselves been globalized. Although he appreciates the usefulness of such political categories and their central role in modern social critiques of injustice and inequality, he is also persuaded that they are inadequate for capturing the complex transformations of postcolonial societies. Thus, he posits that Europe 'is both indispensable and inadequate in helping us think through the various life practices that constitute the political and the historical in India' (Chakrabarty 2000a: 6). Central to this ambivalent relationship with Europe is his critique of historicism. He defines historicism as the perception of the inevitability of the global dissemination 'over time' of European modernity and capitalism (Chakrabarty 2000a: 7, 30–34; see also Chakrabarty 2003: 129). Such an emphasis on inevitability entails a *telos*, a final destination point when the whole world becomes modern in the image of the West (see also **Mignolo**).

The trouble with historicism, claims Chakrabarty, is that it gave birth to a developmental vision of the world outside of the West. This vision placed non-Western societies in the 'waiting room' of history (Chakrabarty 2000a, 2002) until they reach the appropriate stage of development that allows them to be *fully* modern. However, the limits of historicism and of the developmental vision that attends it are clear when one pays attention to the mobilization of groups that have been considered pre-modern and pre-political by traditional social science, such as peasants and *dalits* (untouchables). In his view, subaltern groups' political struggles in colonial and postcolonial India constitute a paradigmatic example of the postcolonial practices of political modernity. The reality of such struggles denies the 'waiting room' version of history, which states that groups such as peasants have to wait to be educated before qualifying for the modern status of 'bourgeois citizen'.

Such a critique is levelled not only at the Eurocentric assumptions of contemporary social science, but also at the 'hyperrationalism' of Indian historians who refuse to transcend these narrow parameters. In Chakrabarty's estimation, they reproduce the development-focused and historicist vision of Indian society by working with an opposition of reason versus emotion, which constructs Indian religious views as irrational and pre-modern and European thought as rational and progressive (Chakrabarty 2002: 24–25). Such an oppositional stance obscures the hybridities that resulted in the postcolonial world (and in Europe itself) from the encounters between science/rationalism, on the one side, and religion/faith, on the other (2002: 28). Furthermore, such an opposition also leads to a more serious obfuscation, which is that of modern colonialism being the fundamental historical condition through which global capital inserted itself in non-Western societies (2002: 13; see also **Mignolo, Spivak**). Following Ranajit Guha in his rejection of the category of the *pre-political*, Chakrabarty claims that an emphasis on the differential trajectories of power in Europe and in the colonies 'pluralizes the history of power in global modernity and separates it from any universal history of capital' (2002: 12). We thus infer that his conceptualization of globalization is inseparable from an understanding of the global processes of colonialism.

Chakrabarty's long-term project of exploring the limits and manifestations of global modernity has significant consequences for any reconsideration of the discipline of history. His analysis is not simply a critique of European political categories and of the discipline of history. Rather, he brings the notion of 'historical difference' to bear on how we conceptualize the globalization of political modernity. 'Historical difference' exposes the gap between nationalist historiography and the *translation* of European modernity into colonial life worlds. The former renders non-Western histories as 'yet another episode in the universal [...] march of citizenship, nation-state, and of the themes of human emancipation' engendered by the Enlightenment (Chakrabarty 2000a: 39). The latter constitutes global modernity as a hybridized sphere where political modernity interacts and coexists with the non-modern and the anti-historical.

Minority histories and the globalization of democratic practices

Chakrabarty's interest in the dynamics of global modernity prompts him to probe the issue of minority histories. More specifically, building on his previous work on peasants as political figures of (post)colonial modernity, Chakrabarty investigates the imaginative political struggles of 'marginal and traditionally-oppressed classes in an age of cultural globalization' (Chakrabarty 2006b: 235) (see also **Appadurai, Roy, Santos, Spivak**). He is particularly intrigued by what he calls 'the globalization of the word "indigenous"', both through UN-based resolutions that allow various groups to make claims to indigenous status and thus to special protection, and through grounded mobilizations of various tribal communities (2006b: 237) (see also **Tsing**). Chakrabarty focuses on the example of India's *adivasi* (tribal) communities to illustrate that 'the global language for claiming indigenous status' has allowed tribal communities to emerge as '*global* subjects and not as *national* citizens' and thus to form transnational solidarity bonds with other groups (Amita Baviskar quoted in Chakrabarty 2006b: 239, 241; see also Chakrabarty 2003, 2006a).

The focus on minority histories in an age of globalization has prompted him to reflect on the impact of forms of 'mass democracy' upon knowledge practices as produced by academia (see also **Appadurai, Santos**). In contemplating political mobilizations by marginal groups around the world, Chakrabarty sees the beginnings of a 'vision [...] of a modern and democratic politics' that contests the linear and self-enclosed character of academic disciplines (Chakrabarty 2003: 140). The reality of India's *dalits* and *adivasis* mobilizing under the global banner of 'race' to contest their marginalization and discrimination flaunts academic definitions of authentic indigeneity. He calls such political tactics 'politics of the multitude' (see **Hardt and Negri**), which contest neatly organized categories such as nation, race, class and gender, and produce more fluid and more empowering political identities (see also Chakrabarty 2005, 2006a).

Humanism in a global world

Aligned with his attention to minority histories is a concern for postcoloniality as a global condition. Such a condition generated various and conflicting formulations of 'anti-colonial humanism', which attempted to negotiate cultural difference and the violence of the colonial encounter (Chakrabarty 2005, 2009b). Chakrabarty thus reflects on types of universalisms that can be articulated out of the postcolonial condition. He suggests that anti-colonial theorists such as Aimé Césaire and Léopold Senghor helped to formulate a new type of the universal – one which does not erase its rootedness in historical specificity but rather depends upon it (2009b: 35). Thus, he does not perceive cultural globalization processes to entail a necessary homogenization of differences and particularities. Rather, by paying attention to postcolonial articulations of hybridized identities, he sees emerging new forms of universalisms that maintain their roots in historical and cultural locales (see also **Mignolo, Tsing**).

Recently, Chakrabarty has turned his attention to the debates surrounding climate change. He raises the following question: how does the climate change crisis help us to foster a sense of 'human universals' while at the same time altering our perception of global history (Chakrabarty 2009a: 201)? His insightful and thought-provoking analysis indicates that such a crisis faces us in two different perceptions of global historical time that are in tension with each other: the planetary and the global (2009a: 213). The former points to a 'deep history' of the planet that precedes the time of humanity; the latter refers to a 'recorded history' that is intimately linked to the movement of capital. Furthermore, the crisis has prompted a reconsideration of our human condition from biological agents to 'geological agents' who are capable of large-scale planetary transformations (2009a: 206–207).

Major globalization writings

Chakrabarty, D. (1989) *Rethinking Working Class History: Bengal 1890–1940*, Princeton, NJ: Princeton University Press.

——(2000a) *Provincializing Europe: Postcolonial Thought and Historical Difference*, Princeton, NJ: Princeton University Press.

——(2000b) 'Universalism and belonging in the logic of capital', *Public Culture*, vol 12, no 3, pp. 653–678.

——(2002) *Habitations of Modernity: Essays in the Wake of Subaltern Studies*, Chicago, IL: University of Chicago Press.

——(2003) 'Globalisation, democratisation and the evacuation of history?', in J. Assayag and V. Bénéï (eds) *At Home in the Diaspora: South Asian Scholars and the West*, Bloomington and Indianapolis, IN: Indiana University Press.

——(2005) 'Legacies of Bandung: decolonisation and the politics of culture', *Economic and Political Weekly*, vol 40, no 46, pp. 4812–4818.

——(2006a) 'A global and multicultural "discipline" of history?', *History and Theory*, vol 45, no 1, pp. 101–109.

——(2006b) 'Politics unlimited: the global *adivasi* and the debate about the political', in B. G. Karlsson and T. B. Subba (eds) *Indigeneity in India*, London, New York, NY, and Bahrain: Kegan Paul.

——(2009a) 'The climate of history: four theses', *Critical Inquiry*, vol 35, no 2, pp. 197–222.

——(2009b) 'Humanism in a global world', in J. Rüsen and H. Lass (eds) *Humanism in Intercultural Perspective: Experiences and Expectations*, Bielefeld: Transcript Verlag.

Further reading

(2000) Chakrabarty, D., Breckenridge, C. A., Pollock, S. and Bhabha, H. K. (eds) *Cosmopolitanism*, Durham, NC: Duke University Press.

See also: **Appadurai, Dirlik, Giddens, Hardt and Negri, Mignolo, Roy, Santos, Spivak, Tsing.**

REY CHOW

Rey Chow grew up in British Hong Kong during the 1960s and 1970s. She characterizes herself as 'probably one of the few "postcolonial" intellectuals working in the North American humanities academy today who can lay claim to having been subjected to a genuinely classic colonial education' (Chow 1998: 161). Her personal experience of colonialism and her unique background (she was born into a Muslim Chinese family) have left an imprint on the way in which she conceptualizes difference and otherness, key themes crucial to understanding contemporary aspects of culture and globalization. Her most significant publications, among which are *Woman and Chinese Modernity* (1991), *Writing Diaspora* (1993), *Primitive Passions* (1995), *The Protestant Ethnic and the Spirit of Capitalism* (2002) and *Sentimental Fabulations* (2007), help us to understand cultural globalizing process by delving into issues pertaining to twentieth-century Chinese literary texts, postcolonial studies, interdisciplinary analyses of film, and cultural and critical theory. Modelling, in exemplary fashion, the conduct of interdisciplinary research, and tracing the global in imaginative and thought-provoking ways and in unconventional locations, it is not surprising that Rey Chow's work has been extensively anthologized and translated into various European and Asian languages. Rey Chow is currently Anne Firor Scott Professor of Literature at Duke University, US.

Chow adopts an uncompromising attitude towards globalization, which she sees as 'Western imperialism [that] has been about aggression and eliminating others' existence so that the empire can expand and enhance its own interests' (Chow 2001: 69). From the perspective of 'colonized subjects', globalization has amounted to, more often than not, exclusion and subordination (2001: 69). Rey Chow's engagement with the various faces, traces and practices of the global is infused with a meticulous concern about nuances and layers. Chow's deeply textured analyses of four themes that reiterate throughout her work – lost origins and modernity, woman and modernity, diaspora, and visuality – are crucial to understanding contemporary cultural processes of globalization.

Lost origins and global modernity

In several of her writings, Chow deals with the link between an eminently *modern* obsession with primitivism, and with authenticity, nativism and the construction of our understanding of modern subjectivity. The importance of this insight for understanding globalization becomes clearer when this modern obsession is regarded as a global practice inflected by class, race and gender signifiers (see also **McClintock**). These signifiers, in turn, have powerful political implications for the ways in which we conceive key cultural practices in contemporary globalizing times: those of cultural translation and representation. In particular, evocations of the figure of the 'native', whether they come from anthropology, cultural studies, geography, history, literary studies, sociology or indigenous studies, serve to redeem the colonial defilement of indigenous/local cultures and realities strategically, and to rescue their authenticity. Such narratives undoubtedly perform a work of memory; but their evocation of the past/present converges around the figure of the 'native' through practices of sanctifying and/or exoticizing the 'native'. These practices speak about a desire to take possession of an authentic experience long lost in a globalized and (post)modernized world, and tend to claim authenticity through the purified image of the 'native'. Chow enquires, in *Writing Diaspora*, into the source of this search for lost origins and for authenticity:

> Why are we so fascinated with 'history' and with the 'native' in 'modern' times? What do we gain from our labour on these 'endangered authenticities' which are presumed to be from a different time and a different place? What can be said about the juxtaposition of 'us' (our discourse) and 'them'? What kind of *surplus value* is created by this juxtaposition?
>
> (Chow 1993: 42; emphasis in the original)

Mediating 'endangered authenticities' constitutes a class- and power-ridden practice. Practices of mediation involve 'first word' and 'third world' intellectuals and activists who assume the mission to retrieve the 'native's' long-lost authenticity from the turmoil of modernization, colonial/imperial and globalizing processes. Chow uses the term 'native' to refer to a state of subalternity, oppression and marginality, to which certain categories of people are assigned (see Chow 1993: 30). Thus, rescuing 'endangered authenticities' is never an innocent practice. Chow points to how categories such as 'the people', 'the real people', 'the populace', 'the peasants', 'the poor' and 'the homeless' function as *signifiers* which 'gesture towards another place [...] that is "authentic" but that cannot be admitted into the circuit of exchange' (1993: 118). Within the context of modernization and globalization, Chow's focus on representations of 'natives' indicates how 'Our fascination with the native, the oppressed, the savage, and all such figures is therefore a desire to hold on to an unchanging certainty somewhere outside our "fake" experience' (1993: 53).

Chow remarks that 'first word' and 'third world' intellectuals seem to constantly attempt to salvage the other as the site of authenticity and true knowledge. In this global era, retrieving the 'native's' voice and subjectivity speaks more about a desire to 'seek security and order in an amorphous [post]modern society' than about a 'genuine' attempt to *see* others and listen to their voices (1993: 52). Such a desire for viewing/seeing the subjects of research as sites of endangered authenticity speaks also about a desire to seize control (see **Mignolo, Santos**).

Chow is thus keen to point out that the practice of exoticizing the oppressed, the marginal, the silent, the everyday man and woman characterizes the formation of cultural production *within a culture* as much as it characterizes the 'writing between cultures', such as orientalism. What is significant about Chow's analysis is the paradoxical manner through which the 'primitive' is located within the discourse of modernity; thus, globalization both as 'culture' (as national identity) and 'nature' (as lost origins) is 'caught between the forces of "first world" imperialism and "third world" nationalism' (1995: 23).

Woman, modernity and globalization

Rey Chow's research has also explored the production of woman as otherness in various discourses and practices, including those pertaining to visuality, diaspora, capitalism and primitivism/nativism. In a critique of the idealism of 'first world' feminists with regards to 'third world' women's oppression, Chow engages, at the same time, in a critical review of postmodernism's tendency to homogenize difference and automatize it into what she describes as a 'postmodern automaton'. Her contention is that 'first world' feminist analyses of women's condition in the 'third world', while subversive of a certain hegemonic masculinity, operate nonetheless with an 'oppressive discursive prowess of the "first world"' (Chow 1993: 67). In this respect, these analyses are consistent with her view of globalization amounting to exclusion and subordination. Her specific concern lies with the manner in which 'first world' feminism disregards the 'local' or 'locality' as a space of *coalitional* politics (1993: 70–71) – a concern of other authors studied in this book, notably **Escobar**. This coalitional politics concretely implies that:

> The task that faces 'third world' feminists is thus not simply that of 'animating' the oppressed women of their cultures but of making the automatized and animated condition of their own voices the conscious point of departure in their intervention.
>
> (Chow 1993: 68)

What Chow is arguing for here is not only the necessity for cross-cultural dialogue, but also for an understanding of how 'third world' feminists' employment of 'the victimhood of women and "third world" cultures is both symptomatic of and inevitably complicitous with the "first world"' (cf. **Shiva**). Ultimately, Chow contends, women's struggle against oppression cannot and should not be disentangled from other forms of struggle against oppression. The 'local' or 'locality' is a space imbued with difference, and woman as otherness is ineluctably woven into multiple productions of otherness, both within and across locality. Challenging globalization thus must begin with action at local places (see also **Dirlik, Escobar**).

Her analysis of woman as a socially oppressed, primitivized other in a modernizing China at the turn of the century illustrates this last point. Exploring visual discourses (cinema, in particular) produced during that time, Chow remarks on the fetishized character of feminine portraits who serve as the connecting points between 'the super-stitious practices of "primitive" cultures' and 'the harsh realities of modernized metropolises' (Chow 1995: 26). Furthermore, when it comes to the production of ethnicity in an age of global capitalism, Chow points to women as 'the most palpable ethnics in the capitalist workforce' (Chow 2002: 34). Woman as otherness is thus produced in and enmeshed within various practices, whether visual, diasporic, modernist or capitalist. Chow's method of investigating marginality and exclusion in an age of global capital, or 'global instrumentalism' as she puts it, is to perceive the various categories of marginal and excluded others in complex and textured interactions. For her, the excluded or the oppressed person's consciousness is inseparable from her reified and commodified existence. To the question 'What can be known of the feminized "object"?', Chow replies that this feminized 'object' is a *social* object, which is 'by nature "ridden with error"', and thus amenable to a critique from within that aims at exposing 'the *social* sources of its formation' (Chow 1993: 66).

Diaspora

Diasporas have become central sites of investigation of cultural globaliz-ations. Writing against a prevalent celebration of 'minority discourse' in diasporas, Chow constructs her position vis-à-vis diasporic practices of identity. She concentrates on the unequal relations, particularly as they bear upon women, operating within societies that are produced and performed in diaspora. She notes that the diasporic male intellec-tual's strategy of identification shifts according to his location: 'They [diasporic Chinese intellectuals] are minors and women when faced with "foreigners"; they are fathers when faced with "insiders", especially women' (Chow 1993: 110). Such a shifting identification exposes the power relations embedded in the discourses of diasporic intellectuals; they subsume women's oppression and subjugation under the 'creation of alternative *official minor positions*' (1993: 111; emphasis in the original). Such positions always imply the construction of oppositional pairs such as tradition/modernity, China/West, China/Japan, communists/nationalists, feudal lords/the people, rich/poor, global/local, which evoke a kind of marginality that inevitably places more value on the centre.

Rey Chow thus warns against the lures of diaspora as a space of unquestioned marginality and subversiveness. Rather, she sees it as a space where the physical alienation under globalization of the diasporic intellectual can and, indeed, many times does intensify the 'aestheticization of the values of "minority" positions' (1993: 118). By 'aestheticization' she means that 'the older visuality [of Chinese culture] is increasingly associated with "*origins*", with notions of the *past*, the *ancient*, and the *lost*' (Chow 1995: 36; emphasis in original). Thus, the lures of diaspora for globalization scholars focusing on culture is a propensity towards a nostalgia for lost origins that effectively conceals the hegemony of the 'third world' intellectuals 'over those who are stuck at home' (1995: 36).

Intimately connected to the notion of diasporic subversiveness of the 'minority' position is her understanding of ethnicity. Chow sees ethnic struggles in an age of global capital not only as signs of emancipation and freedom from oppression, but most importantly as 'an indisputable symptom of the thoroughly and irrevocably mediatized relations of capitalism and its biopolitics' (Chow 2002: 48). Thus to protest, from Chow's perspective, is to be implicated in the commodified relations of global capital, to follow an economic logic that ensures the 'protesting ethnic' the best visibility, worldwide publicity and circulation (2002: 48). She argues that in an age of globalization, ethnic struggles and diasporic 'minority discourse' need to be perceived in their textured complicities with global capital, relations of commodification and local patriarchal hegemonies, among others. After all, as she remarks: 'Resistance and protest [...] are part and parcel of the structure of capitalism; they are the reasons capitalism flourishes' (2002: 47).

Visuality or 'global visibility'

Scholars of contemporary cultural globalization such as **Appadurai**, **Castells** and **Tomlinson** point to the importance of digital technologies and mass media in distinguishing the present period from earlier globalizing eras. Rey Chow's entry into this discussion involves explorations of 'global visibility', perhaps her most fertile and innovative area of research. Her analytical focus on the image does not rely on a linear interpretation of cinematic discourses as mere allegories of 'the lives and histories of "real" cultural groups' (Chow 2007: 12). Rather, she is interested in the productive character of the image itself, and of the ways in which the visual has become a global space where the 'condition of visibility in general' can be produced and performed (2007: 11). For example, she wonders whether it would not be more helpful to conceive of Asianness as 'a commodified and reproducible value', rather than as some authentic experience lying beyond the superficial realm of the visual. This commodified value is sustained and made possible by the global flows of capital; it is also part of something more – namely, of 'a contemporary global problematic of becoming visible' (2007: 12–13).

Chow defines 'global visibility' as a contemporary phenomenon of late capitalism characterized by 'mediatized spectacularization' whereby various groups are engaged in continuous self-production and self-consumption for the purposes of social recognition and visibility. Her theory of becoming visible in an age of global flows rests on the notion that becoming visible is no longer about being seen or perceived as an image, in a visual sense. Rather, it is also about 'participating in a discursive politics of (re)configuring the relation between centre and margins, a politics in which what is visible may be a key but not the exclusive determinant' (2007: 11). Put differently, becoming visible in the global era is also about who and what cannot be seen, and about the ways in which this absence is performed in the realm of the visual. More specifically, she suggests conceiving of 'film as ethnography' because it would allow for a rethinking of 'East' and 'West' that goes beyond retrieving origins. Such a theorization would seek to dismantle '*both* the notion of origin and the notion of alterity' (Chow 1995: 194, emphasis in the original). For example, 'Asianness' translated into visual discourse need not be conceived as the fake copy or the imperfect representation of the original. Rather, it can be seen as 'that "novel anthropology" in which the "object" recorded is no longer simply the "third world" but "the West itself as mirrored in the eyes and handiwork of its others"' (Michael Taussig quoted in Chow 1995: 202).

Major globalization writings

Chow, R. (1991) *Woman and Chinese Modernity: The Politics of Reading between East and West*, Minneapolis, MN: University of Minnesota Press.

——(1993) *Writing Diaspora: Tactics of Intervention in Contemporary Cultural Studies*, Bloomington and Indianapolis, IN: Indiana University Press.

——(1995) *Primitive Passions: Visuality, Sexuality, Ethnography, and Contemporary Chinese Cinema*, New York, NY: Columbia University Press.

——(1998) 'The postcolonial difference: lessons in cultural legitimation', *Postcolonial Studies*, vol 1, no 2, pp. 161–169.

——(2001) 'How (the) inscrutable Chinese led to globalized theory', *PMLA*, vol 116, no 1, pp. 69–74.

——(2002) *The Protestant Ethnic and the Spirit of Capitalism*, New York, NY: Columbia University Press.

——(2006) *The Age of the World Target: Self-referentiality in War, Theory and Comparative Work*, Durham, NC: Duke University Press.

——(2007) *Sentimental Fabulations, Contemporary Chinese Films: Attachment in the Age of Global Visibility*, New York, NY: Columbia University Press.

See also: **Appadurai**, **Dirlik**, **Escobar**, **McClintock**, **Santos**, **Shiva**, **Tomlinson**.

JOHN COMAROFF AND JEAN COMAROFF

Jean and John Comaroff grew up in South Africa and received their Bachelor's degrees from the University of Cape Town in 1968 and 1966, respectively. They subsequently moved to the UK where they pursued doctoral degrees at the London School of economics, obtaining their Ph.D. degrees in 1974 and 1973, respectively. Soon after, they joined the Department of Anthropology at the University of Chicago, where they currently work as distinguished professors of anthropology and social sciences. They have published both independently and collaboratively on topics such as colonialism and postcoloniality in Africa, modernity, capitalism and neoliberalism. We focus here on their collaborative research.

Their main contribution to globalization studies lies in their joint research on 'the making of local worlds in the wake of global "modernity" and commodification' (see http://anthropology.uchicago.edu/people/faculty_member/jean_comaroff). More specifically, over the years, they have examined the social, cultural and political effects of neoliberal globalization on postcolonial societies (with an emphasis on Africa), and the contradictory, paradoxical and unequal character such effects have had on these societies. We focus on two major themes emerging from their joint collaboration: their theorization of 'millennial capitalism' and their analysis of the emergence of the Global South. They characterize the latter as the 'new frontier' space of the 'globally competitive capital' where 'radically new assemblages of capital and labor are taking place, thus [...] prefigure[ing] the future of the global north' (Comaroff and Comaroff 2012: 13).

Millennial capitalism: social and cultural effects of neoliberal globalization

In employing the phrase 'millennial capitalism', Jean and John Comaroff seek to explore two dynamics of global capitalism: its mutations and transformations at the millennium (as the twentieth century ended and the next century began), and capitalism 'as a gospel of salvation' – that is, its 'messianic, salvific, even magical manifestations' in our contemporary world (Comaroff and Comaroff 2001: 2). More specifically, they are interested in examining the correlation between such manifestations and significant shifts in our social world. These changes include the increasing relevance of consumerism and its impact upon identity processes; the waning of 'modernist categories' such as social class; global crises of 'reproduction and community, youth and masculinity'; and the increasing salience of 'generation, race, and gender as principles of difference, identity, and mobilization' (2001: 2). In light of such shifts, they discern three major repercussions on our global world: the transformation of the nation-state (see also Comaroff and Comaroff 2000, 2006, 2012) (cf. **Brenner, Cerny)**; the rise of 'new occult economies' and new religious movements (see Comaroff and Comaroff 2001, 2006, 2012); and the influence of neoliberal discourses on practices of civil society.

Jean and John Comaroff describe consumerism as a constant pre-occupation with material accumulation, fostered by governments and commercial interests especially after World War II (Comaroff and Comaroff 2001: 4). They find that consumption plays a crucial role in contemporary processes of identity formation, and it constitutes one of the prime engines for the emergence of a global neoliberal capitalism (2001: 4). Moreover, as consumption acquires increasing salience, the value of production declines. The secure linkage between workplace and labour, firmly 'rooted in a stable local context', disappears and thus no longer shapes the production of identities (2001: 4). Contemporary capitalism has rendered labour employment much more flexible, particularly as the speculative forms of finance capital have become more dominant in the world economy. The logic of gambling, of assuming more risk, has become as much an economic as a socio-cultural logic. In this context, we witness the popularization of risk-based economic activities, whereby average citizens routinely take up investing in 'stocks, bonds, and funds, whose fortunes are governed largely by chance' (2001: 5). Quoting the work of Susan **Strange** on 'casino capitalism', the authors indicate that the global economic system has become 'a gambling hall' (2001: 7) (see also **Hardt and Negri**). In this sense, precisely because of the increasing fluidity and instability of the global economic system, there has been a steady trend towards the financial economy gaining more and more 'autonomy from "real production"' (2001: 10) (see also **Arrighi, Cox, Harvey, Helleiner**). In these circumstances, capital becomes more and more autonomous from labour with important repercussions for the category of class in an age of neoliberal globalization (2001: 10).

The authors argue that the 'transnationalization of primary production', where the process of manufacturing has been integrated across various countries, has had profound implications for the continuing relevance of the category of class (2001: 12). While the national space was the relevant space for class formation, the 'global dispersal of manufacture is likely to fragment modernist forms of class consciousness [and] class alliance' (2001: 12). More to the point, while certain dynamics of class formation have been projected and replicated at a transnational level (see **Castells**, **Cerny**, **Cox**), the working class or proletarian consciousness has been deeply unsettled by processes of economic globalization (2001: 12). Thus, the authors point to the rise of a transnational capitalist class (see also **Beck**, **Ong**) even as the international contours of the proletariat are quickly vanishing (2001: 12).

This decline of the salience of class partly explains the increasing relevance of other social dimensions such as ethnicity, race, gender and generation as categories around which identity construction takes place. Jean and John Comaroff call this shift a 'boom in the identity economy' through which identity (especially ethnicity) is incorporated within circuits of commodification via the internet, the tourism industry and the media (Comaroff and Comaroff 2012: 18; see also Comaroff and Comaroff 2009). This explosion of identity politics has mixed effects; it can give birth to what has been called 'new social movements' and thus provide new avenues for civic and political mobilization (see also **Castells**). It can also be appropriated by the logic of the market and commodification (Comaroff and Comaroff 2001, 2009, 2012). Moreover, such new forms of collective identity can also lead to xenophobia and racism, when the processes of globalization trigger a reactionary backlash against migrants, refugees and foreigners (see **Appadurai**, **Sen**).

The emergence of the Global South as the new frontier

In their recent joint publication *Theory from the South*, Jean and John Comaroff note that the very shifts and transformations in social and political relations outlined above 'are disrupting received geographies of core and periphery, relocating southward – and of course, eastward as well – some of the most innovative and energetic modes of producing value' (Comaroff and Comaroff 2012: 7). Here, the authors advance two arguments. First, the type of modernity that emerged in Africa (and in other parts of the postcolonial world) is a *vernacular* modernity and, hence, not merely 'a derivative of the Euro-original'. Rather, it is shaped by its 'dialectical relationship with the global north' and with its capitalist expansionism, but also by its linkages with other locales (2012: 9, 19, 7) (see also **Appadurai, Chakrabarty**; for a different counterpoint, see **Dirlik**). Second, they challenge mainstream social science discourse that conceives of the Global South always trailing behind the North and thus in much need of catching up with the latter's developmental progress (2012: 12). The authors counter by arguing that precisely because of the unpredictable dialectic of capitalism and modernity, 'it is the south that often is first to feel the effects of world-historical forces, the south in which radically new assemblages of capital and labor are taking shape, thus to prefigure the future of the global north' (2012: 12).

One of the most significant consequences of this re-ordering of political geographies is the transformation of the role of the nation-state (see also **Brenner, Cerny**). The authors note that the claims to difference and particularism within the nation-state have given rise to 'policulturalism' – a process that entails the 'politicization of diversity' through claims to increased autonomy from the state and even to 'sovereignty against the state' (2012: 24). Citizens no longer see themselves as citizens '*of* the polity' but rather citizens '*in* it'. Accordingly, they no longer claim the national community as their ultimate space for identity construction (2012: 24, 65–89) (see also **Castells, Sen**). This increasing disconnect between state and nation happens both in the Global South and in the North. The responses of nation-states to such challenges are very complex and paradoxical. In a sense, the national border has come to symbolize perfectly the contradictions between 'globalized *laissez-faire* and national priorities, protections, and proprieties' (2012: 27). Thus, borders are paradoxically both closed and open: they are open to business and to flows of goods and cheap labour, and closed to 'alien' workers who are seen as stealing the jobs of *bona fide* citizens (2012: 91–107). This paradox was made painfully acute in May 2008 when the deadly attacks against foreigners and migrant workers in South Africa took place. The disconcerting rise of xenophobia, manifested either as violence against migrants in the South or as racism and discrimination in the North, is part and parcel of the complex process of 'the collapse of the lines of separation between state and market' (2012: 26).

This separation becomes apparent in the paradoxical interplay between limited national legal jurisdiction and enhanced national jurisdiction. Limits occur through the extension of national legal jurisdiction beyond national borders, in cases where states are signatories to various international agreements (such as the International Criminal Court, European Courts of Justice and Human Rights, and others) or members of international institutions (e.g. the World Trade Organization) (2012: 28). Reinforcements of national jurisdiction, in contrast, arise from the hardening of internal borders within countries, which 'reinforce racial and ethnic cleavages, seeking to secure the "homeland" by dividing citizens from outsiders' (2012: 28).

Another significant consequence of the reconfiguration of political geographies under neoliberal capitalism, much explored in their joint research, is 'the turn to law as a site of political contestation' (2012: 34). This turn mimics closely 'the neoliberal propensity to re-situate most domains of life in the market, and, thus, in the realm of contract, right, interest, entitlement' (2012: 34; see also Comaroff and Comaroff 2006). From truth commissions in the Global South to 'recourse to law in repossessing the past' in the Global North (legally redressing past wrongs such as the enslavement of African Americans and the mistreatment of indigenous peoples), 'lawfare' – as the authors call it – has become a powerful contemporary instrument for expressing political subjectivity and agency in an age of neoliberal globalization (Comaroff and Comaroff 2012: 34–35, 133–152).

Elsewhere, Jean and John Comaroff (2006) examine the interpenetration between spaces in the Global South and North with regard to the dissemination of lawlessness and criminal violence in postcolonial societies. Here they make the argument that far from being marginal to the global economy, postcolonial economies are 'entangled in a parallel, pariah economy' of drugs, warlords, precious minerals for global markets, blood diamonds and contraband cultivation (2006: 9–10) (see also **Castells, Cox**). This entanglement between 'illegal' and 'illicit' economic and political activities in the South and various 'legal' and 'licit' economic and political spaces in the North have transformed postcolonial economies in the Global South. They become 'ready and able players in the twilight markets fostered by liberalization' (2006: 10).

Jean and John Comaroff's contribution to on-going globalization debates lies in their investigation of the changing lines between what constitutes 'southern' and 'northern' hemispheres and of the attending structural transformations of their economies (Comaroff and Comaroff 2012: 46). They stress, throughout their joint research, that such an economic reconfiguration entails profound political, cultural, technological and moral rearticulations of societies both in the South and in the North.

Major globalization writings

Comaroff, J. and Comaroff, J. (2000) 'Naturing the nation: aliens, apocalypse, and the postcolonial state', *Hagar: International Social Science Review*, vol 1, pp. 7–40.

——(2001) 'Millennial capitalism: first thoughts on a second coming', in J. Comaroff and J. Comaroff (eds) *Millennial Capitalism and the Culture of Neoliberalism*, Durham, NC: Duke University Press.

——(2006) 'Law and disorder in the postcolony: an introduction', in J. Comaroff and J. Comaroff (eds) *Law and Disorder in the Postcolony*, Chicago, IL, and London: University of Chicago Press.

——(2009) *Ethnicity, Inc.*, Chicago, IL: University of Chicago Press.

——(2012) *Theory from the South: Or, How Euro-America Is Evolving toward Africa*, Boulder, CO, and London: Paradigm Publishers.

Further reading

Comaroff J. and Comaroff, J. (1993) (eds) *Modernity and Its Malcontents: Ritual and Power in Postcolonial Africa*, Chicago, IL, and London: University of Chicago Press.

See also: **Appadurai, Arrighi, Beck, Brenner, Castells, Cerny, Chakrabarty, Cox, Dirlik, Hardt and Negri, Harvey, Helleiner, Ong, Sen, Strange.**

ROBERT W. COX (1926–)

Born in 1926, Robert W. Cox completed a Master's degree in history at McGill University, Montreal, in 1946. Shortly after, he accepted a position at the International Labour Organization (ILO), where he worked until 1972, setting up the International Institute for Labour Studies. He then taught at Columbia University, which he left to accept a position of professor of political science at York University in Canada in 1977. He has been Professor Emeritus at York since 1992. As an academic, Cox is known for his fierce independence, his challenge to orthodoxy and his insistence on understanding global affairs through historical perspectives. He has written: 'Growing up in Montreal during the 1930s and 1940s shaped my outlook. From an early age, I was inclined to see the contradictions in the values of my milieu and to challenge its orthodoxies' (Cox 1996: 19).

Most of Cox's writings on globalization have been compiled into two collections. *Approaches to World Order* includes articles and essays published between 1970 and 1995; *The Political Economy of a Plural World* is a compilation of essays from 1995 to 2002. His book *Production, Power and World Order*, published in 1987, contains a celebrated comprehensive analysis of the concept of hegemony and of the crisis that led to globalization.

Critical theory

Cox's analysis of globalization grows out of what he terms 'critical' theory. Theory is critical when the theorist stands apart from the prevailing order of the world and asks how that order came about. The theorist calls into question institutions and power relations by asking how they emerged and whether they are changing. Critical theory focuses on the social and political complex as a whole; in doing so, the theorist is invariably concerned with history, and with continuing processes of change (Cox 1996: 88–91). Cox goes on to develop a method for critical theory and applies it to three levels of activity: forces engendered by the production process, forms of state and world orders. These levels can be understood as 'particular configurations of forces which successively define the problematic of war or peace for the ensemble of states' (1996: 100).

Cox is interested in explaining the relative stability of successive world orders. He does so by equating stability with *hegemony*, which is based on a coherent overlap between a configuration of material power, a prevalent collective image of world order, and a set of institutions which administers the order by creating a notion of universality (1996: 103). In becoming hegemonic, a state would need to found and protect a world order which is potentially universal – that is, an order which most other states would find compatible with their interests. Hegemony does not speak only to a political order but also to an economic one, one with a dominant mode of production which penetrates all countries and affects other economic structures. Cox summarizes:

> World hegemony [...] is expressed in universal norms, institutions and mechanisms which lay down general rules of behaviour for states and for those forces of civil society that act across boundaries – rules which support the dominant mode of production.
>
> (Cox 1996: 137)

Beginning with the end of World War II, a new period of hegemony termed *Pax Americana* and headed by the US replaced an earlier period that had begun in the nineteenth century under British rule, *Pax Britannica*. The shift to US hegemony involved an intensification of the internationalization of production already begun under the British. Corporations have become ever more international, locating their production in different parts of the world to take advantage of low-cost labour, ever broader markets and new knowledge in the form of technology and market information (Cox 1987: 244ff.) (see also **Arrighi**).

Deeper changes have occurred, however, in the role of the state – changes summarized by Cox in the phrase 'internationalization of the state'. This process involves states revising their policies and practices to take account of the requirements arising from the internationalization of production. Accompanying this change is first a process of consensus-building among states regarding the needs of the world economy and the necessity for a common ideological framework for interpreting events. An important role emerges in this regard for the International Monetary Fund (IMF) and the World Bank set up after the World War II. Second, the process is hierarchically structured with the US and other 'advanced capitalist states' playing a leading role. Third, the internal organization of the state is reconfigured so that governments can translate what is agreed upon internationally into national policy, which leads to increased power for presidents' and prime ministers' offices, treasuries or finance ministries, foreign affairs offices and central banks. The relative importance of civil society actors also changes as multinational corporations increase their structural power while unions and other groups supporting social welfare policies experience a decline.

Cox suggests that two forms of states become dominant under *Pax Americana*. In the advanced capitalist countries, we find 'neoliberal states' whose primary role is to adjust national economic policy so that the state can compete in the world economy (see also **Cerny**). In less wealthy countries where capitalism is less entrenched, there is a move towards a 'neo-mercantilist developmental state'. Such states seek to develop domestic capitalism by limiting foreign capital, taxing resource exports more heavily, and borrowing from abroad in order to invest in strategic domestic industries, which are often nationalized. These developmental states maintain domestic political order and social peace by controlling labour relations and drawing upon extensive national police forces to protect foreign investment.

Globalization

In Cox's thinking, globalization processes emerge with the gradual decline of *Pax Americana* and the end of US hegemony. He identifies the economic crises of the early to mid-1970s as the beginning of this transition. During this period, the system for regulating the world economy, involving the IMF, the World Bank and US economic power, came into crisis as the US moved away from steering the world economy, which led to the collapse of agreements on currency management and on capital controls. Out of the crisis has come the gradual emergence of a 'global economy' – one where trans-border economic flows are no longer subject to the control of nation-states.

'States are, by and large, reduced to the role of adjusting national economies to the dynamics of an unregulated global economy' (Cox 1996: 528). Accompanying the changes in production is a growing problematic relationship with finance capital. During this period, financial transactions become more and more decoupled from funding production and increasingly autonomous from the real economy, feeding on themselves. Global production and global finance come to constitute separate spheres of power relations, placing further constraints on states' policy-making. Competitiveness in the global economy becomes the ultimate criterion of public policy. 'The state retains a function as enforcer of contracts and as instrument of political leverage to secure access to resources and markets worldwide. It is also at times expected to salvage reckless enterprises, if they are big enough' (1996: 529).

Along with the new global economy, Cox suggests that we need to think increasingly of a global society where global elites shape the social order. Segments of populations in both rich and poor countries who are linked to the global economy fare well, but are relatively few in number. The further away populations are from the global economy, whether in rich or poor countries, the worse they fare in terms of well-being, wealth and social protection. These divisions exist not only between states but also, to a greater extent, within states. In Cox's words, the 'North is generating its own internal South; and the South has formed a thin layer of society that is fully integrated into the economic North' (1996: 531).

Cox links these changes in the global economy and global society to the environment, or what he calls the 'biosphere'. He observes that the biosphere suffers the impact of both the expanding global economy and the change in the roles played by states. A global economy, highly focused on profit maximization, faces no constraints to moderate its destructive ecological effects. The new role of states as facilitators of the growth of the global economy leaves them with little incentive and capacity to achieve agreement on avoiding specific 'noxious practices'. He adds that states are themselves responsible for massive ecological destruction through war. He cautions that a 'valid paradigm for the investigation of global change would need to include the historical interaction of human organization with the other elements in nature' (1996: 517).

The rapid expansion of a largely unregulated global economy points in the direction of the 'double movement' identified by Karl Polanyi, but this time on a global scale. Cox draws upon Polanyi's argument that periods of rapid, unregulated growth of capitalism and its extension to land and money prompt the gradual growth of social resistance to this uncontrolled expansion, where social forces advocate for protection of society against rising poverty, for preservation of cultural practices, and for the safeguarding of social stability. Accordingly, Cox anticipates that the forces of global production and global finance will call into being other forces concerned with 'ecology, peace, gender, ethnicities, human rights, the defense of the dispossessed and the advancement of the disadvantaged' (1996: 496). In short, these are the forces that were to be named 'global civil society' in subsequent years by other globalization thinkers.

Covert globalization and resistance

The rapid growth and penetration of globalizing processes across the world provoke two kinds of responses, according to Cox. First, there is a 'covert world' which grows parasitically on globalization. It feeds off the social consequences of globalization (Cox 2002: 135) and includes a heterogeneous set of forces and movements involved in corruption and clandestine activities: intelligence agencies, organized crime and the drug trade, money-laundering banks, the arms trade, paramilitary bands and mercenaries, religious cults, the sex trade, and terrorist organizations (2002: 91) (see also **Castells**). As Cox adds, the 'overt world, through the chaos it generates, gives rise to the covert world' (2002: 125). The forces of covert globalization are decentred, all the while featuring organizations with tight hierarchical authority.

At the same time, globalizing processes have also given rise to global resistance movements (see also **Appadurai, Falk, Scholte**). These include those who are marginalized from the economic benefits of globalization as well as those who fear for the future of the planet and of the biosphere as a result of globalization's fixation on immediate accumulation of wealth. Cox observes that these resistance movements are developing identities that displace the traditional identification with the nation-state (see also **Castells**). He resurrects an old concept, that of 'civilization', to characterize these new forms of identity. He defines a civilization as a fit or correspondence between material conditions of existence and inter-subjective meanings (2002: 161). In this use of the term, civilizations become the media through which people organize themselves materially and mentally to cope with the challenges in their daily living, and to imagine a collective future where those challenges are met. Thus, a global organization such as Via Campesina, which represents peasants and small farmers from across the world who suffer from the globalization of agriculture might be seen as a civilization in Cox's thinking. What they have in common is a shared perspective on the world – a perspective that challenges the focus on materiality and concerns itself with the biological future of the planet – and a project to meet these challenges.

Major globalization writings

Cox, R. (1987) *Production, Power and World Order: Social Forces in the Making of History*, New York, NY: Columbia University Press.
Cox, R., with Schechter, M. G. (2002) *The Political Economy of a Plural World: Critical Reflections on Power, Morals and Civilization*, London: Routledge.
Cox, R., with Sinclair, T. (1996) *Approaches to World Order*, Cambridge, UK: Cambridge University Press.

Further reading

Leysens, A. (2008) *The Critical Theory of Robert W. Cox: Fugitive or Guru?* Houndmills, UK: Palgrave Macmillan.
Polanyi, K. (1944) *The Great Transformation: The Political and Economic Origins of Our Time*, Boston, MA: Beacon Press.

See also: **Appadurai, Arrighi, Castells, Cerny, Falk, Scholte**.

ARIF DIRLIK (1940–)

Arif Dirlik is a Turkish-born Marxist historian well known for his research on modern Chinese history (with a focus on the Chinese Revolution and on the history of Chinese Marxism), but also for his analyses on the link between processes of globalization and those of modernity. Dirlik completed his Ph.D. in history at the University of Rochester in 1973. He spent three decades at Duke University between 1971 and 2001, where he taught in the History Department. He subsequently held the position of Knight Professor of Social Sciences and was a professor of history and anthropology at the University of Oregon until 2006 when he retired. Dirlik held visiting positions at universities in California, Canada, France, China and Hong Kong, and was the recipient of numerous fellowships. His works have been translated into eight languages. Some of his most significant books on modern Chinese history include *The Origins of Chinese Communism* (1989), *Anarchism in the Chinese Revolution* (1993) and *Marxism in the Chinese Revolution* (2005a).

Dirlik's thinking on globalization is shaped by his research on the Chinese shift from communism to post-socialist development, and on the implications of the integration of the Asia-Pacific region within the circuits of global capitalism (Dirlik 1994). In parallel with his interest in Chinese history, he has explored the politics of contemporary intellectual trends, such as postmodernism and postcolonialism, which he sees as 'new ideological formations', parts of which could be associated with the rise of global capitalism (Dirlik 1997: 1; see also Dirlik 2001, 2005b, 2007). It is this longstanding research interest, developed over the last two decades, that informs most directly his work on globalization.

Global modernity

Dirlik began reflecting on 'the reconfiguration of global relations under [...] global postmodernity' in his collection of essays entitled *The Postcolonial Aura: Third World Criticism in the Age of Global Capitalism* (1997). His argument is that with decolonization and the crumbling of communist regimes in Eastern Europe, capitalism has now attained the stage of global capitalism – that is, the globalization of capitalism's logic and processes across the world. While he makes several references to 'global postmodernity' in this work, he does not theorize upon it or provide a detailed explanation for it. Global capitalism (see also Dirlik 1994) arises out of the conjunction of six features. The first of these is the 'new international division of labour', where new technologies have provided capital and production with 'unprecedented mobility', allowing production processes to be relocated to places that maximize profits and minimize political and social intervention (Dirlik 1997: 70) (see also **Harvey**). A second feature concerns the 'decentering of capitalism nationally'; capitalism is no longer centred within a specific nation or region (1997: 70) (see also **Arrighi, Castells**). A third feature of global capitalism is the rise of the transnational corporation, which shifted the 'locus of economic activity' from national markets to corporate actors who now control most decision-making processes regarding production (see also **Beck**). The 'transnationalization of production' has given rise to the fourth feature: the emergence of simultaneous processes of homogenization and fragmentation (see also **Robertson, Scholte**). The former lead to greater economic, social and cultural homogeneity across various regions under the sway of capitalist expansion; the latter entail both the removal of capitalism from a regional centre and 'the fragmentation of production processes' at the local level where localities within the same region compete with each other for attention from investors (1997: 70–71). The fifth feature of global capitalism, which Dirlik sees as the most significant one, is its emergence as a genuinely 'global abstraction', in which, for the first time in its history, capitalism has become divorced from its Euro-American roots (1997: 71). He conceives this process as leading to 'cultural fragmentation' or 'multiculturalism', where various societies inflect capitalism with their own cultural characteristics (1997: 71). The sixth feature refers to the obsolescence of the earlier vision of the globe, one divided into First, Second and Third Worlds (1997: 72). Dirlik suggests that, currently, a more appropriate distinction would be one that focuses on those regions or locales that have become 'pathways of transnational capital' versus those which comprise 'the marginalized populations of the world' (1997: 72) (see also **Castells**).

Dirlik goes on to refine his understanding of 'global modernity' in a series of articles that examine the complex relations between colonialism, modernity, capitalism and globalization. In an article published in 2003, he argues against what he sees as an implied teleology in current discourses of globalization: hailing globalization as the beginning of a development towards global economic and political integration, with the past unfolding inevitably towards the global present. Dirlik places the process of modernity at the centre of globality (see **Beck**, **Giddens**). Modernity is understood to be 'the product of historical interactions', including colonialism, in particular, with Europe playing a central role in its formation and in its dissemination (Dirlik 2003: 289 n1) (see also **Escobar**, **Mignolo**). He argues against the theory of 'multiple/ alternative modernities' (see **Robertson**), whose protagonists posit that modernity is not an exclusively Western phenomenon, but one that includes local processes of modernization emerging in various societies around the world in tandem with the hegemonic European one (see Featherstone *et al.* 1997; Eisenstadt 2000).

In contrast, Dirlik sees modernity being forged in the encounter between European colonial projects of capitalist expansion and various societies around the world. Accordingly, he argues that there is only a 'global modernity' possessing a Euro-American core (see also **Chakrabarty**, **Giddens**, **Mignolo**). Through processes of colonial conquest and domination, which supported the expansion of capitalism to new markets, modernity, too, became global(ized) (Dirlik 2003: 276). In short, Dirlik sees global modernity as the historical process through which capitalist modernity 'has gone global' (Dirlik 2007: 7); global modernity is the endpoint of capitalist modernity, not its beginning. Two obstacles had stood in the way of globalizing capitalist modernity: colonialism and socialism – themselves products of capitalist modernity (Dirlik 2003: 276; 2007: 97–98). With the unfolding of decolonization and with the fall of communist regimes in Eastern Europe – the latter involving the decline and discrediting of socialism as a viable alternative to capitalism – the way was open to the globalization of capital (Dirlik 2003, 2005b, 2007).

Dirlik's vision of global modernity has important ramifications not only for our understanding of colonialism, but also for modernity's continuing role in the contemporary world. What distinguishes modern colonialism or 'the colonial modern', as he phrases it (Dirlik 2005b), as a process of conquest and domination from other such occurrences in human history is capitalism. In his words: 'Without capitalism as the foundation for European power [...] Eurocentrism [...] would have been just another ethnocentrism' (Dirlik 1997: 68). Therefore, the process of global modernity where the formerly colonized were able to make their own claims to modernity is not so much one of decolonization. Rather, it involves the 'reconfiguration of colonialism' as capital is globalized, necessitating the incorporation of new states within its operation that are crucial to global management, as well as providing a voice for the newly created management classes in these states who become the personnel for the expanded capitalist system (Dirlik 2005b: 7; 2007: 98). Dirlik is not persuaded by **Hardt and Negri**'s famous argument that colonialism and imperialism have been replaced by an abstract empire with no centre and no clearly delineated boundaries. He finds that such conceptualizations of contemporary global power relations evade the issue of agency: the existence of privileged classes of transnational elites who advance the interests of capital (2007: 99–100). He also criticizes **Tomlinson**'s notion of 'cultural imperialism' for the same vagueness in theorizing the cultural dimensions of today's imperialism, which is portrayed as being devoid of a centre of power (2007: 102–103). By placing an emphasis on agency and power relations, rather than assuming that modernity is an inescapable condition, Dirlik can point to agents in colonial places who participated in the making of global modernity (see also **Spivak**). Restoring the issue of agency in analyses of globalization is crucial for the formulation of politically emancipatory pedagogies for Dirlik.

In addition to representing the endpoint of globalization, in spite of the vast discrepancies in power, wealth and integration within the global economic system, global modernity 'is characterized by temporal contemporaneity' unlike the previous era of 'Eurocentric modernity' (2007: 94–95). In this theorization, agents in colonized areas 'acquire a history as agents of a colonial modernity that they helped fashion with their participation in its workings' (2007: 113). The fact that 'the globalization of capitalism has reconfigured global relations' (2007: 95) is another intrinsic feature of global modernity. The 'tripartite division of the world' has been reconfigured as economic activity now operates along networks where global cities are crucial nodes of capitalism (see **Brenner, Castells, Sassen, Taylor**). Lastly, global modernity is characterized by 'class structuration' at a global scale with the emergence of the 'transnational capitalist class' and of transnational underclasses fragmented along gender, class and ethnic lines (2007: 96) (see also **Ong**).

The role of 'place' in an age of globalization

Dirlik also enquires into 'the relationship between the emergence of a Global Capitalism and the emergence of concern with the local as a site of resistance and liberation' (Dirlik 1997: 85). Remaining critical of the political implications of what he calls the 'new ideological formations' of global capitalism, postmodernism and postcolonialism, Dirlik notes that their 'repudiation of the metanarrative of modernization' and of the teleology of development have produced significant contemporary consequences (1997: 87). One consequence is a redirection towards the local as a site of emancipation. The local, however, has a paradoxical status in an age of global capitalism; it has become the site that perhaps displays best the complex contradictions of global flows (Dirlik 2007: 96) (see also **Escobar**). On the one hand, the local has become the place from where local movements formulate oppositional politics against the encroachment of global capitalism (see **Santos**). On the other, it has also become a space of capitalist innovation and manipulation through which the local is turned into 'a commodity available for global circulation' (Dirlik 2001: 27). The latter aspect, which Dirlik calls 'the globalization of the local', is the strategy through which capitalism attempts 'to assume localized colourings', making its penetration of local markets more compatible with local cultures and values (2001: 23). This paradoxical status of the local indicates the blurring of the lines between global and local within global modernity (see also **Mignolo**, **Robertson**, **Santos**, **Sassen**), making the two interdependent both for tactics of resistance and for the circulation of global capital (2001: 29). In terms of mobilizing place-based resistance, this paradox demands that place-based social movements must always consider what he calls the global dimension of their mobilizations (Dirlik 1997: 96, 150). Dirlik echoes **Appadurai**'s concern with the need for elaboration of emancipatory pedagogies that enable place-based mobilizations to become aware of the global context of their oppression and their struggle.

'Asia-Pacific as space of cultural production'

In spite of the hybridization between the local and the global, Dirlik advocates both a rethinking of place and a defence of place (Dirlik 2001: 35–42). He has devoted a number of his publications to exploring place-based mobilizations in the Asia-Pacific region. His focus on Asia-Pacific stems from his longstanding interest in modern China. He also seeks to show the invention of 'the Asia-Pacific idea' as a largely 'Euro-American formation', commonly portrayed as the emerging powerhouse of global capitalism. It links 'Western centers of global power' with the new nodes of global capital (Tokyo, Hong Kong, Seoul, Singapore and Taipei) (Wilson and Dirlik 1995: 2). This commonly held vision of Asia-Pacific has resulted paradoxically in the exclusion from this economistic mapping of the region of indigenous peoples' mobilizations that have remained 'staunchly "local" in orientation and resistant in political design' (Wilson and Dirlik 1995: 7). The advent of 'counter-hegemonic and oppositional projects of national identity and cultural location' in regions across Asia-Pacific such as Taiwan, Hawaii, South Pacific islands, New Zealand, Australia and South Korea speaks both to the globalization of local anti-capitalist activism and to indigenous visions of alternative modernities (Dirlik 1997: 139) (see also **Escobar, Tsing**). Dirlik places great hope in these indigenous mobilizations, especially since they coalesce around several notable challenges to current manifestations of globality, including, most importantly, the rejection of 'the fetishism of development' (1997: 139).

Dirlik is ultimately preoccupied with the emergence of viable alternatives to the contemporary global neoliberal orthodoxy. In some of his later writings he discerns the beginning of a 'global consensus against a hegemonic [neoliberal] empire' (Dirlik 2007: 147) (see also **Santos**). In this sense he sees the rise of the Beijing Consensus under the leadership of the post-socialist People's Republic of China to provide hope for alternative possibilities of countering the hegemonic sway of global capitalism (see also **Arrighi**). He sees China not only as an emergent 'new center of gravity of the third world' but also as a potential model of a 'third way of development' (2007: 147). For this potential to be realized, however, post-socialist China needs to attend to the severe contradictions created by its own successes.

Major globalization writings

Dirlik, A. (1994) *After the Revolution: Waking to Global Capitalism*, Hanover, NH: University Press of New England.

——(1997) *The Postcolonial Aura: Third World Criticism in the Age of Global Capitalism*, Boulder, CO: Westview Press.

——(2001) 'Place-based imagination: globalism and the politics of place', in R. Prazniak and A. Dirlik (eds) *Places and Politics in an Age of Globalization*, Lanham, MD: Rowman & Littlefield.

——(2003) 'Global modernity? Modernity in the age of capitalism', *European Journal of Social Theory*, vol 6, pp. 275–292.

——(2005a) *Marxism in the Chinese Revolution*, Lanham, MD: Rowman & Littlefield.

——(2005b) 'The end of colonialism? The colonial modern in the making of global modernity', *Boundary 2*, vol 32, pp. 1–31.

——(2007) *Global Modernity: Modernity in the Age of Global Capitalism*, Boulder, CO: Paradigm.

Dirlik, A. and Wilson, R. (1995) 'Introduction: Asia/Pacific as space of cultural production', in R. Wilson and A. Dirlik (eds) *Asia/Pacific as Space of Cultural Production*, Durham, NC: Duke University Press.

Further reading

Dirlik, A. (ed.) (2006) *Pedagogies of the Global: Knowledge in the Human Interest*, Boulder, CO: Paradigm.
Eisentstadt, S. N. (2000) 'Multiple modernities', *Daedalus*, vol 129, pp. 1–29.
Featherstone, M., Lash, S. and Robertson, R. (eds) (1997) *Global Modernities*, London: Sage.

See also: **Appadurai, Arrighi, Beck, Brenner, Castells, Chakrabarty, Escobar, Giddens, Hardt and Negri, Harvey, Mignolo, Ong, Robertson, Santos, Sassen, Scholte, Spivak, Taylor, Tomlinson, Tsing.**

ARTURO ESCOBAR (1951–)

Arturo Escobar was born in Manziales, Colombia. He completed a B.Sc. in chemical engineering at the Universidad del Valle, Cali, Colombia, in 1975. He went on to obtain a Master's degree in food science and international nutrition at Cornell University and then a Ph.D. in the Philosophy, Policy and Planning of Development programme at the University of California at Berkeley in 1987. He has taught at various universities in the US and also for short periods in other places, particularly Colombia, Finland, Barcelona and England. He has conducted or participated in workshops on development and ecology in Colombia, Ecuador, Mali, Brazil, Denmark, England and Mexico. He is involved with the World Anthropology/ies Network, a network of scholars and activists who question current patterns of knowledge production, opening up anthropology to a plurality of styles, modes of thinking, practices and enquiries about culture and politics worldwide. Currently, he holds the position of Kenan Distinguished Teaching Professor of Anthropology at the University of North Carolina, Chapel Hill.

Escobar's thinking about globalization challenges several important positions in the field. First, he argues that sociological theorizing is wrong in seeing globalization as involving the worldwide diffusion of the institutions of modernity (see **Bauman, Beck, Giddens, Tomlinson**). This thinking overlooks the fundamental relationship between modernity and coloniality. Second, he suggests that we must give more attention to the politics of 'place' in thinking about globalization rather than emphasizing so strongly space, movement, flows and instantaneous communication. When pursuing this line of thinking, he reconsiders another core concept in globalization studies – that of networks. He offers another view of networks that departs from that of thinkers such as **Castells**. This alternative conceptualization, in turn, has implications for how we understand social movements and actions opposing globalizing processes. Finally, he articulates a critique of claims about the universality of scientific knowledge that usually follows from the modernity hypothesis.

Globalization, modernity, coloniality

Escobar questions what he terms the 'Giddens effect' definition of globalization. In brief, **Giddens** argues that the basic institutions of modernity – the nation-state, capitalism, industrialism, military power controlled by the state, surveillance – as well as key processes – reflexivity, time–space distanciation and disembedding – emerged in Western Europe (see also **Dirlik**). Since the late eighteenth century, these institutions and processes are seen to be gradually spreading to encompass increasing parts of the world. For example, the nation-state form of governance became the dominant one in the world by the late twentieth century and capitalism displaced all other economic processes following the collapse of the communist-bloc states. In Giddens' view, globalization thus refers to processes where the whole world becomes 'modern'.

As part of this argument, 'development' is a key imaginary in the processes whereby the world embraces 'modernity all the way' (Escobar 2008: 162). Accelerated economic growth, intensification of natural resource extraction, urbanization and the emergence of 'development enclaves' – all are processes that lead receiving societies to modernity. States, international funding agencies and transnational corporations become vectors of development in the pursuit of modernization.

Escobar adds that the thesis that 'there is no outside to modernity' has implications for resisting or challenging globalization. Citing the thinking of **Hardt and Negri**, he argues that these scholars believe that resistance has to come from *inside* modernity. Hardt and Negri invoke the growth of the 'multitude' and see it as becoming a global force in its own right and, thus, the kind of actor that might bring an end to capitalist globalization. They dismiss local place-based activism as beside the point, if not irrelevant, if 'Empire' is to be challenged. Escobar disagrees fundamentally with this conclusion.

Escobar is a central contributor to a research programme that challenges this modernity-focused understanding of globalization. He articulates several precepts that distinguish his (and other researchers') position from the 'Giddens effect'. First, they see modernity originating with the conquest of America and the control of the Atlantic by Europeans after 1492, and not with the Enlightenment of the eighteenth century. Second, they argue that colonialism and the making of the capitalist world system are constitutive of modernity; economic exploitation of non-European areas makes modernity possible. Third, they view modernity and coloniality as a linked binary; modernity was never just an intra-European process but was always linked to exploiting other parts of the world. Fourth, in requiring the domination of others outside its European core, the spread of modernity violently subjugates the knowledge and cultures of those in its path, and results in their 'subalternization'. In this understanding, Eurocentric knowledge becomes universal, being presented as superior to all other forms of knowledge.

For Escobar, therefore, the proper analytical unit for the analysis of modernity and, thus, an understanding of globalization is *modernity/coloniality* (see also **Mignolo**). By placing these states of being together, he suggests that modernization was only possible because of colonization. In fact, coloniality (the state of being colonized) constitutes modernity. The 'colonial difference' – that is, the distinct way of being that comes with being colonized – makes possible the evolution of a privileged epistemological and political 'modern' space. Those who have had their living spaces 'developed', their knowledge disparaged and attacked, and their cultures classified as primitive or savage or ignorant bring to light the power dimension of the advance of modernity. And their resistance offers a different understanding of globalizing processes.

It is at this point that Escobar introduces the concept of the 'politics of place' as a challenge to conceptions of globalization that emphasize 'space', 'flows' and 'movement'. By place, Escobar refers to 'engagement with and experience of a particular location with some measure of groundedness (however unstable), boundaries (however permeable), and connections to everyday life, even if its identity is constructed and never fixed' (Escobar 2008: 30). In his research, he identifies that the challenges to places arising from colonial modernity take the form of a triple transformation:

> It entails the transformation of local diverse economies, partially oriented to self-reproduction and subsistence, into a monetized, market-driven economy. It involves changes of complex ecosystems into modern forms of nature (often plantations or pasture [...]). And it is changing place-based, local cultures that increasingly (have to) resemble dominant modern cultures, with their individualistic and productive ethos and market orientation.
>
> (Escobar 2006: 7)

For the study of places, Escobar develops a political ecology strategy that involves looking at 'difference' which becomes evident when local communities in places confront modernity/coloniality. He suggests that we think of the politics in such places in terms of practices of economic, cultural and ecological difference, which correspond to the process of economic, cultural and ecological conquest that such communities face (Escobar 2004a: 221). The subaltern experiences and knowledge of the local economy, ecology and culture that come into play in conflicts with 'imperial globality' provide the key to understanding globalization (Escobar 2006: 11). In the process of resistance, it is not only possible for alternative modernities to be suggested, even pursued, but also (and even more importantly) for alternatives to modernity to become the goal. Escobar adds: 'Many subaltern struggles can be seen today in terms of place-based yet transnationalized strategies, or more succinctly, as forms of place-based globalism' (2006: 11).

Networks and social movements

This invocation of 'transnationalism' by Escobar leads to a discussion of two other core concepts in globalization theory – networks and social movements – where he challenges the thinking of other globalization scholars (see, for example, **Castells**). Escobar identifies two theoretical approaches to networks. The first incorporates networks within an existing social theory; these networks often take a hierarchical form, with **Castells'** theorizing of 'spaces of flows' being a well-elaborated theory along these lines. Drawing from self-organization, assemblage and autopoiesis theories, Escobar articulates a second approach. In this thinking, networks emerge in a self-organizational way when multiple agents interact and pursue goals following local rules rather than top-down commands (Escobar 2008: 274). Borrowing from de Landa, he terms these structures 'meshworks', which are based on decentralized decision-making, self-organization, and heterogeneity and diversity. They are non-hierarchical and have no overt single goal. They develop and grow through their encounters with their environments and the challenges that they face in these environments.

Escobar argues that contemporary social movements are often formed in ways consistent with this meshwork model. He adds that contemporary information and communication technologies facilitate the formation of such meshworks, resulting in what might be called 'subaltern intelligent communities' (Escobar 2004a: 210). Based on this self-organizing logic and drawing upon these technologies, such social movements enact a politics of place that contrast with the grandiose politics of 'the Revolution' and with conceptions of anti-imperial politics that require that empire be confronted in its totality (2004a: 221) (see **Hardt and Negri**). Escobar describes these social movements as 'place based', all the while engaging with 'transnational networks'. The same technologies have made it possible for broader social entities to emerge as 'always unfolding intermeshed sites' (Escobar

2008: 290). The actions of these place-based meshworks across the world create possibilities for overcoming the disempowerment of place embedded in global-centric thinking through struggles to create an emergent order that might be an alternative to modernity (2008: 303–305) (see also **Mignolo, Santos**).

In addition to these social changes, Escobar observes that such interlinked meshworks lead to the questioning of modern science (as part of modernity), resulting in a 'plural landscape of knowledge forms' (Escobar 2004b: 17). The recovery of subaltern knowledges from the cracks emerging in neoliberal globalization creates openings for the possible reconstruction of local and regional places on different logics, leading, perhaps, to alternative worlds that leave modernity behind (see also **Santos**). Admittedly, these possibilities cannot be realized without translation capacities. The worldviews, life worlds and concepts inherent to place-based politics and meshworks are not necessarily intelligible to those in other places, even though they share goals in a common meshwork. These difficulties suggest an important need for a theory of translation: processes that make understanding and intelligibility possible across knowledges and cultures (see also **Santos**). Such translation capacities are increasingly recognized as essential for the advancing of 'counter-hegemonic globalization' (Escobar 2004a: 224).

Major globalization writings

Escobar, A. (2001) 'Culture sits in places: reflections on globalism and subaltern strategies of localization', *Political Geography*, vol 20, no 2, pp. 139–174.
——(2004a) 'Beyond the third world: imperial globality, global coloniality and anti-globalisation social movements', *Third World Quarterly*, vol 25, no 1, pp. 207–230.
——(2004b) 'Development, violence and the new imperial order', *Development*, vol 47, no 1, pp. 15–21.
——(2006) 'Difference and conflict in the struggle over natural resources: a political ecology framework', *Development*, vol 49, no 3, pp. 6–13.
——(2007) 'Worlds and knowledges otherwise: the Latin American modernity/coloniality research program', *Cultural Studies*, vol 21, nos 2–3, pp. 179–210.
——(2008) *Territories of Difference: Place, Movements, Life,* Redes, Durham, NC: Duke University Press.

See also: **Beck, Castells, Dirlik, Giddens, Hardt and Negri, Mignolo, Santos, Tomlinson**.

RICHARD A. FALK (1930–)

Richard A. Falk is the author or co-author of 20 books and the editor or co-editor of another 20 books. Falk obtained a B.Sc. in economics from the Wharton School,

University of Pennsylvania, a Bachelor of Laws from Yale University, and a Doctor of Laws (SJD) from Harvard University, US. He is Albert G. Milbank Professor Emeritus of International Law and Practice at Princeton University, and was Visiting Distinguished Professor in Global and International Studies at the University of California, Santa Barbara (2001–2004). During 1999 to 2000, Falk worked on the Independent International Commission on Kosovo. In 2001 he served on a three-person Human Rights Inquiry Commission for the Palestine Territories. On 26 March 2008, the United Nations Human Rights Council (UNHRC) appointed Falk to a six-year term as a United Nations Special Rapporteur on 'the situation of human rights in the Palestinian territories occupied since 1967'.

In his long career as a legal scholar concerned with world order, Falk became increasingly convinced that 'humane governance' was necessary if the world's serious social, cultural, economic and political problems were to be addressed. By the early 1990s, he had identified globalization both as a crucial obstacle to realizing humane governance and as a potential force for moving towards that goal. In the process of analysing competing forms of globalization, he also came to highlight human rights, particularly economic and social rights, regionalism, inter-civilizational dialogue, inter-temporal equity and moral globalization.

Humane governance

Falk's association with the concept of humane governance grew out of his participation in a research project entitled The Global Civilization: Challenges, for Democracy, Sovereignty, and Security Project (GCP), sponsored by another longer-running effort, The World Order Models Project (WOMP), established in 1968. The GCP had a steering committee of people from across the world when it began operating in 1987, including representation from the rapidly changing Soviet Union. After five years of intense work and meetings in different parts of the world, Falk, as the rapporteur for the project, was asked to arrange and compose a volume based on insights from the project, but in his own voice. *On Humane Governance: Toward a New Global Politics* (Falk 1995) was the result of that undertaking.

He describes humane governance as the preferred form of 'geo-governance', or global governance as it later came to be called. Such governance emphasizes:

> [...] the achievement of comprehensive rights for all peoples on earth. It accords priority to those most vulnerable and abused, providing an alternative source of security to that associated with geopolitics and seeking to resolve conflict and establish order with a minimum reliance on violence [... It] presupposes environmental quality to protect the health and well-being of those now alive and those as yet unborn.

> (Falk 1995: 9)

Humane governance is to be based on 'global constitutionalism', thus involving the democratizing agenda of bringing law and popular participation to bear upon economic and political matters (1995: 46). His book ends with the identification of problematic dimensions of governance that need to be changed: taming war, abolishing war, making leaders accountable, collective security, rule of law, non-violent revolutionary politics, human rights, stewardship of nature and cosmopolitan democracy (see also **Held**, whose thinking influenced Falk).

Globalization from above

In Chapter 6 of *On Humane Governance*, Falk identifies 'globalization from above', or 'corporate globalization', as an important obstacle to achieving humane governance. It is important to note that he does not believe that globalization is inherently bad or good. He sees its core elements to include the compression of time and space on a planetary scale, the intensification of cross-border activity, networking, information technology, and global markets (Falk 2004: 18; 2009: 192). For Falk, however, problems arise when these processes are harnessed and controlled by transnational corporations (TNCs) and supportive states for their own ends.

The economic well-being inherent to humane governance is less and less possible in Falk's view as neoliberal ideology comes to shape state policy. Policy ideas based on liberalization, privatization, minimizing economic regulation, reducing expenditures on public goods, tightening fiscal discipline in favour of freer flows of capital and so on are implemented by states. In the process, states themselves become 'globalized' in the sense that their policies are drawn away from citizens to focus on supporting 'non-territorial regional and global market forces', which, in turn, are manipulated by transnational corporations and financial conglomerates (Falk 1999: 39) (see also **Harvey**). Over time, Falk adds, the ideological atmosphere arising from the dominance of neoliberal thinking leads to fewer and fewer challenges to these policies. Capitalism, as a consequence, can pursue its market logic with a relentlessness not seen since the beginning of the Industrial Revolution (1999: 129).

Consequently, the societal mood shifts to beliefs that governments are incompetent and are obstacles to well-being. Public policy becomes more business focused and the power of organized labour diminishes. The fiscal imperatives of debt and deficit reduction in the interests of transnational monetary stability open the door to ever increasing economic inequality and diminishing social welfare policies (see also **Cerny**). From the perspective of human rights, Falk notes that economic, social and cultural rights become less and less of a concern and discussions of human rights focus primarily on political and civil rights. The notion of human solidarity at the heart of humane governance suffers deeply under this form of globalization.

Globalization from below

Falk does not believe that globalizing processes can be stopped or rolled back. To move towards humane governance, therefore, would require an alternative globalization to the corporate form. By 1995, Falk had identified global civil society as a possible source for this alternative. He notes the challenges mounted by various groups to corporate globalization's adverse effects on social policies, human rights and the environment. He also welcomes initiatives in the international community, particularly from arenas in the UN system 'not fully subordinated to the imperatives of geopolitics' (Falk 1995: 199). At the same time, he notes that moving towards change will be difficult because conventional electoral politics at the nation-state level are futile, opposition to ecological change is strongly resisted by TNCs, and right-wing extremism has flourished under the auspices of globalization from above.

Accordingly, to be successful, civic globalization will need to come up with a common theoretical framework sufficiently sophisticated that it can persuade people to move beyond neoliberalism. This framework will need to be able to clearly address poverty, social marginalization and environmental decay (Falk 1999: 145). Falk goes on to offer the idea of 'normative democracy' as a potential unifying ideology to meet these problems. Influenced by both **Bello** and **Held**, Falk's conception argues that 'security' must extend to include environmental protection and economic viability for citizens. Human rights should comprise economic and social rights, as well as the rights to development, to peace and to self-determination (see also **Howard-Hassmann**). Normative democracy is conceived as 'extending beyond constitutional and free, periodic elections, to include an array of other assurances that governance is oriented toward human well-being and ecological sustainability, and that citizens have access to arenas of decision making' (1999: 147).

The consensus in the emerging globalization from below is that 'normative democracy' would include consent of citizenry, rule of law, human rights, participation, accountability, public goods available in a restored social agenda, transparency and non-violence (1999: 148–149).

Falk adds that globalization from below is not opposed to the application of contemporary technologies to productive processes in ways that would achieve economic growth, social gains in health and well-being, and in education. He notes that the support of civic globalization for institutions such as the International Criminal Court, a global people's assembly and the international rule of law is encouraging and builds on efforts to eliminate anti-personnel land mines and related campaigns (Falk 2004: 29).

Like other globalization authors (see **Amin, Arrighi, Cox**), Falk reflects on the possible role of the growing number of regional units of organization in the world order and their increasing importance. Thinking optimistically, Falk outlines four potential roles for such regional bodies in the pursuit of a more civic globalization (Falk 1999: 64). First, they could function to contain 'negative globalism' – that is, the worst effects of corporate globalization. Second, they could mitigate 'pathological anarchism' exemplified by the outbreaks of violence when weaker states break down in the face of corporate globalizing pressures. Third, they could promote 'positive globalism' – that is, the ideas being articulated more generally by global civil society as part of civic globalization. Fourth, they could work directly to build an alternative economic and social order within their region to challenge the neoliberal global order. In short, Falk writes:

> [...] one crucial contribution of regionalism is to help create a new equilibrium in politics that balances the protection of the vulnerable and the interests of humanity as a whole (including future generations) against the integrative, technological dynamic associated with various forms of globalism.
>
> (Falk 2004: 63)

The concepts of 'humane', of 'humanity' and of 'human rights' reflect the idea that all human beings share certain common characteristics, wherever they live and whatever the culture in which they are immersed (cf. **Howard-Hassmann**). Falk is conscious that the use of these terms may reflect a particularly 'Western' understanding of the human condition and thus that his promotion of civic globalization might be interpreted as Western centric if not imperialist. He challenges these claims (Falk 1999: 106; 2000: 149–163) while acknowledging that history reveals a false universalism that has obscured Western hegemony. In contrast, he submits, a true universality would acknowledge significant difference as well as sameness 'in constituting a world order based on procedures and norms explicitly designed to ensure equitable participation by each major world civilization' (2000: 149). He adds that inter-civilizational equality has to be a constitutive principle of any new world order and, thus, a part of global governance.

He suggests that the first truly inter-civilizational critique of prevailing human rights discourse in contemporary times came from indigenous peoples in their struggles for recognition of their rights (see also **Dirlik, Escobar, Tsing**). These struggles exposed the 'radical inadequacy of a civilization-focused "blind" approach to human rights' (2000: 151). As a consequence, their activism has given rise to an alternative conception of rights (now formalized in the 2007 Declaration on the Rights of Indigenous Peoples at the UN). In any framing of global human rights, therefore, Falk advocates that there has to be the right for participation at an inter-civilizational level, adding that such participation by representatives of the Islamic world would be an 'enlightening education process' (2000: 163). He adds that a sustainable world community can only 'result from a combination of secular and spiritual energies' (Falk 2009: 78).

Falk concludes these reflections by reaffirming the importance of 'humanity' as an ethical and spiritual ideal. He stresses that the human rights movement expressed claims that were based on the identity of 'human' and not on the basis of some 'fragmentary sense of privileged or denigrated identity associated with religion, race, nation' (2009: 197). It will be necessary that sentiments of solidarity create 'a vibrant *human* identity' that supports 'strong institutions and networks of cooperative endeavor, but certainly not of an exclusivisit or homogenizing nature that repudiates other identities' (2009: 200). It is with these ideas in mind that he speaks of 'moral globalization'.

Major globalization writings

Falk, R. (1995) *On Humane Governance: Toward a New Global Politics: The World Order Models Project Report of the Global Civilization Initiative*, University Park, PA: Pennsylvania State University Press.

——(1999) *Predatory Globalization: A Critique*, Malden, MA: Polity Press.

——(2000) *Human Rights Horizons: The Pursuit of Justice in a Globalizing World*, New York, NY: Routledge.

——(2004) *Declining World Order: America's Imperial Geopolitics*, New York, NY: Routledge.

——(2009) *Achieving Human Rights*, New York, NY: Routledge.

See also: **Amin, Arrighi, Bello, Cerny, Cox, Dirlik, Escobar, Harvey, Held, Howard-Hassmann, Tsing**.

ANTHONY GIDDENS (1938–)

Anthony Giddens was born in England and grew up in a lower middle-class family in north London. The first member of his family to go to university, he obtained his BA in sociology and psychology at the University of Hull, followed by a Master's degree from the London School of Economics. He began his teaching career at Leicester in 1961, giving courses in social psychology. He completed a Ph.D. from King's College, Cambridge, in 1974, where he already had an academic appointment beginning in 1969.

A prolific author, his early works focused on articulating a new theoretical and methodological view of the field of sociology. He followed that project by proposing a theory of structuration where he argued that social research should not give primacy to either agency or structure. Both macro-structural factors and micro-behaviours must be considered in understanding societies and individual behaviour. A third phase of his work began in the late 1980s where he focused on the emergence of modernity and its revolutionary characteristics when compared to pre-modern societies. By the end of the 1990s, he had moved away from elaborating upon theories of society to proposing ideas and programmes for helping citizens, particularly those in the UK, to navigate their way in an increasingly globalized world.

Giddens' thinking about globalization grows out of the third principal focus of his research, that on modernity. For Giddens, the changes entailed in the shift from pre-modern or traditional societies to modern ones are the most deep-seated and fundamental ones; his understanding of globalization is built upon a theory of modernity. Therefore, he does not see globalization as being a rupture or a break in societal development, but a 'radicalization' of modernity or as characteristic of 'high modernity'. He also sees the institutions of modernity as being first developed in the West and then spreading to other parts of the world. For similar reasons, therefore, globalization refers to a set of processes that also originated in the West, but are now globally distributed (for an alternative perspective on modernity, see **Escobar**, **Mignolo**).

Modernity

Giddens begins with the argument that modern institutions are unique; they are distinct in form from all the societies that came before them. In fact, he suggests that modernity has swept aside all previous forms of society. The depth of these changes comes from their extensionality and their intensionality. With respect to the former, they have led to forms of social interconnection that span the world; to the latter, they have penetrated deeply into people's daily lives, altering their most intimate and personal features. These concepts of extensity and intensity are picked up by other globalization thinkers, such as **Held**. When comparing modernity to earlier societies, Giddens argues that the pace of change is more rapid by far and the scope of change is more encompassing.

The dynamism of modernity arises from three distinct processes: the separation of time and space, the disembedding of social systems, and the reflexive ordering and reordering of social relations. Speaking to the first of these processes, Giddens suggests that pre-modern societies linked time with place. They 'told' time by looking at physical features, often related to the sun or the seasons, and these understandings would vary widely from one place to another and one society to another. He argues that the invention of the mechanical clock and its widespread diffusion in society during the early eighteenth century changed this linkage between time and place. Gradually, time became 'emptied' of place and more abstract. Something as simple as a schedule for when trains would arrive and depart was not possible without this emptying process.

Giddens gives particular emphasis to the process of disembedding that becomes important with the separation of time and place. By disembedding, he means the lifting of social relations out from local contexts of interaction and their restructuring across indefinite spans of time and space. He refers to 'symbolic tokens' and 'expert systems' as examples of disembedding. The most prominent example of symbolic tokens is money. The development of money and its increasing separation from place permits commercial relations to become more extensive and intensive on a world scale. Something as simple as a traffic system – use of signal lights, divided roads, common symbolic signs, speed limits – exemplifies an expert system. Again, such systems take the practice of driving or transportation and separate it from particular places and times. Whether one drives a car in New York or in Kuala Lumpur, the system is essentially the same.

The third process of importance is reflexivity: social practices are constantly examined and reformed in light of incoming information about those very practices, thus constitutively altering their character. Cigarette smoking might be a good example. For a period of time, smoking was not seen as particularly harmful to one's health. Gradually, as the chemical structure of tobacco smoke was analysed and knowledge improved of the relations between chemicals and cancer, the conclusion was drawn that smoking was potentially harmful to one's health. Research continued further and showed that even the inhaling of second-hand smoke had these unwelcome impacts upon health. Consequently, over time, in the face of this accumulating evidence, the act of smoking in many societies became sufficiently socially condemned that workplaces and then many public spaces became 'smoke free' by law. Modernity is replete with this examination and re-examination of what we do, whether by social, physical or life sciences.

Giddens identifies four 'organizational clusters' as being built upon and giving force to these three processes and, thus, of modernity itself. These include capitalism, industrialism (the use of inanimate sources of material power in producing goods accompanied by a central role for machinery in the production process), the nation-state and its surveillance capacities (capacity to supervise the activities of its population), and monopoly control of the means of violence. For Giddens, then, the three processes noted above are necessary for these institutional forms to develop and be linked together. At the same time, these processes themselves are conditioned by the four institutional dimensions of modernity.

Globalization

Giddens describes globalization as the 'radicalization' of modernity leading to a period that he refers to as 'high modernity'. If we return to his concepts of extensionality and intensionality, we might say that radicalization refers to the spread of the four modern institutional complexes as a system from the West to every part of the world (extensification). And in the course of this expansion, more and more people's lives are affected in intimate ways by this system (intensification). No one, in a sense, is left untouched. He writes that high modernity is a period when humankind becomes a 'we': we are all facing problems and opportunities that arise from the globalization of modernity itself.

In reflecting upon how high modernity has come into being, Giddens points to the three key processes which, by separating time and place and by creating spaces 'emptied' of place, have the potential to restructure the world into a global modern one. He adds that institutional clusters such as capitalism, industrialism and the state itself are also inherently globalizing. They gain their dynamism by placing themselves everywhere. In addition, although he does not theorize the connection as much as some other globalization scholars (see also **Castells**), he notes the importance of communication and information technologies. He observes how satellite technologies make it possible to have instantaneous communication from one side of the world to the other. He sees the extensiveness and intensiveness of the global spread of modernity as being built upon the use of electronic communication. Even here, however, he sees continuity, noting that the role of electronic communication today is analogous to the role played by printing in the birth of modernity.

Accordingly, he describes globalization as a 'stretching process' where connections between social factors become networked across the world (Giddens 1990: 64). He writes that globalization is an 'intensification of worldwide social relations which link distant localities in such a way that local happenings are shaped by events occurring many miles away and vice-versa' (1990: 64). As such, he stresses, *local transformation* is as much a part of globalization as the extension of social relations across the world. This point is elaborated upon by other globalization scholars such as **Sassen** and **Tomlinson**.

In his various writings on globalization, Giddens discusses two themes in particular that have influenced other globalization scholars. First, he comments at length about the related notions of risk and trust (see also **Beck**). He argues that they become key social variables with the arrival of modernity. Trust refers to confidence in the reliability of a person or a system regarding a given set of outcomes or events. Clearly, this social act becomes crucial given the disembedding of many aspects of living from place. Thus, to return to an example above, when we proceed through a green light in a traffic system, we trust that those people sitting at the red light will remain stopped until the light changes. In this situation there is also risk: the danger that might emanate from an expert system breaking down by individual or technological acts. Thus, when we are going through the green light, we know that there is some danger that another driver might proceed through the red light at the same time.

Under globalization, Giddens sees the balance of dangers and risks shifting significantly: hazards created by us become more threatening on a global scale whether these are environmental degradation, nuclear proliferation or a global economic collapse (see **Beck**). Some of these risks are very intense, such as the consequences of a nuclear war. Others result from the infusion of human knowledge into the environment (genetically modified organisms), the expansion of institutionalized risk environments (world capital markets) and awareness of the limitations of expertise. In short, although the very notion of risk is one that emerges only with modernity, the scale of the dangers we face and, thus, the levels of risk we confront become more dangerous as modernity itself is globalized (see also **Beck**).

Second, Giddens offers commentary throughout his writings on the transformation of intimacy (the direct transfer of trust with large elements of mutuality) that comes with high modernity, particularly as it concerns the role of women. He proposes the concept of a pure relationship as a tool for analysing these changes: a relationship based upon direct face-to-face communication of emotions, where the rewards gained from that communication are the main basis for the relationship to continue. To use his earlier analysis, relationships become disembedded from family structures involving person-to-person direct contacts and from cultural values based on particular concepts of the role of women. He reviews the presence of this emotional communication in sexual and love relationships, parent–child relationships and friendships. He suggests that as relationships become disembedded from traditional family and community structures, person-to-person intimacy gradually takes on an importance that it did not have in the past. And as this notion becomes globalized, it destabilizes views about marriage, women's roles in society, homosexuality and child-rearing across the world.

In reading Giddens, one concludes that he believes that we are fated to live in a world where modernity has itself become global. His political activity, including the promotion of a 'third way' between socialism and market fundamentalism and, more recently, his concern with environmental degradation, suggests that he also believes that globalizing processes have both positive and negative impacts upon the world. The task, it would seem, is to build on the positive contributions while making social, political and economic changes to counter the harms being experienced through modernization by so many people across the world.

Major globalization writings

Giddens, A. (1990) *The Consequences of Modernity*, Stanford, CA: Stanford University Press.

——(1991) *Modernity and Self-identity: Self and Society in the Late Modern Age*, Stanford, CA: Stanford University Press.

——(1999) *Runaway World: How Globalization Is Reshaping Our Lives*, New York, NY: Routledge.

See also: **Beck, Castells, Escobar, Held, Mignolo, Sassen, Tomlinson.**

ULF HANNERZ (1942–)

Born in 1942, Ulf Hannerz received his Ph.D. in social anthropology from Stockholm University in 1969, where he became an acting professor from 1976 to 1980, and then Professor of Social Anthropology beginning in 1981 until he retired in 2007. He has also taught at several American, European, Asian and Australian universities. He is a member of the Royal Swedish Academy of Sciences and the American Academy of Arts and Sciences, an honorary fellow of the Royal Anthropological Institute of Great Britain and Ireland, and an honorary member and former chair of the European Association of Social Anthropologists. His research areas of specialization include urban anthropology, media anthropology and transnational cultural processes. He has undertaken field studies in West Africa, the Caribbean and the US, as well as multi-sited field research in four continents on the work of news media foreign correspondents. He has also directed an interdisciplinary research project on cosmopolitanism.

Globalization, culture and creolization

Hannerz has focused his study of globalization on culture. He investigates how cultural globalization follows different tracks from economic and political forms. He defines globalization 'as a process in which people get increasingly interconnected, in a variety of ways, across national borders and between continents, and in which their awareness of the world and of distant places and regions probably also grows' (Hannerz 2001: 57). He adds that globalization in this sense is not new, it has a history. He also argues that it can go 'back and forth' – that is, there can be histories of 'deglobalization' as well. The participation of people in globalizing processes is remarkably uneven across the world. In different places, there have been 'different globalizations'. What is characteristic of the present era, however, is that when it comes to culture, there is greater interconnectedness between people across the world than in any time during the past. And more people are experiencing globalization in more significant ways in their daily lives (see **Held**). In the face of such developments, we can no longer assume that a person's culture is largely determined by her or his nation. Rather, the various relationships and connections in which people engage permit the development of different cultural repertoires. Hannerz suggests that we use the term 'habitats of meaning' to refer to the cultural tools used to build these habitats and to engage with the world. Accordingly, with contemporary globalization, individuals' habitats of meaning have the potential to become dramatically enlarged, depending upon personal circumstances.

In developing this understanding of how individuals engage with cultural processes, Hannerz, like **Tomlinson** and **Escobar**, stresses the continued importance of local places. The 'everyday life' of the local place involves face-to-face relationships, inclusive long-term relationships, shared understandings that are worked out in detail, and redundant and practical activities. What changes is that more and more of this experienced reality that constitutes habitats of meaning is 'shaped from outside. We are just giving up the idea that the local is autonomous' (Hannerz 1996: 27). The choices people make are more diffuse and free. In this respect, local places become areas 'where people's habitats of meaning intersect and where the global, or what has been local somewhere else, also has some chance of making itself at home' (1996: 28).

Hannerz identifies four different 'frames' through which culture flows. The 'market' frame involves flows from sellers to buyers, which might involve music, film, literatures, art or modes of dress. With contemporary globalization, the economic power of transnational corporations selling cultural products has the most influence on cultures (Hannerz 1992: 234). Cultural influences also move from the rulers of states to their citizens; this constitutes the second frame. Social and religious movements and institutions provide a third kind of flow of culture, one greatly enhanced through contemporary information and communication technologies (see **Castells**). Finally, forms of life such as workplace relationships, agricultural production, marriage and divorce constitute a fourth frame through which cultural practices move.

Hannerz observes that often these cultural flows travel from centres of power in the world to those countries and places that have less power and fewer resources. He cautions against a conclusion, however, that assumes these influences are simply adopted or assimilated by these populations. He writes that cultural flows do not enter into a vacuum or imprint themselves upon a *tabula rasa*. Rather, they interact with people's habitats of meaning that are already present. Those living on the periphery gain access to a wider cultural inventory, providing them with new resources of technology and symbolic expression 'to refashion and quite probably integrate with what exists of more locally rooted materials' (1992: 241).

He suggests that the cultures resulting from these changes are 'creole' ones. Intrinsically of mixed origin, they involve the coming together of two or more widely separate historical cultural currents. Not artificial or lacking in authenticity, these cultures develop over time and move towards a degree of coherence. Creolization, he adds, entails a highly specific, complex relationship between social structures and cultural forms, not just a simple mixing of cultures. In these ways, cultural processes of creolization are not simply a matter of pressures from the centre overwhelming cultural practices of those living on the periphery, but involve a much more creative interplay (1992: 264). Creole cultures put things together in creative ways; increasingly, they permit those on the periphery to 'talk back' to those living in the dominant centres of power.

Global cultural ecumene, transnationalism and cosmopolitanism

Hannerz argues that scholars must move away from thinking of the world as a cultural mosaic – that is, one composed of cultures with hard, well-defined edges or boundaries. What is emerging, he argues, is a global 'ecumene'. In ancient Greece, this term referred to the inhabited world. Hannerz adapts the term to suggest a world where there is persistent cultural interaction and exchange (Hannerz 1992: 18). What might formerly have been termed 'cultures' are more like subcultures within this larger ecumene. Boundaries between cultures have become fuzzy, if not arbitrary. Perpetual cultural interconnectedness is taking place in the world – cultural globalization if you will; the global ecumene becomes a very large social network or a network of networks (Hannerz 2001: 61). He writes: 'the notion of culture, in the singular, as a global pool of meanings and meaningful forms, suggests that in principle, at least, anything cultural can indeed move from anywhere to anywhere, from anybody to anybody' (Hannerz 1996: 50).

In reflecting further upon the global ecumene, Hannerz argues that two major meta-cultures coexist and play a part in shaping present-day cultural flows. The first of these emphasizes similarity in the form of modernity and tends to work from the top down (see also **Beck, Giddens**). 'Modernity was not originally everywhere, and it has spread everywhere, or is at least making itself felt everywhere' (1996: 55). The organized large-scale reflexivity characteristic of modernity is spread unevenly in the world. In the periphery, this meta-culture is often 'imported from the center and still controlled by the center, with the political and cultural consequences that this may have' (1996: 55). The meta-culture of difference, in contrast, works from the bottom up, manifesting itself in the creativity of creolization and similar processes. It is here that we see challenges to the 'neoliberal cultural complex' form of modernity that has emerged since the early 1990s (Hannerz 2010: 7).

In order to understand the implications of the increasing back and forth movements of people on a global scale, Hannerz suggests using the concept of 'transnational cultures':

> [...] structures of meanings carried by social networks which are not wholly based in any single territory. The people of the transnational cultures tend to be the frequent travelers, the people based in one place but routinely involved with others in various places elsewhere. The people combine involvements with one transnational culture or possibly more than one and one or more territorially based cultures.
>
> (Hannerz 1992: 249)

Transnationalism emerges from the condition that a great many real relationships to people and places may cross boundaries. These new relationships do not fit easily with established ideas of 'nation'; among some people involved in transnational ties, there may be a weakening of the nation as an imagined community and source of identity. Hannerz stresses here that he is referring to the nation as a cultural community and not to the state. Consequently, for people in transnational relationships, deep feelings of rootedness in a nation are replaced by an equally intense experience of discontinuity and rupture (Hannerz 1996: 88). In becoming involved in more transnational ties, there may be:

> [...] a kind and a degree of tuning out, a weakened personal involvement with the nation and national culture, a shift from the disposition to take it for granted; possibly a critical distance to it. In such ways, the nation may have become more hollow than it was.
>
> (Hannerz 1996: 88)

In becoming immersed in transnational cultures, an increasing number of people are systematically and directly involved with more than one culture. In living in such cultures, new mediating possibilities emerge: 'one can use the mobility connected with transnational cultures to make contact with the meanings of other rounds of life, and gradually incorporate this experience into one's personal perspective' (1996: 104) (see **Appadurai**). In such circumstances, these individuals are more likely to adopt a cosmopolitan orientation, a willingness to engage with the other, an openness towards diverging cultural experiences, and a personal readiness to make one's way into other cultures. In experiencing such changes, a person gains more personal autonomy from the culture in which he or she originated (1996: 103). Accordingly, living in a transnational culture opens up new mediating possibilities. A person can 'use the mobility connected with transnational cultures to make contact with the meanings of other rounds of life, and gradually incorporate this experience into one's personal perspective' (1996: 106).

'World cities' have a particular role in supporting transnationalism. By this term, Hannerz identifies cities that are engaged in transformations and re-combinations of meanings and meaningful forms. Such changes lead to 'changes in how we think about the relationships between culture and territory' (1996: 127). Hannerz's emphasis on cultural change distinguishes his discussion from those of 'global cities', which focus more on the role of cities in the global economy (see **Abu-Lughod**, **Brenner**, **Sassen**, **Taylor**). World cities incubate transnational relationships; significant parts of their populations 'are physically present in the world cities for some larger or smaller parts of their lives, but they have also strong ties to some other place in the world' (1996: 129). He identifies four categories of people who are more likely to be transnational: international business persons, immigrants from middle- and low-income countries living in wealthier countries, people engaged in cultural activities (dancers, musicians, film makers, artists), and tourists (see also **Bauman**). He writes that large numbers of 'expressive specialists' help to shape these cities' roles as transnational cultural marketplaces (1996: 135).

In working through the implications of the concepts of global ecumene and transnationalism, Hannerz posits that there is now one world culture (1996: 110). By this conclusion he is referring to the fact that all the variously distributed structures of meaning and expression are 'becoming interrelated, somehow, somewhere' (1996: 110). He adds that, those living in transnational spaces with cosmopolitan perspectives have a special role in bringing about a degree of coherence in this global ecumene.

Major globalization writings

Hannerz, U. (1992) *Cultural Complexity: Studies in the Social Organization of Meaning*, New York, NY: Columbia University Press.

——(1996) *Transnational Connections: Culture, People, Places*, London: Routledge.

——(2001) 'Thinking about culture in a global ecumene', in J. Lull (ed.) *Culture in the Communication Age*, London: Routledge.

——(2008) 'Afterword: anthropology's global ecumene', in A. Boskovic (ed.) *Other People's Anthropologies: Ethnographic Practice on the Margins*, New York, NY: Berghan Books.

——(2010) *Anthropology's World: Life in a Twenty-first-century Discipline*, London: Pluto Press

See also: **Abu-Lughod, Appadurai, Bauman, Beck, Brenner, Castells, Escobar, Giddens, Held, Sassen, Taylor, Tomlinson.**

MICHAEL HARDT (1960–) AND ANTONIO NEGRI (1933–)

Michael Hardt was born in Washington, DC, in 1960 and is a political philosopher and literary theorist currently based at Duke University, North Carolina. He received an MA in 1986 and a Ph.D. in 1990 in comparative literature from the University of Washington, US. His recent writings deal primarily with the political, legal, economic and social aspects of globalization. In his books with Antonio Negri, he has analysed the functioning of the current global power structure, as well as possible political and economic alternatives to that structure based on new institutions constituting a shared commonwealth.

Antonio Negri is an Italian Marxist sociologist, scholar, revolutionary philosopher and teacher. He was born in 1933 in Padua, Italy, and became a political militant as a young man, working towards significant societal change. He was jailed by the Italian government in 1979 for his work with a group called the Autonomy Movement. He escaped Italy in 1983 and fled to France, where he became active among French intellectuals. After negotiating a plea bargain, he returned to Italy in 1997 to finish his sentence. Many of his most influential books were published while he was behind bars. He now lives in Venice and Paris with his partner, French philosopher Judith Revel.

Hardt and Negri have collaborated on three highly influential books (2000, 2004, 2009). They see globalizing processes to be intimately linked with profound changes in the world order. These changes include the development of a new system of governance that is profoundly global, termed 'Empire'; a new system of production and form of capitalism intimately linked to information technologies; the constitution of a global base for resistance termed the 'multitude'; and the increasing importance of spaces and activities that are neither private nor public but 'common'.

Globalization, production, capitalism

Hardt and Negri argue that 'Globalization involves multiple processes that are not unified or univocal' (Hardt and Negri 2000: xv); nothing is fixed or finalized. They add that it is not simply a matter of resisting these processes but reorganizing them, redirecting them, and even giving rise to new processes that help move towards new ends. The vast numbers of global flows pierce through existing boundaries, bringing an end both to colonialism and to modernity as led by imperial powers: 'The age of globalization is the age of universal contagion' (2000: 136).

Drawing from and then building on these processes, we can increasingly speak of 'global markets' and 'global circuits of production'. Hardt and Negri speak of the 'postmodernization of the global economy' (2000: xiii). In commenting upon the global character of corporations, they observe that 'only in the second half of the twentieth century did multinational and transnational industrial and financial corporations begin to structure global territories biopolitically. Corporations [...] now tend to make nation-states merely instruments to record the flow of commodities, monies and populations that they set in motion' (2000: 31) (see also **Arrighi**, **Bello**, **Harvey**).

These changes are intimately linked to the forms of communication, language and symbolism arising from new digital technologies. These forms permit the development of communication networks essential to the constitution of global markets and production relations. These networks, in turn, have 'an organic relationship to the new world order, it is cause and effect, product and producer' (2000: 31). They facilitate new mechanisms of control that are more 'biopolitical', on the one side, and that involve 'the creation of new circuits of cooperation and collaboration that stretch across nations and continents and allow an unlimited number of encounters', on the other (Hardt and

Negri 2004: xiii). These new circuits make possible the production of languages, knowledges, codes, information and affects that are necessary for resistance and for formulating alternative worlds (Hardt and Negri 2009: viii) (see also **Chakrabarty**).

Hardt and Negri observe further that these networks and flows constitute a regime for the production of identity and difference as homogenization and heterogenization (see also **Bauman**, **Robertson**). They stress that local identities for resistance are not established outside of globalizing processes and the global economy. Rather, local resistance gives priority to 'reterritorializing' boundaries while the global movements prioritize the mobility of 'deterritorializing flows' (Hardt and Negri 2000: 46). Resistance that is only focused on local factors can never succeed without engaging in global links and confronting global institutions (for a counter-argument, see **Escobar**, **Santos**).

Rule through Empire

Hardt and Negri use the term 'Empire' to suggest a form of governance that is imperial on the one side, where some powerful groups control the lives of many others in pursuit of their own interests. On the other side, this emerging form of governance marks a transition from old forms of imperialism, including the period of US domination, to a new world order whose form is currently unknown. The contemporary global order, they suggest, is 'characterized by a distribution of powers, or more precisely a form of network power, which requires the wide collaboration of dominant nation-states, major corporations, supranational economic and political institutions, various NGOs, media conglomerates, and a series of other powers' (Hardt and Negri 2009: 205). In contrast to earlier forms of imperial rule, therefore, Empire is decentred; it establishes no territorial centre of power and does not rely on fixed boundaries (Hardt and Negri 2000: xii). The shift to Empire makes possible the realization of the capitalist goal of bringing together economic and political power, thereby creating a proper global capitalist order (see **Dirlik**).

In the newly globalized world, no state can pursue its interests and dominate without collaborating with the other major powers and organizations that make up Empire. Hardt and Negri thus challenge the arguments of those who hold that after the end of the Cold War, the US was building a stronger, more globally entrenched empire. They see the US's 'adventures' in Iraq and Afghanistan, among other places, as the last gasp of traditional forms of imperialism. While the US remains a strong contributor to Empire, other international powers, including corporations, have arrived at the conclusion that the US no longer advances their global interests, nor does it have the capacity to do so. They point to difficulties experienced by the US in getting its own way in the Doha Round of trade negotiations at the World Trade Organization and in attempts to set up a Free Trade Area of the Americas as indicative of its decline (Hardt and Negri 2009: 16). They conclude: 'We are living today in a period of transition, an interregnum in which the old imperialism is dead and the new Empire is still emerging' (2009: 18) (see also **Cox**).

The paradigm shift in the new form of rule takes several forms. First, drawing from Foucault, they note that the system of rule works through controlling the brains and bodies of the ruled. They describe this paradigm of power as 'biopolitical'. The pre-eminence of intellectual, immaterial and communicative labour power in the present era over the physical labour power characteristic of the previous one leads to the control of labour by inducing workers to discipline themselves and their bodies (see also **Ong**).

At the same time, Empire works towards a new juridical order, a system of rule anchored in global laws and norms. Moral and juridical force is anchored in laws and forms such as human rights frameworks. Hardt and Negri argue that many non-governmental organizations help to enforce these rules by framing the opposition to Empire in terms of violations of human rights (for alternative perspectives, see **Falk**, **Howard-Hassmann**). These moral arguments thus create rationales for 'intervention' by the dominant imperial institutions in the new order. The right of intervention is based on an appeal to universal values, the essential values of justice. Such appeals create the basis for the 'right of police' to intervene (Hardt and Negri 2000: 18).

Under old imperial thinking, interventions through war were the exception; they took place only after politics failed. Influenced by Deleuze and Guattari's conceptualization of the 'war machine', Hardt and Negri argue that under Empire, war no longer occurs only when politics fails, but becomes normalized. War enters into general discourse in phrases such as the 'war on terror' or the 'war on drugs'. These phrases are not simply metaphors but refer to real wars against indefinite enemies. The limits to the use of war become indeterminate. All the while war becomes indistinguishable from police activity. The shift in language from 'defence' to 'security' 'leads to an active and constant shaping of the environment through military and/or police activity' (Hardt and Negri 2004: 20).

The multitude and the common

Consistent with their thinking about production and capitalism, on the one hand, and the nature of rule, on the other, Hardt and Negri argue for a new consideration of the oppressed, the impoverished and the poor. Rather than referring to 'labour' or labour organizations, which were concepts developed to talk about resistance in state-based former imperial rule, they suggest a new term: the multitude. What globalization has gradually produced is a large population of the poor and the disenfranchised that live in close proximity to the wealthy everywhere in the world. Such populations exist not only in the former colonized areas of the world, but in the very heart of the most prosperous countries as well. Some of this movement involves forced migration as capital demands cheap disposable bodies needed to run the engines of the global economy. Other aspects of migration arise in response to the deepening inequalities and to the lack of social support experienced by the impoverished. They need to move to survive.

Accordingly, Hardt and Negri argue that the multitude 'calls Empire into being'. A new decentralized global system of rule is needed to control the movements of the multitude and to ensure that these movements facilitate the on-going growth of the global economy and not challenge its existence. In response to Empire, the multitude seeks global citizenship – the right to move anywhere in the world at any time. 'Global citizenship is the multitude's power to reappropriate control over space and thus to design the cartography' (Hardt and Negri 2000: 400). More generally, Hardt and Negri see the project of the multitude as building a world of equality and freedom and an open and inclusive global society. The principal obstacle to this goal is the current global state of war (Hardt and Negri 2004: xi). They speak to the rise of antagonistic subjects 'from below' that challenge this permanent state through the expression of 'indignation' in the face of the lack of freedoms and the injustices of power. When they invoke the need for an alternative cartography, they stress that 'the breakdown of borders does not determine nomadism, but instead nomadism itself breaks down borders and threatens the territorial stability of capitalist control' (Hardt and Negri 2009: 244).

The multitude might be thus conceived as: 'an open and expansive network in which all differences can be expressed freely and equally, a network that provides the means of encounter so that we can work and live in common' (Hardt and Negri 2004: xiii). In their view, a primary effect of globalization is the creation of a common world, 'a world that for better or worse, we all share, a world that has no "outside"'

(Hardt and Negri 2009: vii). They argue that the binary of public (state actions) versus private (capitalism) fits the old imperial order. However, globalization confounds this binary by making the 'common' more apparent. They emphasize the need 'to institute and manage a world of common wealth, focusing on and expanding our capacities for collective production and self government' (2009: x). They conclude their analysis by suggesting that the 'metropolis' will increasingly become the site for these struggles because 'it is the space of the common, of people living together, sharing resources, communicating, exchanging goods and ideas' (2009: 250). Open to 'aleatory encounters', metropolitan life is becoming a general planetary condition, but also a dangerous place, especially for the poor.

Major globalization writings

Hardt, M. and Negri, A. (2000) *Empire*, Boston, MA: Harvard University Press.

——(2004) *Multitude: War and Democracy in the Age of Empire*, New York, NY: Penguin Group.

——(2009) *Commonwealth*, Boston, MA: Harvard University Press.

Further reading

Deleuze, G. and Guattari, F. (1987) *A Thousand Plateaus: Capitalism and Schizophrenia*, trans. B. Massumi, Minneapolis, MN: University of Minnesota Press.

See also: **Arrighi, Bauman, Bello, Chakrabarty, Cox, Dirlik, Escobar, Falk, Harvey, Howard-Hassmann, Ong, Robertson, Santos**.

DAVID HARVEY (1935–)

David Harvey was born in 1935 in Gillingham, Kent, in England. Starting from his Ph.D. (on hop production in the nineteenth-century), Harvey's attention to history has been an important component of his research as he has gradually shifted his scholarship to focus on issues of social injustice and the nature of the capitalist system. After teaching at the University of Bristol from 1961 to 1969, he moved to Johns Hopkins University in the US where he positioned himself centrally in the newly emerging field of radical and Marxist geography. He returned to the UK to teach at the University of Oxford between 1987 and 1993. Since 2001, he has been Distinguished Professor of Anthropology at the City University of New York. Perhaps most famous for his bestselling work *The Condition of Postmodernity* (1989), he has also engaged critically with the globalization literature over the past 20 years.

Capitalism and globalization

In order to understand contemporary globalization, Harvey argues, one has to begin with capitalism and the logic of capitalist accumulation (see also **Brenner**). Since the fifteenth century, this logic has led to the gradual incorporation of most parts of the world within the capitalist system. With such global processes in play, the question then becomes: why has the word 'globalization' been used to characterize these processes and their effects since 1970? Harvey (2010: 157) draws our attention to the following statement by Karl Marx from *The Communist Manifesto* in 1848:

> All old established industries have been destroyed or are daily being destroyed [...] In place of the old wants, satisfied by the productions of the country, we find new wants, requiring for their satisfaction the products of distant lands and climes. In place of the old local and national seclusion and self-sufficiency, we have intercourse in every direction, universal interdependence of nations.

Harvey adds, 'what we call "globalization" has been in the sights of capital all along'.

Beginning with the fifteenth century, Harvey argues, there has been an inexorable trend for capitalism to expand geographically, producing what he calls 'time-space compression': 'a world in which capital moves faster and faster and where distances of interaction are compressed' (2010: 158) (see also **Brenner, Giddens, Scholte**). Like other scholars influenced by Marx (**Amin, Arrighi, Cox**), Harvey identifies two competing logics of power related to capitalist expansion: territorial and capitalist. Whereas capitalism operates in continuous time and space, politicians function in territorialized spaces. The anchoring of supportive institutions for capitalism in particular places is necessary for its expansion. But when the spatial range of capitalism becomes hampered by the territorial logic institutionalized at a given time, a crisis develops leading to changes in both the capitalist and territorial logics (Harvey 2005b: 183) (see also **Arrighi**).

Harvey pays particular attention to what he terms 'capitalist imperialism' or the 'imperialism of capital'. This form of capitalism became dominant in the latter part of the nineteenth century and is distinguished by the subordination of the territorial logic to the capitalist logic. At this point, the bourgeoisie (capitalist class) became the ruling class for the first time, with Britain acting as the hegemon – a period of domination that lasted approximately from 1870 to 1945. The second stage in the political rule of the bourgeoisie lasted from 1945 to 1970 under US hegemony and dominance. As other scholars have noted (**Amin**, **Arrighi**, **Bello**, **Cox**), this period was one of remarkable economic growth across the world. With the US clearly in the leadership role, the major capitalist countries avoided internecine wars and shared in the benefits of impressive capitalist growth in their regions. The geographical expansion of capitalism was eased by decolonization and by 'developmentalism' as a generalized goal for the rest of the world (2005b: 57–58). This period came to an end as a result of the US overreaching politically (the Vietnam War) and economically, while facing more intense competition from other capitalist powers (Germany and Japan).

Neoliberalism and contemporary globalization

Accordingly, Harvey situates many of the changes labelled 'globalization' by other scholars in the context of the history of capitalist imperialism and refers to them as the 'production of uneven temporal and geographical development' (Harvey 1995: 8). Contemporary globalization is a response to a crisis in capitalist over-accumulation (excess capital due to a lack of investment possibilities). But a crisis in capitalism also brings with it a crisis of the organization of territory: existing territorial arrangements are seen as preventing the full exploitation of the capital available. Specifically, this crisis is one linked to the territorial organization of US hegemony and domination of the world economy in the period between 1945 and 1970.

Normally, to address such crises in an imperialist era, processes termed 'accumulation by dispossession' need to take place. Borrowing from Marx's notion of 'primitive accumulation', Harvey says that these processes involve securing the release of assets, including labour power, at very low cost (or, in some instances such as slavery, zero cost). Once released, capitalists can invest their excess capital to exploit these assets for profit (Harvey 2005b: 149). For Harvey, then, many of the new trans-planetary processes that emerge beginning in the 1970s, and that are termed 'globalization', involve accumulation by dispossession.

Neoliberalism provides the ideological framework for justifying the violence needed for releasing new assets for capital investment and for making these changes appear to be 'common sense'. The change in territorial logic accompanying this ideology is embodied in the neoliberal state (see also **Brenner**). Harvey defines neoliberalism as a 'theory of political economic practices that proposes that human well-being can best be advanced by liberating individual entrepreneurial freedoms and skills within an institutional framework characterized by strong private property rights, free markets, and free trade' (Harvey 2005a: 2). The proponents of this ideology take the political ideals of human dignity and individual freedom as fundamental, ideals that are compelling and persuasive. These values, neoliberal proponents argue, are threatened by any form of state intervention that substituted collective judgements for those of individuals who had the freedom to choose (2005a: 5).

Based on this thinking, the fundamental mission of the state must be to facilitate conditions for the profitable accumulation of capital through investment whether the sources of capital are domestic or foreign. To achieve these ends, the neoliberal state:

> [...] should favour strong individual private property rights, the rule of law, and the institutions of freely functioning markets and free trade [...] The state must therefore use its monopoly of the means of violence to preserve these freedoms at all costs.
>
> (Harvey 2005a: 64)

The neoliberal state thus creates and protects the conditions for accumulation by dispossession in the contemporary globalization period. In fact, the globalization of neoliberal thinking and of the neoliberal form of the state are two of the most important changes distinguishing the current era from the two earlier ones of capitalist imperialism.

Harvey discusses several different processes for pursuing accumulation by dispossession. 'Financialization' is the first of these and refers to the taking of steps to create fully global financial markets through the reduction, if not elimination, of state regulation and control of financial transactions. The wave of innovations in financial services not only improved trans-world financial connections, but also led to new kinds of markets for securities, derivatives and futures trading. 'Neoliberalization has meant, in short, the financialization of everything' (2005a: 33) (see also **Arrighi**, **Cox**, **Helleiner**). At the same time, this set of changes weakened the dominance of the US, which had controlled the world financial and monetary system through the International Monetary Fund (IMF) and the World Bank in the immediate period after World War II.

A second key process is privatization: the transfer of productive public assets from the state to the private sector. In the period after 1970, capitalist states gradually moved to privatize more and more of the distribution of public goods and services. In the wealthier states, these changes involved more private investment in education, social welfare, health and culture. In addition, traditional parts of the public domain – forests, water, air – become available for sale or lease (see also **Cerny**).

An even more strict form of neoliberal thinking came to inform the IMF and the World Bank during the 1980s and 1990s. Acting through Structural Adjustment Programmes, many weaker states were required to privatize large parts of their public sectors in exchange for loans to address balance of payment difficulties (see **Amin, Bello**). Through the creation of the World Trade Organization (WTO), they were also compelled to reduce obstacles to foreign direct investment in their territories. Accordingly, during this period, most of the state economies in the world became more 'open', giving rise to the rapid growth of the numbers of transnational corporations doing business in all parts of the world. At this time, there is also a shift of investment in industrialization to many of these same areas due to lower labour costs and worker protections. Privatization also involved the enshrinement of intellectual property rights in global law through the Trade-Related Aspects of Intellectual Property Rights (TRIPS) agreement of the WTO.

With this thinking as his departure point, Harvey interprets the innovations in, and rapid growth of, information and communication technologies differently from other globalization scholars. He sees reductions in time and cost of transportation, improved trans-world communication tools and the ability to compress large amounts of information both as enabling financialization and privatization, and as responses to these various processes. He adds that these technologies also enable individualization, particularly individual consumption, so necessary to capitalist expansion. They also reinforce the idea of the free and autonomous individual at the core of neoliberal thinking and the individual as a consumer of culture (Harvey 2002).

He summarizes: 'Neoliberalism became, in short, hegemonic as a universalistic mode of discourse as well as a foundation for public policies worldwide. It increasingly defines the common sense way many of us interpret, live in, and understand the world. We are, often without knowing it, all neoliberals now' (Harvey 2009: 57). Despite its close association with the US, however, Harvey sees a diminishing of that country's global dominance and hegemony in this globalizing period. Financialization, extensive military expenditures particularly in Iraq and Afghanistan, and relocation of manufacturing to other parts of the world have opened the door to new sites of power, notably China, but also other East Asian countries, Brazil and India (see also **Amin, Arrighi, Cox**). He argues, in particular, that the neoliberal policies on international trade opened up the world to new market forces, most notably China's 'tumultuous entry' into the world market. The policies in place in the 1945 to 1980 era, particularly the US control of currency markets, would not have permitted China's emergence (Harvey 2005a: 121). When it comes to challenging these changes, Harvey speaks briefly about the potential of 'subaltern cosmopolitanism', building on the activities of social groups everywhere fighting neoliberalism in local places (Harvey 2009: 95–97) (see also **Santos**).

Major globalization writings

Harvey, D. (1990) *The Condition of Postmodernity: An Enquiry into the Origins of Cultural Change*, Oxford, UK: Blackwell.

——(1995) 'Globalization in question', *Rethinking Marxism*, vol 8, no 4, pp. 1–17.

——(2002) 'The art of rent: globalization, monopoly and the commodification of culture', *Socialist Register*, vol 38 pp. 93–110.

——(2005a) *A Brief History of Neoliberalism*, Oxford, UK: Oxford University Press.

——(2005b) *The New Imperialism*, Oxford, UK: Oxford University Press.

——(2009) *Cosmopolitanism and the Geographies of Freedom*, New York, NY: Columbia University Press.

——(2010) *The Enigma of Capital and the Crises of Capitalism*, New York, NY: Oxford University Press.

See also: **Amin, Arrighi, Bello, Brenner, Cerny, Cox, Giddens, Helleiner, Santos, Scholte.**

DAVID HELD (1951–)

David Held was born in the UK and spent most of his childhood there. He was educated in the UK, France, Germany and the US. He holds a Ph.D. from the Massachusetts Institute of Technology (MIT), an M.Sc. from MIT and a B.Sc. from the Manchester University Institute of Science and Technology. David Held's main research interests include rethinking democracy at transnational and international levels and the study of globalization and global governance. He has strong interests both in political theory and in the more empirical dimensions of political analysis. During the last five years he has lectured regularly on questions of democracy, international justice and globalization to audiences in many countries. Two decades ago David Held co-founded Polity Press, which is now a major presence in social science and humanities publishing. In 2011, he resigned his position as Graham Wallas Professor of Political Science at the London School of Economics and Political Science and took up the position of Master of University College, Durham University, UK.

Defining globalization

Held began writing about globalization during the early 1990s and these writings culminated in his highly influential book *Democracy and the Global Order.* In this book, he provides an initial definition that draws from his earlier articles: 'the stretching of social relations across space and time, via a variety of institutional dimensions (technological, organizational, legal and cultural) and their intensification within these domains' (Held 1995: 98). Working then with frequent co-author Anthony McGrew and two other scholars, David Goldblatt and Jonathan Perraton, Held wrote a second highly influential book, *Global Transformations*, which built systematically on this earlier definition (Held *et al.* 1999: 16): 'a process (or set of processes) which embodies a transformation in the spatial organization of social relations and transactions – assessed in terms of their extensity, intensity, velocity and impact – generating transcontinental or interregional flows and networks of activity, interaction, and the exercise of power'. By 'flows', Held *et al.* include movements of physical artefacts, people, symbols, tokens and information. His reference to 'networks' draws, in part, from **Castells**' analysis.

During the late 1990s, as Held was building on this definition, he was also participating in a debate over how best to conceptualize globalization, how scholars should think about its causal dynamics and its history, and what are its wider structural consequences, if any. Working with McGrew, he discussed two positions on these issues that he found wanting. The first, 'hyperglobalism', presented globalization as a new epoch in human history where nation-states are being largely eclipsed by the private sector operating in a single competitive global market, while the second position, 'scepticism', held that contemporary levels of economic interdependence had occurred earlier in human history; accordingly, the contemporary era did not involve a new world order (see **Hirst, Thompson and Bromley**). Held contributed a third position to this debate, 'transformationalism'. He argues that globalization is bringing profound change to societies and governments around the world and adds that the direction of these changes remains uncertain. By the early 1990s, Held had already taken up this transformationalist view and pointed out that this position allowed scholars to avoid an economy-centred and, thus, limited view of globalization. Globalization brings dramatic changes not only to the economy but also to political, cultural, military, technological, ecological and migratory spheres. As these processes unfold, he stresses, the power, functions and authority of national governments are being reconstituted, but not necessarily weakened, as suggested by the hyperglobalist position.

In developing an analytical framework for supporting this argument, Held stresses that the first characteristic of globalizing processes to observe is their *extensity* (see also **Scholte**) – that is, the changes they bring to 'spatio-temporal' processes in order to transform human living by linking together and expanding human activity across the world. Second, analysis should take into account the *intensity* of these processes: the degree to which they penetrate and change the daily living of people everywhere in the world. Third, scholars should assess the *velocity* of these connections: how rapidly they are being formed and made. With these processes taken into account, scholars will then be well prepared to analyse a fourth dimension of change: the degree to which local and global changes are enmeshed in ways that heighten the *impact* of global events locally and that magnify the worldwide consequences of local developments.

Putting together these four spatio-temporal dimensions permits Held and his colleagues to distinguish four different types of globalization. *Thick globalization* represents a world where extensity, intensity and velocity are high and reciprocity between local and global events is frequent and important. *Diffused globalization* is similar to the thick version except that the reciprocity between local and global events is low. *Expansive globalization* has high extensivity of global connections, while the intensity and velocity of these connections are low. Nonetheless, when these connections occur, the impact locally and globally is high. Finally, *thin globalization* involves high extensity of connections; but these might be fewer in number and the intensity, speed and impact of those connections locally and globally are weak.

This analytical framework paved the way for Held to enter the debate that began during the late 1990s over the novelty or the singularity of contemporary globalization when compared to similar processes in earlier periods. He notes that there were important examples of globalizing processes before the sixteenth century, but that these tended to be 'thin'. The period between 1500 and 1850 brought important accelerations in the four dimensions of globalization as key European institutions of modernity developed. Alongside important innovations in communications and travel technologies, European empires became a catalyst for significant increases in global connections. The period of modern globalization, 1850 to 1945, brought a further change in extensity, intensity and velocity of global connections, with even deeper effects on local communities and larger numbers of people. Finally, he carries out a review of the importance of global connections in the domains of politics, law and governance; military affairs; cultural linkages and human migrations; shared global environmental threats; and finally all dimensions of economic activity. Based on this analysis, Held argues that a distinctive historical form of globalization began to emerge after 1945. For the first time in history, globalization has some of the attributes of 'thick' globalization (for similar arguments, see also **Hopkins, Rosenau, Sassen, Scholte, Tomlinson**).

Political communities

Of the many implications that arise from this understanding of globalization, Held stresses the significance of the transformations that occur in political communities (Held 1995; Held *et al.* 1999; Held and McGrew 2007). To an extent not seen in history before, political communities can no longer be viewed as self-enclosed political spaces. Although previously somewhat enclosed within nation-states, communities are changed by globalizing processes that enmesh them in complex structural arrangements of overlapping relationships and networks with other communities in the world (Held and McGrew 2007: 211–213). The growth in trans-border political issues erodes familiar distinctions between domestic and foreign affairs, internal and external political issues, and traditional understandings of state sovereignty. What develops under these circumstances is what Held terms *overlapping communities of fate*. People are bound together by processes no longer controlled by nation-state governments. Such communities of fate include, among others, those affected by the management of nuclear waste; rising water levels due to climate change; levels of regulation of global banks and financial markets; the militarization of outer space; sharing a common culture in a globally extensive diaspora or a religious sect; the building of foreign military bases; and the spread of diseases such as HIV/AIDS, severe acute respiratory syndrome (SARS), tuberculosis and malaria.

The rapid growth of such communities of fate means, according to Held, that it is anachronistic to think that nation-states and longstanding international relations involving states can remain the dominant centres of decision-making. 'Political communities today are locked into a diversity of processes and structures which range in and through them, linking and fragmenting them into complex constellations. Moreover, national communities themselves by no means make and determine decisions and policies exclusively for themselves when they decide on such issues as the regulation of sexuality, health and the environment' (Held *et al.* 1999: 445). Accordingly, questions are raised about the very idea of political community and about the appropriate space where political goods might be articulated and pursued. Of even greater importance for Held is the significance of these questions for democracy itself.

Cosmopolitan democracy

As a political theorist and a scholar committed to democracy as a mode of governance, Held has sought to explore in depth the implications for governance of globalization and of the accompanying changes in political community. In the last two parts of *Democracy and the Global Order*, Held (1995) lays out a compelling theoretical argument for a new governance approach entitled cosmopolitan democracy. In subsequent writings, he has expanded upon, simplified and linked his theoretical corpus to on-going political problems and debates about the contemporary world. For example, in 2004, he published the well-received and often-read book *Global Covenant: The Social Democratic Alternative to the Washington Consensus*. He has been consistently willing to speak about the implications of his understanding of globalization and about these possibilities for democratic governance in ways accessible not only to academics but also to the informed public.

The basic values of cosmopolitanism espouse the idea 'that human beings are in a fundamental sense equal, and they deserve equal political treatment, that is, treatment based upon the equal care and consideration of their agency, irrespective of the community in which they were born or brought up' (Held 2010: 537). Cosmopolitan values can be expressed in terms of a set of eight principles: equal worth and dignity; active agency; personal responsibility and accountability; consent; collective decision-making about public issues through voting procedures; inclusiveness and subsidiarity; avoidance of serious harm; and sustainability. Held argues that these eight principles are interrelated and together provide the basis of an orientation that helps to illuminate what human beings have in common. He discusses these interrelationships in considerable detail in an article on law (Held 2002).

In making the case for cosmopolitan democracy, Held (1995, 2002) examines at length the concept of sovereignty and how that concept has gradually changed in nature in the period following World War II. During this period, he argues, classical sovereignty was dislodged and replaced by a regime that he terms 'liberal international sovereignty'. He systematically surveys legal developments since 1945 as they bear on rules of warfare and weaponry; war crimes and the role of the individual; human rights, democracy and minority groups; and environmental law (2002: 6–17). Based on this review, he shows that national sovereignty and autonomy are now embedded within broader frameworks of governance and law. As a consequence, states have become but one site for the exercise of political power and authority (see also **Howard-Hassmann**, **Sassen**, **Scholte**). Moreover, states gain legitimacy to the extent to which they support human rights and democratic standards. In addition, the boundaries between states, nations and societies can no longer claim the deep legal and moral significance they possessed in the past (2002: 20). The changes to sovereignty that occurred in this liberal internationalist period are important, on the one hand, but increasingly inadequate, on the other. The inadequacies arise from their continuing state-centric character and, hence, their inability to accommodate the effects of globalizing processes that increasingly enmesh in changing political communities, or what he terms overlapping communities of fate. With globalization, the degrees of mutual connectedness and vulnerability are growing rapidly. What is needed now, Held argues, is a common framework of action informed by cosmopolitan values. Cosmopolitanism thus builds on such strengths of the liberal internationalist order as human rights and democratic values by framing what is to be done in terms of the eight principles noted above.

When these principles are followed through to their logical conclusion:

> [...] people would in principle come to enjoy multiple citizenships – political membership, that is, in the diverse political communities that significantly affect them. In a world of overlapping communities of fate, individuals would be citizens of their immediate political communities and of the wider regional and global networks that impact upon their lives.
>
> (Held 2002: 33)

Held details the implications of these ideas in many of his later works, but the bedrock analysis is found in Section 4 of *Democracy and the Global Order*. He argues consistently that a fundamental rethinking of global governance is necessary if symmetry between decision-makers and decision-takers is to be restored, having been lost ever more rapidly since 1945 as contemporary globalization has continued apace. Such symmetry, of course, is a necessary condition for democracy.

Major globalization writings

Held, D. (1991) 'Democracy, the nation-state and the global system', *Economy and Society*, vol 20, no 2, pp. 138–172.

——(1995) *Democracy and the Global Order: From the Modern State to Cosmopolitan Governance*, Stanford, CA: Stanford University Press.

——(2000) 'Regulating globalization? The reinvention of politics', *International Sociology*, vol 15, no 2, pp. 394–408.

——(2002) 'Law of states, law of peoples', *Legal Theory*, vol 8, no 1, pp. 1–44.

——(2003) 'Cosmopolitanism: globalization tamed?', *Review of International Studies*, vol 29, no 4, pp. 465–480.

——(2004) *Global Covenant: The Social Democratic Alternative to the Washington Consensus*, Oxford, UK: Polity Press.

——(2009) 'Restructuring global governance: cosmopolitanism, democracy and the global order', *Millennium: Journal of International Studies*, vol 37, no 3, pp. 535–547.

——(2010) *Cosmopolitanism: Ideals and Realities*, Cambridge, UK: Polity Press.

Held, D. and McGrew, A. (2007) *Globalization/Anti-globalization: Beyond the Great Divide*, Cambridge, UK: Polity Press.

Held, D., McGrew, A., Goldblatt, D. and Perraton, J. (1999) *Global Transformations: Politics, Economics and Culture*, Stanford, CA: Stanford University Press.

See also: **Castells, Howard-Hassmann, Rosenau, Sassen, Scholte, Tomlinson.**

ERIC HELLEINER (1963–)

Eric Helleiner received his BA in economics and political science from the University of Toronto in 1986, and his M.Sc. and Ph.D. from the Department of International Relations of the London School of Economics in 1987 and 1991, respectively. He taught at York University and held a Canada Research chair at Trent University before taking up a CIGI chair in international political economy at the University of Waterloo in 2007. He was named a fellow/lauréat of the Pierre E. Trudeau Foundation in 2007. He has also won the Donner Book Prize for his research on currencies and the Marvin Gelber Essay Prize in International Relations. He oversaw the design and implementation of the joint interdisciplinary Ph.D. programme in Global Governance at the University of Waterloo and Wilfrid Laurier University, and of the MA Programme in Global Governance, now based at the Balsillie School of International Affairs. In the first 20 years of his career, he has gained a global reputation for his outstanding research and publications on international finance, globalization, currencies and global governance.

Helleiner has explored in depth the role that states play in the contemporary globalization period, which began, in his view, during the 1970s. More specifically, he challenges arguments that claim that market developments, particularly the growth of transnational corporations, as well as technological innovations, are the best explanatory factors. He makes his case by focusing on what many people believe is the deepest example of globalization: changes in financial markets. By showing that states are the principal creators of global financial markets, his analysis becomes particularly compelling.

Globalization

Helleiner provides a broader discussion of globalization than some authors who have focused on economic globalization (such as **Hirst,**

Thompson and Bromley, **Weiss**). He writes: 'economic globalization is an "intensification of world-wide economic relations" that can be seen as an economic, political, social and cultural process taking place at several different historical speeds and involving a compression of space, time and hierarchy' (Helleiner 1997: 102). He reaches this definition by drawing on the thinking of **Braudel**, who suggested that key historical changes be studied from various observation points along four distinct axes: space, time, 'social orders' and hierarchy. From the *space* perspective, globalization can be viewed as a process of 'spatial compression'. As such, it has been going on for over 500 years, continually reconfiguring the world in varying ways and, in particular, presenting challenges to the territoriality of the nation-state over the past 40 years. From the perspective of *time*, we see how globalization as a historical process has gone through three phases: fifteenth to the eighteenth century, from 1850 to 1914, and the present era beginning in the 1970s. **Braudel**'s four social orders include the economic, political, social and cultural. Here Helleiner outlines changes in globalization from the perspective of each of these orders. His analysis of hierarchy suggests that globalization began as a process principally involving societal elites and over time has penetrated ever more deeply into societies (at varying speeds across the world) to affect more and more people directly.

Financial globalization

In his first book, *States and the Reemergence of Global Finance*, Helleiner (1994) notes that financial markets in the period between 1850 and the 1920s had become highly liberalized and increasingly global. These liberal arrangements collapsed beginning in 1931 and most definitely after the outbreak of World War II (Helleiner 1995: 317). As victory in this war became ever more clear, the Allied powers, led by the US and the UK, developed plans for a new international order based on the concept of 'embedded liberalism': financial markets would be strongly controlled by states to permit them to build effective social welfare safety nets (see **Howard-Hassmann**, **Ruggie**). Such financial markets would enable states to reconstruct their economic and social structures after the war and to ensure that prosperity benefited the large majority in societies, not just a highly wealthy financial elite. The 1944 Bretton Woods Agreement granted countries the explicit 'right' to use capital controls and almost all of the advanced industrial states did employ extensive controls in the early post-war years (1995: 317–318). The world hegemon, the US, did not itself employ capital controls initially, but was very accepting of their use by other states.

The first break in these arrangements came when the UK government, with the tacit support of the US, permitted the development of a 'Euromarket': the buying and selling of US dollars and the trading of securities in US dollars based in the City of London, the UK's principal financial district. Facing inflation and rising costs from the Vietnam War, the US imposed its own capital controls during the late 1960s. These two events, among others, were preliminary to the US deciding to push for the liberalization of financial markets, thus setting the stage for the globalization of finance. As the world economy faced new challenges, the Japanese and then West German governments pushed for cooperative action to control financial markets (1995: 322). The US blocked this arrangement, preferring to move in a liberal direction. It announced in 1973 that it would eliminate its own capital controls. US-based transnational corporations were also increasingly frustrated by capital controls and had begun to support more openly thinkers advocating a neoliberal approach (see also **Harvey**). The UK was to follow the US in 1979 by abolishing its own capital controls. Helleiner details three events during the late 1970s and early 1980s that might have led back to more controlled financial markets. When these failed, wealthy governments gradually moved to abolish capital controls one by one, signalling the full arrival of financial globalization.

In concluding his discussion of the steps taken by states to create a global liberal financial order, Helleiner stresses that factors noted by other scholars such as technology (see **Castells**) and market changes (see **Arrighi**) were also linked to these state decisions. Transnational corporations were growing rapidly in number and in size and operating on an increasingly global scale. These operations, in turn, drew heavily upon the innovations in information and communication technologies. Helleiner is not interested in downplaying markets and technological innovation. Rather, he argues that the decisions of states have been often ignored as important contributing factors to financial globalization.

Accompanying the globalization of financial markets was the gradual development of the regulation of financial markets at the international level. Beginning in the mid-1970s, in response to the collapse of two banks with global ties, an emerging regime began to regulate banks (Committee on Banking Supervision), securities markets (International Organization of Securities Commissions), insurance markets (International Association of Insurance Supervisors) and payments systems (Committee on Payment and Settlement Systems) (Helleiner and Pagliari 2010: 2–3). After the financial crisis in 1997 to 1998, these arrangements expanded further as dominant OECD states promoted their rules across the world. At the same time, these arrangements were generally quite fragmented and weak. In comparison with the highly integrated and legalized trade regime (after the creation of the World Trade Organization in 1994), for example, international financial governance was weak. And also in contrast to trade, the organizations involved tended to be very exclusive, having a narrow membership drawn from the principal capitalist powers. Helleiner and Pagliari also note that after the 1997 to 1998 crisis, rather than reinforcing these regulatory bodies, states assigned more and more of the responsibility for regulating financial and securities markets to private market actors (in essence, the global banks and securities houses) (2010: 3–4).

These observations are important because Helleiner underlines the importance of states in driving financial globalization in two other respects. First, states have played the leading role in resolving financial crises. He observes that this role has been no more evident than in the financial crisis that began in 2007 to 2008. Public authorities not only provided massive emergency assistance to support the financial system but also nationalized various leading global banks (Helleiner 2009: 67). He writes: 'And it has been *national* officials above all that have played the most decisive role [...] If it was not clear before, it is now hard to ignore the fact that nation-states, backed up by national taxpayers, provide the ultimate foundation of international financial markets' (2009: 67). Second, states have benefited directly from financial globalization. Over the last decade, in particular, states have become significant investors in their own right in global financial markets through the creation of sovereign wealth funds. Particularly active here have been oil exporting countries and East Asian exporters (particularly China and Singapore) (2009: 63). In addition, financial globalization has increased the structural power of the US, and permitted it, for example, to finance its own large fiscal deficits through investments by other, particularly East Asian, states (see also **Strange**).

Over the past decade, Helleiner has extended his research on global finance to include a close look at currencies, with a particular concern for the role of the US dollar. Based on his historical research, he demonstrates that territorial currencies linked to nation-states, such as the US dollar, are relatively recent phenomena with their influence expanding since the nineteenth century. He also suggests that globalization is affecting these currencies by weakening the link between national identities and territorial currencies (Helleiner 2003: 242). Other contemporary challenges include the rise of 'electronic money', the widespread use of foreign currencies in poorer countries, and a growing interest in local currencies due to the internet and the interests of the environmental movement (2003: 243). With respect to the US dollar in particular, he observes that the dollar's economic attractiveness increased as financial globalization intensified due to the unique depth, breadth and efficiency of US financial markets (Helleiner 2008: 367). Helleiner remarks that the US currency shifted temporarily from a 'negotiated' position to a more predominantly 'top' one (Susan **Strange**'s terminology). The increased economic difficulties of the US in the first decade of the twenty-first century, however, have shifted the currency back to a 'negotiated' position and have even raised questions about it falling even further in influence.

Major globalization writings

Helleiner, E. (1994) *States and the Reemergence of Global Finance: From Bretton Woods to the 1990s*, Ithaca, NY: Cornell University Press.

——(1995) 'Explaining the globalization of financial markets: bringing states back in', *Review of International Political Economy*, vol 2, no 2, pp. 315–341.

——(1997) 'Braudelian reflections on economic globalisation: the historian as pioneer', in S. Gill and J. Mittelman (eds) *Innovation and Transformation in International Studies*, Cambridge, UK: Cambridge University Press.

——(2003) *The Making of National Money: Territorial Currencies in Historical Perspective*, Ithaca, NY: Cornell University Press.

——(2008) 'Political determinants of international currencies: what future for the US dollar?', *Review of International Political Economy*, vol 15, no 3, pp. 354–378.

——(2009) 'The politics of global finance: does money make the world go round', *The Trudeau Foundation Papers*, Montreal, Pierre Elliott Trudeau Foundation, vol 1, pp. 46–66.

Helleiner, E. and Pagliari, S. (2010) 'Crisis and the reform of international financial regulation', in E. Helleiner, S. Pagliari and H. Zimmermann (eds) *Global Finance in Crisis: The Politics of International Regulatory Change*, London: Routledge.

——(2011) 'The end of an era in international financial regulation? A postcrisis research agenda', *International Organization*, vol 65 (Winter), pp. 169–200.

See also: **Arrighi**, **Braudel**, **Castells**, **Harvey**, **Hirst**, **Thompson and Bromley**, **Howard-Hassmann**, **Ruggie**, **Strange**, **Weiss**.

PAUL HIRST (1947–2003), GRAHAME THOMPSON (1945–) AND SIMON BROMLEY

Paul Hirst studied at the University of Leicester and the University of Sussex, UK, before taking up a lectureship at Birkbeck College, University of London, in 1969. In 1972, he was one of the founding members of the Department of Politics and Sociology at Birkbeck. Grahame Thompson, an economist, was originally a member of the Department of Economics at the Open University in the UK. Hirst and Thompson published the first edition of *Globalization in Question* in 1996, in which they challenged many of the claims made about globalization during the early 1990s. Their book generated tremendous debate and discussion to which they responded in 1999 with a second edition containing an updated and expanded analysis. Unfortunately, Professor Hirst passed away in 2003. Thompson recruited another colleague, Simon Bromley, to co-write a third edition, published in 2009. Bromley holds a first-class degree in social and political sciences from Cambridge (1983) and a Ph.D. also from Cambridge (1988). He is currently a professor at the Open University. The book (in its three editions) has been a classic in globalization studies for nearly two decades owing to its systematic analysis of economic globalization, its up-to-date observations of economic change over the past 15 years, and the sharpness and clarity of the authors' scepticism regarding many claims about globalization.

Models of the world economy

Hirst *et al.* enrich our understanding of globalization by arguing that states remain central actors in the global economy (see also **Brenner, Helleiner, Weiss**). At the same time, states have undergone important, if not profound, changes leading to limitations in policy capacity (see also **Cerny, Strange**). To pursue domestic economic growth and stability, they must collaborate ever more with other states if they are to be successful. They also argue that regional linkages between states have become more crucial and outweigh the significance of global ties.

Hirst *et al.* thus distinguish between the ideal types of an 'inter-national' and 'globalized economy'. An 'inter-national' economy is:

[...] one in which the principal entities are national economies. Trade and investment produce growing interconnections between these still national economies. These interconnections, in turn, lead to the increasing integration of more and more nations and economic actors into world market relationships.

(Hirst *et al.* 2009: 19)

The interdependence between states is strategic: there is a continued separation between areas of domestic and international policy-making, with these two policy fields remaining relatively distinct levels of governance. States retain control of the speed at which, and the degree to which, they adjust to international economic forces.

In contrast, in a globalized economy:

[...] national economies and their international interactions are subsumed and rearticulated by genuinely global processes and transactions into a new structure. Economic actors and activities become disembedded from national societies and domestic policies [...] and must routinely take account of the potentially global determinants of their sphere of operations.

(Hirst *et al.* 2009: 20)

In a globalized economy, corporations become fully transnational and are no longer rooted in a particular national economy and society. Capital mobility leads to important shifts of investment and employment to less wealthy countries, trade and investment are no longer concentrated in wealthy countries, and no country can regulate economic flows on its own.

In each of the three editions of their book, Hirst *et al.* draw on extensive empirical analysis to demonstrate that there is little fit between the working of the contemporary world economy and the 'globalized' model (for a counter-argument, see **Hopkins, Rosenau, Scholte**). They stress that the changes that have taken place in the economy are not at all unprecedented and point to economic developments in the period between 1870 and 1914 that are as important changes to the international economy as those that have occurred over the past 30 years. In making this historical comparison, they also note that the opposite of a globalized economy is not a nationally inward-looking one. Rather, the contemporary international economy is an open one 'based on trading nations and [is] regulated to a greater or lesser degree by both the public policies of nation-states and supra-national agencies' (2009: 21).

Changing roles of states

By presenting, revising and adding to their analysis over 13 years, Hirst *et al.* also contribute to globalization studies in detailing the ever-growing changes in states' interactions with the world economy. They begin by noting two aspects of states that have not changed much. First, states retain a large measure of control over the regulation of populations, including immigration, the flow of refugees and the movements of 'illegal migrants'. This control contributes to the legitimacy of states to speak internationally for their 'national' populations and on policies controlling the movement of people (Hirst *et al.* 2009: 225). Second, the vast inequalities in the distribution of power and social goods between wealthy and less wealthy states have not changed. If anything, these inequalities have deepened.

At the same time, Hirst *et al.* demonstrate that, over the 13 years spanned by the three editions of their book, states are becoming less autonomous, are losing control over economic and social processes within their territories, and are less able to sustain strong national identities. The evidence for these losses is particularly evident in questions of war. States will be less and less able to mobilize their societies and to build the degree of social solidarity and the common sense of national purpose necessary to pursue the total wars that occurred over the twentieth century (2009: 228). The emergence of new information communication technologies (ICTs) during the 1970s (see **Castells**) has led to a more integrated 'international' civil society in which people from a wide range of countries discover common interests. In their view, ICTs also open up the possibility of 'cosmopolitan' cultures (see also **Beck, Held**), whether elite or popular, scientific or artistic, 'linked through English as a universal rather than a national language' (2009: 231). With the possibility of an exclusive and self-sufficient 'national' culture thus threatened, states lose some control over their national territories, national culture and national homogeneity.

Over the same period, major multilateral institutions such as the World Trade Organization, the World Health Organization and other institutions in the United Nations system have become more globally inclusive. As a consequence, their roles in governance have become more important. Conversely, Hirst *et al.* add:

> [...] states will come to function less as all-purpose providers of governance and more as the authors and legitimators of an international 'quasi polity'; the central functions of the nation-state will become those of providing legitimacy for, and ensuring the accountability of, supranational and subnational governance mechanisms which exercise various forms of 'private' authority.
>
> (Hirst *et al.* 2009: 220)

Supranational regionalism

Over the 13 years that Hirst *et al.* have studied and expanded their analysis of economic change and its consequences, the rapid economic growth of economies in East Asia, particularly China, has begun to alter the geography of the world economy (see also **Arrighi, Brenner, Cox, Taylor**). Successive waves of Asian industrialization have led to the region accounting for over 35 per cent of world output and over 25 per cent of world exports. Since the start of the new millennium, the region has accounted for over 50 per cent of the world's economic growth. China has emerged as the most important contributor to this shift in the global economy towards Asia. Its economy has been the fastest growing in the world since 1979 with the consequence that China has become perhaps the 'dominant part of a general shift in the historical geography of industrial capitalism to emerging Asia' (Hirst *et al.* 2009: 143). Hirst *et al.* conclude that the combination of industrialization in North-East Asia and the prospect of sustained growth in South Asia indicate that the forces of convergence between these regions and the 'advanced capitalist economies' are very strong (2009: 156–157).

In assessing these changes, Hirst *et al.* are reluctant to see them as part of globalization. Rather, they argue that the trajectory for the international system is towards 'supranational regionalization' defined as a 'geographically contiguous area composed of the territories of nation-states that have either combined in an integrative economic or monetary union, or whose economies have evolved into a closely interdependent entity, or who can empirically be shown to be advancing along these routes' (2009: 159). Examples of these processes include the European Union (EU), the North American Free Trade Agreement (NAFTA), the Association of South-East Asian Nations (ASEAN) and the West African Economic and Monetary Union, among others. They suggest that the international system is showing strong tendencies towards forming into supra-regional blocs of this kind rather than intensifying globalization processes. Thus, 'under current conditions, the supranational regionalism/regionalization process looks to be more robust and convincing than full globalism/globalization' (2009: 189). Other scholars have commented on similar processes (**Amin**, **Arrighi**, **Cox**, **Strange**) but tend to see them as part of globalization rather than distinct from it.

Major globalization writings

Hirst, P. Q. and Thompson, G. (1996) *Globalization in Question: The International Economy and the Possibilities of Governance*, Cambridge, UK: Polity Press.

Hirst, P. Q. and Thompson, G. (1999) *Globalization in Question: The International Economy and the Possibilities of Governance*, 2nd edition, Cambridge, UK: Polity Press.

Hirst, P. Q., Thompson, G. and Bromley, S. (2009) *Globalization in Question: The International Economy and the Possibilities of Governance*, 3rd edition, Cambridge, UK: Polity Press.

See also: **Amin**, **Arrighi**, **Beck**, **Brenner**, **Castells**, **Cerny**, **Cox**, **Held**, **Helleiner**, **Hopkins**, **Rosenau**, **Scholte**, **Strange**, **Taylor**, **Weiss**.

A. G. HOPKINS (1938–)

Antony Gerard Hopkins was born in the UK and completed his BA in history in 1960, followed by his Ph.D. in the same discipline in 1964 at the University of London. After holding positions at the University of Birmingham and at the Graduate Institute of International Studies at the University of Geneva, he took up the Smuts Professorship in Commonwealth History at the University of Cambridge in 1994.

He left the UK in 2002 to accept the Walter Prescott Webb Chair in History at the University of Texas at Austin. Hopkins' outstanding reputation as a historian is due to his extensive work on African and imperial history, and, more recently, to his efforts to interest historians in the history of globalization. His principal works include *An Economic History of West Africa* (1973) and, with Peter Cain, *British Imperialism, 1688–2000* (2001), which won the Forkosch Prize of the American Historical Association. The latter is one of the most influential interpretations of British expansion offered in the last half century.

Having observed the debates about globalization taking place in the second half of the 1990s and having read much of the literature, Hopkins drew two important conclusions. First, he found the discussion to be too Western-centric in the sense that it spoke mainly about changes in the wealthier countries, particularly those in Europe and North America, while failing to recognize potentially distinct globalizing processes occurring in other parts of the world (see also **Chakrabarty**). Second, the absence of systematic study of the history of globalization contributed to these weaknesses. In reaching the latter conclusion, Hopkins noted that history as a discipline had yet to move away from its state-centric framework to consider systematically how the history of globalization might be studied.

History and globalization

In considering whether contemporary globalization is a new phenomenon, Hopkins argues that scholars need to investigate its historical roots and be prepared to make judgements about turning points in the historical past. He observes, for example, that universalism, cosmopolitanism and the cosmopolitan ideal became prominent during the eighteenth century in Europe. But this ideal lost ground during the nineteenth and the first part of the twentieth centuries as the nation-state became the dominant form of political organization. And it was in the nineteenth century that the academic discipline of history developed in a significant way. Consequently, universal precepts were applied to the history of nation-states. The resulting focus on writing national histories became entrenched even further in the twentieth century through the development and implementation of national education curricula (Hopkins 2002a: 13).

When international themes became important, historians usually treated them 'as spare parts that have to be bolted onto the national story' (2002a: 14). In writing history this way, historians contributed to the nationalizing of international events:

> In these ways historians of the nation state have played their part both in nationalizing internationalism, by treating the wider world as an extension of narrower interests, and in internationalizing nationalism by exporting the blueprint of the nation state and its

attendant historiography to newly independent countries in outer Europe and the non-Western world.

(Hopkins 2002a: 14)

Accordingly, for Hopkins, the historical study of globalization provides a powerful way for moving the study of history forward. In particular, the emergent field of 'world history' is seen to offer a counter-perspective to the nation-state focus.

Hopkins makes his own contribution to this study, beginning with a definition of globalization as 'the extension, intensification and quickening velocity of flows of people, products, and ideas that shape the world. It integrates regions and continents; it compresses time and space; it prompts imitation and resistance' (Hopkins 2006: 2). He observes that this definition, like other accounts, has both a quantitative and a qualitative component. Quantitatively, the transformations of economic, political, social and cultural relationships are spread broadly across 'countries, regions and continents' ever more rapidly and become more important to the daily lives of more and more people (see also **Held**). Qualitatively, these kinds of changes are different in kind from those that came before, such that the 'internet is not just a faster telegraph' (Hopkins 2002a: 18).

Historic forms of globalization

In proceeding to define different forms of globalization over time, Hopkins has several goals. Most importantly, he stresses the need to move away from seeing globalization as the 'rise of the West and the decline of the rest' (Hopkins 2002b: 2). He seeks to demonstrate that the world orders that emerged at different periods over the past 800 years were jointly created by different regions of the world, even if some regions had more influence than others at given times (see also **Braudel**; for a critique of this view, see **Dirlik**). Second, he emphasizes the importance of non-state actors as contributors to globalization in each historical period. Finally, he stresses the limitations that come from focusing predominantly on economic dimensions at the expense of political, social and cultural ones.

With these goals in mind, Hopkins outlines four forms or categories of globalization: archaic, proto, modern and postcolonial. In doing so, he proceeds very cautiously, stressing that these categories should be viewed 'as a series of overlapping and interacting sequences rather than as a neat process' (2002b: 3). He adds that in all periods, 'globalization remains an incomplete process: it promotes fragmentation as well as uniformity; it may recede as well as advance; its geographical scope may exhibit a strong regional bias; its future direction cannot be predicted with confidence' (2002b: 3).

The first form, archaic, occurred before the sixteenth century. Hopkins does not state explicitly how far back this period goes; but his main discussion seems to focus on the twelfth and thirteenth centuries, where he cites **Abu-Lughod**'s work favourably. He points out that this period had some rather 'modern' features: the importance of cities; the key contributions of migrants and diasporas; the specialization of labour; and the presence of systems of religious belief that made universal claims while extending across continents (see also **Braudel**). Archaic globalization was not globally extensive in the sense that it did not include the Americas, Australasia and important parts of Africa.

Perhaps the period most extensively discussed by Hopkins is proto-globalization, which he dates roughly from 1600 to 1800. During this period, international connections grew in geographical extensiveness and in intensity, assisted by rather porous state borders, giving the period a fluidity that is reminiscent of circumstances at the start of the twenty-first century. In this environment, there was found a growing symbiosis between emerging state systems and growing cosmopolitanism (Hopkins 2002a: 24), suggesting that non-national loyalties coexisted with emerging national identities. Place, family, religion and polity all exerted claims to varying degrees in this period. Hopkins adds that the creation of a cosmopolitan ideology in the late eighteenth century was unique and a phenomenon not to emerge again until the contemporary period (2002a: 25).

Hopkins regrets, however, that much of the historical studies of this period fail to take account of non-European perspectives on the world order (2002a: 27) (see also **Abu-Lughod, Arrighi**). He suggests that the revitalized and competing state systems in Asia made important contributions to the nature of world order and must be brought into historical discussions of proto-globalization. In addition, he argues that non-state actors (groups often featured in discussions of contemporary globalization) were very important in this period. He singles out for special mention the continued spread of universal religions such as Buddhism and Islam across borders penetrating deeply into Asia and (in the case of Islam) into sub-Saharan Africa. He also points to the importance of the extending geographic reach of great cultural and trading diasporas such as the Chinese in South-East Asia (2002a: 27).

The 'modern' form of globalization gradually displaces the proto form during the nineteenth century, with Hopkins taking 1850 as a starting point. Characteristic features of this period include the globalization of the nation-state as a form of rule, a shift from state mercantilism to freer trade, and far-reaching improvements of technology, including railroads, telegraphs, weaponry and radio communication, among others. Greater economic integration of the world became possible through constant technological innovations. Accompanying these economic and political changes was an expanding sense of nationality. Whereas global civil society actors in the proto period had a somewhat cosmopolitan stamp, those in the modern form manifested the 'imprint of nationality' (2002a: 31). At the same time, the continued vitality of the 'borderless world of diasporas', particularly the Chinese diaspora, but also the Indian one, played a central role in the strengthening of global economic systems (2002a: 32–33).

Not surprisingly, Hopkins spends less time discussing contemporary ('postcolonial') globalization. His concern with the contemporary period lies in pointing out its historical roots. He also draws our attention to aspects of the contemporary period that move away from the 'modern' form: the expanding world trade in services, the size and velocity of world financial markets, the expanding role of transnational corporations, the massive growth of remittances from expatriate communities, and the continuing decline in the cost of communications, among others. He regrets at the same time the lack of analysis of non-Western influences and a perhaps excessive focus on the US and its role in characterizations of this period.

Major globalization writings

Hopkins, A. G. (2002a) 'The history of globalization – and the globalization of history?', in A. G. Hopkins (ed.) *Globalization in World History*, London: Pimlico.
——(2002b) 'Introduction: globalization – an agenda for historians', in A. G. Hopkins (ed.) *Globalization in World History*, London: Pimlico.
——(2006) 'Introduction: interactions between the universal and the local', in A. G. Hopkins (ed.) *Global History: Interactions between the Universal and the Local*, New York, NY: Palgrave Macmillan.

Further reading

Bennison, A. K. (2002) 'Muslim universalism and western globalization', in A. G. Hopkins (ed.) *Globalization in World History*, London: Pimlico.
Brook, T. (2008) *Vermeer's Hat: The Seventeenth Century and the Dawn of the Global World*, Toronto: Viking Canada.

See also: **Abu-Lughod, Arrighi, Braudel, Chakrabarty, Dirlik, Held.**

RHODA E. HOWARD-HASSMANN (1948–)

Rhoda E. Howard-Hassmann is Canada Research Chair in International Human Rights at Wilfrid Laurier University, Waterloo, Ontario, Canada, where she holds a joint appointment in the Department of Global Studies and at the Balsillie School of International Affairs. She is also Professor Emerita at McMaster University in Hamilton, Ontario. Howard-Hassmann holds a Ph.D. in sociology from McGill University (1976), and is a fellow of the Royal Society of Canada. In 2006 she was named the first Distinguished Scholar of Human Rights by the Human Rights Section, American Political Science Association. From 1987 to 1992, she was editor of the *Canadian Journal of African Studies*, and she remains on its editorial board. She is also a member of the editorial boards of the following journals: *Citizenship Studies, Human Rights and the Global Economy, Human Rights and Human Welfare, Human Rights Quarterly, Human Rights Review, Journal of Human Rights* and the *Netherlands Quarterly of Human Rights.*

Building her thinking on the work of Karl Polyani, Howard-Hassmann argues that contemporary globalization entails a second 'great trans-formation' involving the expansion of capitalism. As this current phase of globalization has intensified over the past 20 years, in parti-cular, many pundits have argued that economic globalization is bad for the exercise of human rights; in fact, human rights may need to be suspended in deference to the expansion of capitalism. Howard-Hassmann challenges this view, arguing that the relationship between economic globalization and human rights is variable, depending upon the characteristics of states and how these states act. In addition, she suggests that an international human rights regime has expanded over the same period and is a globalizing phenomenon in its own right. An example of political and legal globalization, this development may influence economic globalization just as much as be curtailed by it.

Globalization as a second 'great transformation'

In his classic work *The Great Transformation*, published in 1944, Karl Polanyi explained the vast social, economic and political changes that took place between the end of the eighteenth century and the first four decades of the twentieth century. The expansion of industrial capitalism at that time undermined social protections in place and led to massive exploitation of labour and eventually the rise of labour-based social movements in sometimes violent protests. Howard-Hassmann argues that the current era has seen a second remarkable expansion of capitalism. It is now penetrating all those areas of the world where it had not systematically reached: communist and socialist countries, states that had high levels of protection against trade, and still others that had withdrawn from the world economy (see also **Arrighi, Harvey**). As part of this expansion, capitalism has triggered the impetus for develop-ment of most of the new information and communication technologies (Howard-Hassmann 2010: 7). By using these technologies, transnational corporations have been able to extend their global economic reach and to increase their market penetration by drawing upon investments from growing capital markets to penetrate new market opportunities the world over (Howard-Hassmann 2005: 5–6; 2010: 33).

Howard-Hassmann defines globalization 'as a process by which local states, economies, cultures, and social actors are increasingly drawn into a global polity, economy, culture, and civil society' (2010: 8). Included in this definition, then, are: the expanding world market and international trade and capital flows; transnational corporations; institutions of global governance, including the international human rights legal regime; international financial institutions such as the International Monetary Fund (IMF) and the World Bank; migration; travel and tourism; global culture; and global civil society organizations (2010: 8). Her focus is on the most recent stage of globalization, which she sees as beginning in the mid-twentieth century and intensifying over the 1990s and 2000s. By the end of this period, she observes that there has emerged an almost universal international world market economy and a system of global economic governance (2010: 10).

In her reflections on globalization, Howard-Hassmann resists simple arguments such as those that say economic globalization is bad for human rights. In response, she outlines two complex models: the first suggests how economic globalization might promote human rights and the second points to how the same processes might undermine human rights. In the first instance (2010: 57), if the economic investments of transnational corporations respect corporate law, property law and the general rule of law, they are likely to support the growth of an educated middle class. Such a class would build a competent civil society and see the need for a liberalized political sphere supported by civil and political rights. Under these political and economic conditions, governments are likely to develop effective social welfare policies and respect economic, social and cultural rights. In the second instance (2010: 71), where the economy survives on the basis of financialization (see **Arrighi**, **Braudel**, **Cox**, **Helleiner**) and 'hot money' (extremely volatile short-term capital that moves on short notice to any country providing better returns), it will likely be accompanied by a weakening of the rule of law, particularly as it bears on economic matters, leading to a declining middle class, lower tax revenue for the state, a downsizing of the state and political unrest. These latter developments are more likely to result in authoritarian governments, controls on civic and political rights, and, ultimately, disrespect, if not abandonment, of economic and social rights.

Specifically, Howard-Hassmann reflects on these models in the context of reparations for Africa. Drawing on a series of interviews she conducted with African elites, she notes that 'Africans are the least able of any group of people to interact as equals in the new supraterritorial world. They have the least capacity to travel, the least access to the Internet, and the least capacity to influence others' (Howard-Hassmann 2009: 242–243). For these elites, colonialism, neocolonialism, international institutions and globalization were one and the same thing. As one interviewee observed, globalization arrives in Africa like an 'airborne disease'. In contemplating these difficulties, Howard-Hassmann rejects the view that reparations are the route to justice for Africans; rather, she prefers distributive justice made possible by respect for economic, social and cultural rights. And based on her modelling, she stresses the rule of law: respect for political and civil rights (see also **Falk**), space for the growth of an educated middle class, and the maintenance of a public sphere for free debate and discussion as the prerequisites for achieving distributive justice and economic, social and cultural rights.

International human rights as a globalizing force

Howard-Hassmann defines human rights as those 'to which human beings are entitled merely by virtue of being biologically human; they are individual rights not tied to group, communal, national or any other membership. Human rights do not have to be earned, nor are they dependent on any particular social status, such as whether one is male or female' (Howard-Hassmann 2010: 3–4). When comparing the first with the second 'great transformation' involving capitalism, she observes that the existence of a human rights regime and an international human rights movement is crucial. The world has moved from 'almost human rights lawlessness' to 'universal human rights law' (2010: 83).

This change, Howard-Hassmann argues, has occurred relatively rapidly. A historically short 60 years after the United Nations Declaration, 162 countries had ratified the International Covenant on Civil and Political Rights, and 159 countries the International Covenant on Economic, Social and Cultural Rights (2010: 87). In addition, by the late twentieth century, most countries had included some statements about human rights in their national constitutions. Having done so, it becomes much more difficult for political leaders to argue that human rights need not be respected. Howard-Hassmann's research does show, however, that these rights are not binding on transnational corporations (TNCs), and even international organizations such as the World Bank pay weak deference to these rights.

Globalization has sped up these advancements in the international human rights legal regime. The global communications networks that are part of contemporary globalization have made it easier for people in all parts of the world to acquire information and to communicate with one another on human rights issues. The interactive character of these technologies means that these individuals are no longer simply consumers of information. They can generate knowledge of difficult situations and debate social issues involving rights. Abuses of human rights become subject to worldwide scrutiny and critique in the global public sphere (Howard-Hassmann 2005: 35).

These same technologies permit those involved in popular struggles for recognition and implementation of human rights law in one place to link with, support and receive encouragement from those in other places involved in similar struggles. In these respects, globalized communication channels erode geographical remoteness. The rights available in international human rights law provide a basis for demands for justice by local actors in more and more parts of the world. Non-governmental organizations promoting human rights, such as Amnesty International, or transnational social movements, such as the World Social Forum, enter into global human rights networks through the use of digital technologies (see also **Santos**). Such networks, in turn, permit them to channel and focus intense political pressure in given places where human rights abuses occur (2005: 35–7). 'In principle', Howard-Hassmann writes:

> the [human rights] regime means that neither rich nor poor countries may ignore their citizens' economic rights. The argument that economic growth requires a free hand for governments and private entrepreneurs without regard to the well-being of citizens or those affected by corporate activities has little purchase in the early twenty-first century.
>
> (Howard-Hassmann 2010: 86)

Howard-Hassmann also recognizes that the globalization of the human rights legal regime is potentially fragile. During the first great transformation, there were reactions, sometimes violent, to the spread of market capitalism, both by trade unions endeavouring to establish rights for workers and by political reactionary movements promoting fascist ideas. Similarly, Howard-Hassmann points to the 'politics of resentment' as presenting a challenge to the global human rights regime. Such resentment arises out of the declining autonomy of nation-states, an increasingly powerful transnational class structure, important changes in social living, and a weakening of national cultural autonomy. It comes in the form of anti-Americanism, armed private militias and religious fundamentalism. In a way, Howard-Hassmann comes back to Polanyi in the end. Her discussion of social democracy is consistent with his view that social protection must be provided for citizens when capitalism brings fundamental changes to ways of life. In a globalized world, states must still be protectors, if not promoters, of economic, social and cultural rights, as well as civil and political rights, if social justice is to be realized.

Major globalization writings

Howard-Hassmann, R. E. (2005) 'The second great transformation: human rights leapfrogging in the era of globalization', *Human Rights Quarterly*, vol 27, no 1, pp. 1–40.
——(2009) 'An airborne disease: globalization through African eyes', in S. Bernstein and W. D. Coleman (eds) *Unsettled Legitimacy: Political Community, Power, and Authority in a Global Era*, Vancouver, BC: University of British Columbia Press.
——(2010) *Can Globalization Promote Human Rights?*, University Park, PA: Pennsylvania State University Press.
Howard-Hassmann, R. E. and Lombardo, A. P. (2008) *Reparations to Africa*, Philadelphia, PA: University of Pennsylvania Press.

See also: **Arrighi, Braudel, Cox, Falk, Harvey, Helleiner, Santos.**

NAOMI KLEIN (1970–)

Naomi Klein is a Canadian award-winning journalist and an internationally established anti-globalization spokesperson. She is a syndicated columnist, writing regularly for the *New York Times,* the *Guardian* and *The Nation*. She previously worked for the Toronto-based newspaper the *Globe and Mail* and *This Magazine*. Her first book, *No Logo*, published in 2000, was an international bestseller and was translated into over 25 languages. Her book *The Shock Doctrine*, published in 2007, became an international and *New York Times* bestseller, translated into over 30 languages and printed into over one million copies. Klein's work launches a vehement critique against corporate globalization, similar to that of Arundhati **Roy**, Vandana **Shiva** and Joseph **Stiglitz**. Her book *No Logo* criticizes the emergence of corporate branding as a marketing technique that revolves not around the specific product being marketed, but around an obsession with developing a brand that appropriates surrounding ideas, peoples and cultures, and commercializes them for corporate profit. *The Shock Doctrine* launches an even deeper critique of capitalism, more specifically of the current stage of neoliberal capitalism, which Klein characterizes as 'disaster capitalism'. Disaster capitalism operates by using moments of crises or shocking events to push through economic agendas and policies, which would otherwise be rejected by citizens.

No Logo

Klein states that 'the brand [is] the core meaning of the modern corporation, and [...] the advertisement [is] one vehicle used to convey that meaning to the world' (Klein 2000: 5). There are important differences between the type of advertisement that was undertaken in the first mass marketing campaigns of the nineteenth century and the contemporary global frenzy with corporate advertising. The former were quite literally campaigns advertising a new product, the emphasis of the message falling on the product itself and on its specific characteristics. These early mass marketing campaigns emphasized the newness of the products advertised and their superior qualities by comparison to traditional ones (2000: 5). With contemporary mass marketing campaigns there is a shift from the product to the 'brand-name version of a product' (2000: 6). Today's marketing is not simply about advertising but about branding, where the brand represents 'an experience', a 'lifestyle', 'a set of values' and not simply a product (2000: 21, 24). Branding assumes that 'advertising and sponsorship [should be] about using imagery to equate products with positive cultural and social experiences' (2000: 29). But as **McClintock** shows, some brands developed by imperialist powers in the late nineteenth century involved more than the product, emphasizing the superiority of doing things in the colonizer's (obviously superior) way.

Klein, however, sees a still more substantive change emerge during the 1990s in the ways that logos are promoted by corporate globalization. Since the 1990s, it is no longer enough to associate a brand with a positive experience; what becomes more important in the on-going competition to out-brand others is the notion that the brand can be taken out of 'the representational realm and [made into] a lived reality' (2000: 29). For example, the ESPN sports channel, owned by Disney, launched a line of ESPN Sports Bars, which embodied the masculinist sports-obsessed culture it tried to nurture via its channel. Another example is the well-known Canadian clothing company Roots, which built a Roots country lodge that attempted to become 'a 3-D manifestation of the Roots brand concept' (2000: 29). One of the effects of this shift from mere representation to performance is that the brand becomes the star, and the sponsored event or culture becomes the mere background, the canvas on which the brand writes its message (2000: 30). Klein notes a worrying trend whereby branding can strip 'the hosting culture of its inherent value and [treats] it as little more than a promotional tool' (2000: 39). She gives the example of Nike's sponsorship of Michael Jordan, through which both Nike and Michael Jordan become global brands in themselves. She notes that Nike's sponsorship of Michael Jordan aimed to highlight not his athletic skills but rather the synonymy between Nike and athleticism (2000: 54). Klein sees the examples of Nike and Michael Jordan as 'emblematic of a new paradigm that eliminates all barriers between branding and culture, leaving no room whatsoever for unmarketed space' (2000: 59).

In an age of corporate globalization, the process of branding might be abstract and representational, but the processes of manufacturing the actual products are very much real. They are rooted in a reality of exploitation and oppression of women and children in the Global South who work in appalling conditions to produce the glamorous products being advertised. However, resistance is being mounted in such locales and such resistance many times uses the brand as a counter-tactic of activism. Targeting high-profile corporations such as Shell, McDonald's and Coke can be a very effective way of exposing labour and human rights abuses precisely because of the global visibility of these brands and the ubiquity of their logos everywhere in the world. Klein notes, however, that this form of resistance creates a problem when trying to publicize abuses by companies that do not brand themselves, such as those multinationals involved in the natural resource industries (2000: 424). Because the exploitation undertaken by these companies is unbranded (meaning is not associated with a highly visible brand), the plight of exploited people becomes less visible and certainly less mediatized (2000: 424).

Nonetheless, even in these circumstances, there are tactics for shaming unbranded corporations by targeting the branded companies who are their clients (2000: 425–427). For example, while Monsanto might be a tough target for a boycott because of its manufacturing of genetically modified organisms (GMOs), targeting branded supermarkets such as Tesco, Marks & Spencer and Safeway who carry GMO products has been effective (2000: 427). The irony here is that the only type of activism visible and powerful enough seems to be 'brand-based activism', which might be considered 'the ultimate achievement of branding' (2000: 428). Klein contrasts this type of activism with the grounded activism that takes place in and around the export-processing zones, factories and sweatshops that manufacture the branded products. Ultimately, Klein notes, the most effective and enduring form of action should be taken politically on a global level 'through the enforcement of existing International Labour Organization treaties' (2000: 436).

Disaster capitalism and The Shock Doctrine

The Shock Doctrine engages in a more comprehensive critique of the contemporary manifestations of capitalism and the inextricable connections between contemporary wars, economic doctrines and corporate takeovers of post-disaster zones. Klein notes that the shock doctrine of disaster capitalism can be traced back to Milton Friedman's work, the guru of neoliberalism. In his *Capitalism and Freedom*, Friedman remarks that 'only a crisis [...] produces real change. When that crisis occurs, the actions that are taken depend on the ideas that are lying around' (quoted in Klein 2007: 6). Friedman's ideas, which glorified a *laissez-faire* capitalism unfettered from governmental intervention, were disseminated while he was a member of the University of Chicago's Economics Department. This department attracted students from Latin America and other parts of the Global South with the purpose of moulding them into advocates for unrestrained capitalism (see also **Harvey**). The first neoliberal experiment was carried out in Chile in 1973, when the democratically elected Salvador Allende was ousted in a military coup (sponsored by the CIA) led by General Augusto Pinochet, a fervent believer in Friedman's ideas. Indeed, the economic advisers put in place by Pinochet were educated at the University of Chicago under the mentorship of Milton Friedman. Pinochet unleashed a series of neoliberal economic policies whose ruthless implementation required the formation and establishment of an extremely brutal apparatus of torture and repression. He was attempting to eliminate those seen as obstacles to the implementation of this new economic agenda.

In fact, Klein devotes a copious amount of space in her book to the practice of torture 'as a silent partner in the global free-market crusade' (Klein 2007: 15). More than a tool for the implementation of unpopular economic programmes, torture is also 'a metaphor of the shock doctrine's underlying logic' (2007: 15). In a harrowing account of some of the first techniques of torture sponsored by the CIA during the Cold War (more specifically, a torture experiment carried out at McGill University), Klein remarks that torture includes a set of techniques intended first to shock the subject into a state of disorientation and, hence, erase their connections to their earlier perceptions of the world (2007: 16, 25–48). Second, the state of shock allows the interrogator/torturer to extract information from the victim or to make the victim compliant and non-resistant. Throughout her book, Klein draws a parallel between the development of the CIA's techniques of torture and the 'shock and awe' economic therapies that are applied to various societies around the world in moments of crisis. She claims that 'The shock doctrine mimics this process [of torture] precisely, attempting to achieve on a mass scale what torture does one on one in the interrogation cell' (2007: 16).

Klein surveys various crises in our contemporary world: from the first neoliberal experiment in Chile, to the shock of the Tiananmen Massacre and the economic liberalization that ensued in China, to the economic shock therapy applied to Russia during the 1990s, to the trauma of 9/11 and the subsequent securitization of American society, to the shock of the 2004 tsunami in South-East Asia and the immediate massive privatization of affected coastlines of Sri Lanka and Thailand, all the way to the shock of the 2003 invasion of Iraq and the selling out of Iraq to private corporations. In all these contemporary crises:

> [...] the original disaster – the coup, the terrorist attack, the market meltdown, the war, the tsunami, the hurricane – puts the entire population into a state of collective shock. The falling bombs, the bursts of terror, the pounding winds serve to soften up whole societies much as the blaring music and blows in the torture cells soften up prisoners.
>
> (Klein 2007: 17)

In these traumatic conditions, 'shocked societies give up things they would otherwise fiercely protect', such as their democratic freedoms, their developmental goals, their welfare programmes and their ways of life (2007: 17). The central goal of her book is to demolish the long-cherished assumption of Milton Friedman's theory that unfettered and deregulated capitalism equals the triumph of individual freedom (2007: 18). On the contrary, she demonstrates, the aggressive deregulation and privatization that followed these moments of crises could only be sustained through the establishment of a set of repressive and anti-democratic measures. These measures, in turn, made it possible for vested corporate interests to amass colossal fortunes and to expand at unprecedented rates (see, for example, her discussion of the massive proliferation of the homeland security industry in the US and abroad after 9/11) (2007: 283–307).

Perhaps surprisingly, the shock therapy administered by disaster capitalism failed to erase resistance in societies affected by it. As the shock wore off, people developed various collective strategies of resisting the policies of the shock doctrine – from protests, mass demonstrations and riots, to community-based reconstruction and mobilization, to less positive consequences such as the rise of inward-looking nationalist and xenophobic movements, as well as various religious fundamentalisms (see **Castells**). Some governments in the Global South managed to recover economically from the shock therapy imposed by institutions such as the International Monetary Fund (IMF) and the World Bank, and even turn down renewals of agreements with the former (especially in Latin America) (2007: 450–457) (see also **Bello**). Klein concludes by vesting hope in the paths forged by community-based mobilizations around the world (such as in post-tsunami Thailand and in post-hurricane New Orleans) to show the way towards alternatives that steer clear of various fundamentalisms (whether economic, nationalist or religious) (see also **Escobar, Mignolo, Santos**).

Major globalization writings

Klein, N. (2000) *No Logo: Taking Aim at the Brand Bullies*, New York, NY: Picador.

——(2007) *The Shock Doctrine: The Rise of Disaster Capitalism*, New York, NY: Metropolitan Books.

Further reading

Klein, N. (2002) *Fences and Windows: Dispatches from the Front Lines of the Globalization Debate*, New York, NY: Picador.

See also: **Bello, Castells, Escobar, Harvey, McClintock, Mignolo, Roy, Santos, Shiva, Stiglitz.**

KELLEY LEE (1962–)

Kelley Lee completed a BA at the University of British Columbia, Canada, in international relations/English literature in 1984, followed by a Master's in public administration in 1986, an MA at the University of Sussex in 1987 in international relations and a D.Phil. at the same institution in international political economy in 1992. She has been honoured with a Doctor of Letters, *honoris causa*, from the British Columbia Open University in 2003, and as a Fellow through Distinction, Faculty of Public Health (FFPH), Royal College of Physicians, in the UK in 2007. She currently holds positions as Professor of Global Health Policy, Department of Global Health and Development; co-director, World Health Organization Collaborating Centre on Global Change and Health at the London School of Hygiene and Tropical Medicine in the UK; and Director of Global Health, Associate Dean, Research Professor, Faculty of Health Sciences, Simon Fraser University, British Columbia, Canada. She has authored over 70 scholarly papers, 40 book chapters and 7 books. Lee's research focuses on the impacts of globalization upon communicable and non-communicable diseases (notably tobacco-related diseases), and the implications for emerging forms of global governance.

Lee has provided important intellectual leadership in the study of the relationships between globalization and health, and their implications for global governance. Her work has ranged widely, including theorizing these relationships, exploring changes to health policy and health governance, and carrying out detailed empirical research on these matters. Her studies of tobacco control and of the relationships between global trade and health regimes have been particularly influential.

Globalization and health

Lee defines globalization in the following terms:

> [...] a set of processes that are changing the nature of human interaction by intensifying interaction across certain boundaries that have hitherto served to separate individuals and population groups. These spatial, temporal, and cognitive boundaries have become increasingly eroded, resulting in new forms of social organization and interaction across these boundaries.
>
> (Lee 2003: 12)

She notes that historically there have been relationships between the movement and settlement of peoples, their lifestyles, their cultural practices including their food choices, and patterns of health and disease. The question that she poses relates to how the more intensified and globally extensive interactions in the contemporary period have affected health outcomes. Her analysis focuses on the three forms of boundaries in her definition: spatial, temporal and cognitive.

Changes in spatial boundaries arising from globalization include the emergence of new forms of community that are much more independent of territorial space. In this respect, she speaks of de-territorialized social spaces (see also **Held**). One of two contrasting examples would be the communities of persons working in transnational corporations (TNCs) and moving frequently from one part of the world to another. In contrast, often in the same parts of the world, where TNCs are influential, there are movements of migrant labour in search of employment and which often find it in building infrastructures for the factories and communities associated with the TNCs. In this respect, there are also processes of re-territorialization in the creation of new trans-border social spaces (see **Sassen**). Lee adds that populations such as undocumented migrants, the poor in shanty towns gathering around TNC investments, and commercial sex workers are particularly vulnerable to health risks owing to their ways of living in these new transnational spaces in the 'global' economic order. Although state-defined geographies remain important, providing services within state boundaries are increasingly insufficient for ensuring the protection and promotion of human health.

The temporal dimension of global change concerns how we perceive and experience time. Globalization is changing the timeframe of many types of social interaction. Lee notes that our capacity to promote and protect public health is affected by the time available to us: 'How long does it take for health risks and opportunities to manifest themselves? How quickly can we mobilize the appropriate decisions, resources and actions to respond to a health need?' (2003: 109). Of particular concern is the time involved in the spread of infections: 'The movement of people via modern transportation systems, rapid urbanization without adequate water, sanitation and public health facilities, human-induced environmental changes, and the increased speed with which infectious agents can arise and spread worldwide' (2003: 112). In order to address these health challenges effectively, it becomes incumbent upon health officials to mobilize and exploit the same information and communication technologies that are changing the temporal parameters of health risks.

Finally, Lee identifies five aspects of cognition that have changed with the intensification of globalization. First, there has been a rapid spread of policy ideas based on neoliberalism targeted at how health-sector reforms should be carried out (see also **Cerny, Harvey**). Second, certain globalized neoliberal discourses involving economic rationality and promoted by health economists have come to play central roles in defining how priority-setting in health policy takes place. Third, a growing number of epistemic communities surrounding scientific research are being penetrated by vested interests in the private sector, which have impacts, in turn, upon how health funding is structured. Fourth, the globalization of marketing and advertising related to health are changing lifestyles that, in turn, have significant health implications. The globalization of certain processed foods and use of baby formula are examples that have definitive implications for health outcomes. Finally, Lee analyses and notes the growing emergence of a consensus around global health ethics raising the level of what is seen as acceptable behaviour in health research, policy and practice.

From international to global health

The onset of globalization and its interaction with health outcomes raises further questions about the relationships between nation-states, risks and disease, and health outcomes. Lee observes that the growth of cooperation between states on public health issues began to grow in systematic ways during the nineteenth century. In 1851, the first of a series of International Sanitary Conferences was held to address cooperation among mainly European and Middle Eastern states and colonies facing cholera outbreaks. Between 1850 and 1938, 14 such conferences were held, putting in place the institutional foundations for fuller international health cooperation (Lee 2009: 2). During the same period, the first of a number of regional health organizations were formed, most notably the Pan American Health Bureau. In 1907, growing out of the Sanitary Conferences, a nascent international organization was set up, the Office International d'Hygiène Publique in Paris, which was joined, in turn, by the League of Nations Health Organization in 1920. Over the same period, however, the medical profession and others interested in health outcomes pointed to an international need for addressing not only the spread of infectious disease, but also the social determinants of health such as sanitation, housing, nutrition and education (2009: 6).

When the United Nations agreed to create a new coordinating body, the World Health Organization (WHO), in 1946, it was given responsibility for both infectious diseases and 'social medicine', or the study of the social determinants of health. Over the first three decades of its existence, the WHO continued to focus on 'international health' – that is, facilitating cooperation between nation-states on infectious diseases and social determinants. With the onset of contemporary globalization during the 1970s, the WHO came to be faced with a rapidly changing environment, where states were no longer alone or even dominant when it came to health cooperation.

During this period, Lee notes, the WHO had to shift its focus from international to 'global' health (Lee and Holden 2009: chapter 5). Global health refers to the effects on social determinants that arise from globalization and thus are effects not well addressed by states acting on their own. With globalization, new actors enter the global health field, including transnational corporations, international non-governmental organizations and an increasing number of privately funded non-profit philanthropic foundations such as the Bill and Melinda Gates Foundation. In addition, other international organizations such as the World Bank (WB) and the International Monetary Fund (IMF) became prominent in the global health field. By the beginning of the new millennium, the WB had a larger health budget than the WHO, and the IMF had used its Structural Adjustment Programmes and neoliberal thinking to require the privatization of many health services in middle- and lower-income countries.

In navigating this highly complex globalized environment, the WHO illustrates the changes that take place when a formerly 'international organization' becomes a 'global' one. As Lee observes, at the end of the first decade of the new millennium, the WHO 'faces continued pressure to become leaner and meaner, given strong dependence on major donors and the powerful economic interests who influence them'. At the same time, this pressure must somehow be reconciled with its role as the world's health organization created to ensure 'the attainment by all peoples of the highest level of health' (Lee and Holden 2009: 128). In essence, Lee observes, the WHO is now functioning in an environment of 'elite pluralism' (Lee 2003: 264–265), where other global institutions, both private and public, are also claiming jurisdiction.

Global health governance

Throughout her career, Lee has deepened her knowledge of globalization and health with often innovative empirical studies in cooperation with an impressive number of scholars from many different disciplines. She has done research on HIV/AIDS, cholera, avian influenza, pharmaceuticals and the World Trade Organization (WTO), among others. Her most extensive research in the field, however, has focused on tobacco control and global health. In this research, she has explored in depth both the WHO and the new actors in global governance that arise from globalization. A crucial event in this research area was the directive by the World Health Assembly (WHA), the governing body of the WHO, to the director-general to exercise the organization's longstanding authority to convene negotiations towards a public health treaty on tobacco control. When Gro Harlem Brundtland became director-general in 1998, she made this directive one of her two highest priorities. In 2003, the WHA formally adopted the Framework Convention on Tobacco Control (FCTC), which acquired the force of international law in February 2005, when 40 member states had ratified it. As of 2012, the treaty had 168 signatories, with the US and the Russian Federation the most prominent states yet to ratify the agreement.

The most important of Lee's contributions to the study of this key event in global health governance focus on the roles played by the dominant large transnational tobacco corporations, which have fought to undermine this international legal framework. She argues that globalization increases the 'structural power' of corporations in their relations with states (see also **Helleiner**). This power derives from their capacity to exit from national economies, where the growing of tobacco and/or the manufacturing of tobacco products are major industries (Lee 2009: 333–335). The corporations also have strong agency power: highly effective lobbying organizations and extensive resources to undermine scientific evidence on tobacco and health. Lee has also noted the importance of international non-governmental organizations in countering the structural and agency power of the tobacco TNCs, most notably a network of such organizations under the umbrella of the Framework Convention Alliance.

In short, Lee's research over the past 15 years underlines the changes to global health governance that arise from globalization, including the growth in influence and structural power of transnational corporations. Her highly detailed observations and careful research have led to key insights about the elite pluralism of international organizations such as the WHO, the World Bank and the IMF, the emergence of powerful private global funders, and the growing importance of transnational corporations and of global civil society. Her scholarship models exceptionally well the kinds of analytical thinking and creative conceptualization needed for studying globalized policy-making.

Major globalization writings

Lee, K. (2003) *Globalization and Health: An Introduction*, Houndmills, UK, and, New York, NY: Palgrave Macmillan.

——(2009) *World Health Organization (WHO)*, Abingdon, UK: Routledge

Lee, K. and Holden, C. (2009) 'Corporate power and social policy: the political economy of the transnational tobacco companies', *Global Social Policy*, vol 9, no 3, pp. 328–354.

Lee, K., Buse, K., Drager, N. and Fustukian, S. (2002) 'Globalisation and health policy: trends and opportunities', in K. Lee, K. Buse and S. Fustukian (eds) *Health Policy in a Globalising World*, Cambridge, UK: Cambridge University Press.

See also: **Cerny, Harvey, Held, Helleiner, Sassen**.

ANNE McCLINTOCK (1954–)

Anne McClintock is currently Simone de Beauvoir Professor of English and Women's and Gender Studies at the University of Wisconsin-Madison, US. She previously taught at Columbia University, where she completed her doctoral degree in 1989. McClintock has authored two short biographies of Simone de Beauvoir and Olive Schreiner, and a monograph entitled *Double Crossings*, in which she explores the links between madness, sexuality and colonialism. Her best-known work is *Imperial Leather: Race, Gender and Sexuality in the Colonial Contest*. Published in 1995 by Routledge, it was chosen to be one of 300 books published online by the American Council of Learned Societies (ACLS) History E-book Project. In the book, McClintock examines the categories of gender, race and class and their intertwined manifestations within the European colonial projects of the nineteenth and twentieth centuries. She argues that these categories did not exist in isolation from each other; rather, they emerged together in the violence that accompanied imperialism. These themes also inform the volume she co-edited with Ella Shohat and Aamir Mufti, *Dangerous Liaisons: Gender, Nation and Postcolonial Perspectives* (1997).

McClintock's work adds to our understanding of the history of globalization by focusing on the linkages between imperialism, colonialism and culture. Moving away from mainstream historical writing to focus on cultural objects and visual representations, she is able to offer important understandings of the complex interplay between gender, race and class that remain crucial to understanding globalizing processes today.

McClintock uses the term 'global' more often than 'globalization'. She associates the former with imperial articulations of race and gender, with the intersections between the globalized industry of sex trade/sex work and practices of sexuality (McClintock 1993a, 1993b), and with past and current expressions of social power and identity. Her work is crucial to arriving at a better understanding of the global dimensions of race and sexuality in the construction of nationalism, and of the complexities of European imperialism as a global politics of violence (see also **Chow, Mignolo**). In these respects, her work informs studies of contemporary globalization and its violence.

Race, gender and class in the colonial contest

In *Imperial Leather*, McClintock begins with the argument that 'imperialism and the invention of race were fundamental aspects of Western, industrial modernity' (McClintock 1995: 5) (see also **Escobar, Mignolo**). Scientific race theories, the 'cult of domesticity', national/imperial bureaucracies, and the global trade of commodities are part and parcel of the Western industrialization project. The connections between such ventures are not trivial or insignificant. Rather, they speak to complex relations between the racialized and gendered formations of power within the Western colonial/modern project. Her meticulous and elaborate analysis of race, gender and class in the context of imperialism complements the analyses of other key globalization thinkers, notably **Escobar, Mignolo** and **Santos**. Like them, McClintock argues that understanding the political, social and cultural dynamics of industrial modernity requires an exploration of the racialized and gendered dimensions of imperial power in its global dimensions.

In her work, McClintock traces the global contours of a field of studies that aims to bring forward marginalized knowledges, voices and perspectives (cf. **Santos**). In looking at the contemporary period, she emphasizes the continuities of imperialism/colonialism in 'the international imbalances of imperial power' (1995: 13). She is intrigued by the workings of imperial power, past and present, and its material, ideological, affective and textual dimensions.

Using a theoretical framework that combines postcolonial, feminist, socialist and psychoanalytical perspectives, McClintock claims that the myth of the colonial discovery of 'empty lands' was a male fantasy, but it also represented a 'crisis in male imperial identity' (1995: 27). Through an analysis of various paintings and drawings portraying the moment of colonial 'discovery', the author remarks that the explorers felt both threatened and emboldened by their encounter with otherness. On the one hand, they projected their male fantasies onto a territory they considered 'virgin', passive and awaiting their penetration. On the other hand, they feared the difference that lay ahead and dreaded the prospect of being 'engulfed' by a culture which they perceived as archaic, backward and heathen. Gender, McClintock observes, is crucial to understanding the global scope of European exploratory ventures because it illuminates not only the identities of those who explored, settled and colonized, but also the manner through which they related to those colonized.

She posits the idea of *anachronistic space* to capture the perception of colonial journeys moving forward geographically into a territory, while travelling backwards in historical time (1995: 30). This concept remains important to contemporary analyses of globalization where such spaces are seen to encapsulate binaries such as modern/traditional, developed/underdeveloped, advanced/emerging, globalized/not globalized. The contradictions to be found in anachronistic spaces throw light on the devastating colonial policies implemented by Western European explorers against local populations. These peoples were viewed as remainders from a prehistorical past inhabiting the modern world (see **Mignolo**, **Tsing**). Such denials of indigenous populations' contemporaneity entail a denial of their humanity – a process that would be transferred to other groups within the imperial metropolis, seen to embody the same atavistic characteristics:

> According to this trope, colonized people – *like women and the working class in the metropolis* – do not inhabit history proper but exist in a permanently anterior time within the geographic space of the modern empire as anachronistic humans, atavistic, irrational, bereft of human agency – the living embodiment of the archaic 'primitive'.
>
> (McClintock 1995: 30; our emphasis)

Another crucial concept employed by McClintock is that of *panoptical time*, where 'the image of global history [is] consumed – at a glance – as a single spectacle from a point of privileged invisibility' (1995: 37). She illustrates this concept by drawing our attention to the emergence of racial typologies during the nineteenth century, which were meant to elucidate the evolution and the hierarchy of 'the family of man'. The idea of 'historical progress' was represented by a scale or by a genealogical tree with European man as the apogee of human evolution and the other races positioned below him. McClintock notes that the metaphor of 'racial progress' understood as 'evolutionary' time was a time without women, insofar as most images were of men (1995: 39). Contemporary human development indexes that rank order countries' achievements in terms of 'standards of living' may reflect similar constructions.

The argument McClintock makes about global modernity follows on Walter Benjamin's suggestion that what was distinct about nineteenth-century industrial capitalism was its obsession with archaic images. Such images were crucial in explaining and illustrating the newness and uniqueness of modernity. Other races, women, the mentally ill and the working class were seen as the embodiments of the archaic and the pre-modern. As she illustrates in her extensive analysis of domesticity and maids' labour in Victorian Britain, those women who transgressed the boundary between the public and the private, 'labour and leisure, paid and unpaid work became increasingly stigmatized as specimens of *racial* regression' (1995: 42; original emphasis). This point brings us to the second part of her argument – namely that global modernity, as it emerged from the imperial/colonial European enterprise, should be understood as a 'triangulated discourse' that relies profoundly on the construction of racial, gendered and class categories. The triangulation between race, gender and class became 'a critical element in the formation of the imperial, modern imagination' (1995: 56). From McClintock's perspective, it is through the strict policing of racial, gender, sexual and class boundaries that imperial modernity comes into being.

Mass commodity spectacle, visuality and the boundaries of 'civilization'

In *Imperial Leather*, McClintock (1995) also examines the central role of visuality in the constitution of imperialism and of global modernity. This examination is important because it foreshadows the more extensive commodification and use of the visual, made possible by the communication and information technology revolution of the current period (see **Appadurai**). She argues that visuality is instrumental in projecting the relations between money, domesticity and racism on a global scale. An important characteristic of the Victorian middle class, she explains, was its obsession with rigid boundaries and with the enforcement of particular rituals. These rituals of cleaning and absolution are interpreted by McClintock to have been essential in 'the policing of social hierarchies' because they attempted to transcend the attendant confusion and identity crises that stemmed from colonials' travels across the boundaries of their known world. What distinguished Victorian cleaning rituals from other cultural traditions of boundary rituals was their 'peculiarly intense relation to money' in the context of the capitalist expansion of European colonial empires (1995: 33).

McClintock claimed that the Pears Soap advertisement, which appeared in *McClure's Magazine* in 1899, marked an 'epochal shift' in the culture of imperialism from scientific racism to *commodity racism*. The manifestations of *commodity racism*, she asserts, were particularly acute in the Victorian practices of advertising and photography, the imperial Expositions and the emergence of the museum. Both the museum and imperial Expositions and 'World Fairs' – wildly popular in France and Great Britain and later in the US between the middle of the nineteenth century and the first three decades of the twentieth century – can be considered modern institutions that embodied two paramount functions. On the one hand, they were meant to archive and preserve the archaic through a visual display that suggested the linear progression from 'primitive' to 'civilized'. In so doing, they also sanctified a Western conception of history as 'evolution' and 'progress' – as a linear and unidirectional narrative that was meant to signal both the newness of modernity and the imperative of its global dissemination. The use of visuality during the nineteenth century aided in the marketing of evolutionary racism and imperial power on an unprecedented and unimaginable scale, a scale not to be reached again until the late twentieth century.

In her analysis of the Pears Soap advertisement, McClintock draws attention to its narrative, which reads: 'The first step towards lightening The White Man's Burden is through teaching the virtues of cleanliness. Pears Soap is a potent factor in brightening the dark corners of the earth as civilization advances, while amongst the cultured of all nations it holds the highest place – it is the ideal toilet soap' (1995: 32). The advertisement suggests that domesticity was one of the key practices that sustained imperialism. She also points to the ad's depiction of a shipboard admiral dressed in an immaculate white uniform and washing his hands with a bar of Pears Soap. Surrounding the central image are scenes of imperial progress: overseas travels and commerce, and the typical civilizing tableau where a scantily dressed 'native' kneels as he receives with gratitude the bar of soap from the hands of a missionary.

To McClintock, the Pears Soap advertisement is representative of an entire genre of Victorian advertising that served to enhance the civilizing narrative, but also to commodify the imperial venture at an unparalleled global scale. In exploring the instrumental role of photography and advertising in the success of the European imperial projects, she delineates how visuality became both a technology of representation and a technology of power (see also **Klein**). The violence of the colonial encounter was thus domesticated through representations found among postcards, family albums, pornography, commercial advertising, encyclopedic documentations and others. It was with the nineteenth-century projects of imperial expansion that domesticity met colonialism. In summary, 'as domestic space became racialized, colonial space became domesticated' (1995: 36). McClintock's rich analyses substantiate the thesis that an understanding of contemporary processes of globalization cannot be pursued outside of an exploration of the racial, gendered and class dynamics of European colonialism (see also **Mignolo**).

Major globalization writings

McClintock, A. (1993a) 'Maid to order: commercial fetishism and gender power', *Social Text*, vol 37, pp. 87–116.

——(1993b) 'Sex workers and sex work: introduction', *Social Text*, vol 37, pp. 1–10.

——(1995) *Imperial Leather: Race, Gender and Sexuality in the Colonial Contest*, New York, NY, and London: Routledge.

See also: **Appadurai, Chow, Escobar, Klein, Mignolo, Santos, Tsing.**

WALTER D. MIGNOLO

Walter D. Mignolo was born in Argentina where he completed his pre-doctoral studies at the Universidad de Córdoba in the field of modern literature, specializing in Latin American writers. He completed a doctorate in semiotics and literary theory at the École des Hautes Études en Sciences Sociales in Paris, France. He taught romance languages and literature at the University of Michigan from 1975 to 1992, when he moved to Duke University, NC, where he is a professor in romance studies and cultural anthropology and director of the Center for Global Studies and the Humanities. He has also been named permanent researcher at large at the Universidad Andina Simón Bolívar in Quito, Ecuador.

Mignolo defines globalization as a set of processes dating to the fifteenth century that give rise to modernity achieved through coloniality. These processes start with imperial European powers colonizing the Americas, followed by other parts of the world. He divides the past approximately 600 years into four periods, where globalization takes particular forms. In discussing the characteristics of these periods, he puts particular emphasis on epistemic colonization, the violent suppression of forms of knowledge other than those dominant 'sciences' imposed by Europeans. As he reflects on contemporary times and the possibilities of breaking free of modernity, he notes the importance of 'border thinking'. He argues that such thinking points to a path to a 'pluri-versal' world.

Modernity/coloniality/globalization

Mignolo's starting position is that there is no coloniality without modernity because coloniality is constitutive of modernity (see also **Escobar**). As Europeans, the originators of modernity, have continued to modernize the world over the past 600 years, they have had to colonize others to reach their goals. They have followed an embedded logic that 'enforces control, domination and exploitation disguised in the language of salvation, progress, modernization and being good for everyone' (Mignolo 2005: 6). The logic of coloniality works through four wide domains of experience: the economic appropriation of land, exploitation of labour and control of finance; political control of authority through vice-royalty, colonial states and military structures; the control of gender and family through notions such as the 'Christian family'; and the control of subjectivity and knowledge (Mignolo 2010a: 332).

Under these circumstances, the West, starting with Europe, positions itself as the locus of 'enunciation': it ascribes to itself the right to describe, conceptualize and rank the rest of the world (see also **McClintock**). In this role, Europeans saw themselves as the centre of political and economic organization, a model of social life, the exemplar of human achievement and, most importantly, the point for observing and classifying the rest of the world:

> The West was, and still is, the only geo-historical location that is both part of the classification of the world *and the only perspective that has the privilege of possessing dominant categories of thoughts from which and where the rest of the world can be described, classified, understood, and 'improved'*.
> (Mignolo 2005: 36, emphasis in the original)

The resulting uneven distribution of knowledge is referred to as the geopolitics of epistemology and the uneven distribution of wealth as the geopolitics of economy.

Mignolo refers to globalization as processes in which global designs are imposed in local places with the goal of 'civilizing' the peoples in those places. In the course of these impositions, European ways of knowing and thinking, and, thus, 'science', are imposed on the colonized with their own ways of thinking and knowing being attacked and disparaged first as 'barbarian' and later as 'primitive' (see also **Santos**). He divides globalization into four periods, each of which constitutes a particular 'moment', with a specific form of 'civilizing mission'.

The first is the 'early modern and early colonial' period, which occurred between 1500 and 1700, with Spain and Portugal being the driving forces. In this first period, the spreading and imposition of Christianity was the civilizing mission and 'global design' at the centre of coloniality. The second moment, the modern and colonial era, took place between 1700 and 1945, involving new dominant states: Britain, France and eventually Germany. Becoming 'like us' – that is, 'European' – emerges as the new global design and civilizing mission which, over time, comes to stress secularization rather than Christianity. The third period begins in 1945 under US domination, where the global design shifts again, this time to 'development', with the civilizing mission becoming one of advancing the 'developing' and 'underdeveloped' parts of the world. Finally, Mignolo identifies a fourth period beginning gradually during the 1980s in pursuit of the global design of neoliberalism whose civilizing mission is the realization of the 'world market' (see also **Brenner, Harvey**). Mignolo also perceives certain cracks in this most contemporary phase of globalization which might lead to an alternative world and the end of the modernity/coloniality dynamic.

Border thinking and pluri-versality

Challenging the Western form of domination – that is, modernity/coloniality – proves immensely difficult given the West's hegemonic position in the economic, political and epistemological domains: 'You cannot envision alternatives *to modernity* if the principles of knowledge you hold, and the structures of reasoning you follow, are molded by the hegemonic rhetoric of modernity and the hidden logic of coloniality working through it' (Mignolo 2005: 114, emphasis in the original). In the contemporary phase of globalization, however, Mignolo sees new potential for reversing domination arising in what he calls 'border spaces'. He defines the border as follows:

> The border lies where [...] Western knowledge and subjectivity, control of land and labour, of authority, and ways of living gender and sexuality have been 'contacting' other languages, memories, principles of knowledge and belief, forms of government and economic organization since 1500.
>
> (Mignolo 2010a: 351)

'Border thinking' then emerges in local settings with local histories and where the communities involved still speak and have access to vernacular languages, as well as imperial ones. The people living in such situations are able to think not only about alternative modernities but also alternatives *to* modernity. In such circumstances, people are more likely to be able to 'delink' their thinking about alternatives from the dominant modernity/coloniality system. With his knowledge of Latin America, Mignolo comments on the potential of indigenous peoples such as the Aymara to articulate alternative ways of living. In confronting the oppression of coloniality, such peoples are able to draw on longstanding ways of knowing, or epistemologies, to envision alternative futures.

More generally, the individuals and peoples most likely to be in this situation are part of 'political society'. Political society is usually counterpoised to civil society: those persons belonging to the civil service, founding and directing non-governmental organizations, teaching in schools and universities, running businesses and corporations, and so on. In contrast, members of political society are outside civil society, without access to the state or to markets. Living on borders, they are better placed to engage in 'epistemic decolonization': bringing to the foreground other epistemologies, other principles of knowledge and, thus, other economies, polities and ethics (2010a: 307). Having knowledge relevant to living on the borders of modernity, they also have the potential to think of different futures 'outside' modernity.

Part of Mignolo's optimism about the importance and the potential that such subaltern communities have for delinking themselves from modernity/coloniality arises from what he terms 'technological globaliz-ation'. The information and communication technologies currently available make it more possible for subaltern communities to create transnational alliances beyond the state to fight for their social and human rights (Mignolo 2000: 298). He also notes the potential of these same subaltern groups to link up with migrants from the non-European–US world currently living in the Western countries as further allies in their struggles (see **Santos**). What all these commu-nities with highly diverse local communities have in common is the need to deal with the power differentials of the modern/colonial world in their pursuit of epistemic decolonization.

Mignolo suggests that there are three scenarios in which global futures might unfold: *re-Westernization*, or the restoration of US hegemony after the damage caused by the military adventurism and financial chaos under the George W. Bush presidency; *de-Westernization*, or a shift in world dominance to economically powerful emerging countries such as China, Singapore, Brazil and Turkey; and *decoloniality*, or a movement led by a globally linked political society pursuing various projects anchored in local communities having in common their delinking from modernity in a search for trans-modern lives (see also **Escobar**). He describes this latter future as pluri-versal: 'Thus the pluriversality of each local history and its narrative of decolonization can *connect* through that common experience and use it as the basis for a new common logic of knowing: border thinking' (Mignolo 2010a: 351; see also 2011a: 330–331, emphasis in the original). Accordingly, he describes the emerging post-globalization world as 'polycentric' (see also **Amin, Arrighi, Cox, Harvey**).

Major globalization writings

Mignolo, W. D. (2000) *Local Histories/Global Designs: Coloniality, Subaltern Knowledges, and Border Thinking*, Princeton, NJ: Princeton University Press.

——(2005) *The Idea of Latin America*, Oxford, UK: Blackwell Publishing.

——(2010a) 'Delinking: the rhetoric of modernity, the logic of coloniality and the grammar of de-coloniality', in W. Mignolo and A. Escobar (eds) *Globalization and the De-colonial Option*, Abingdon, UK: Routledge.

——(2010b) 'Introduction: coloniality of power and de-colonial thinking', in W. Mignolo and A. Escobar (eds) *Globalization and the De-colonial Option*, Abingdon, UK: Routledge.

——(2011a) *The Darker Side of Western Modernity: Global Futures, Decolonial Options*, Durham, NC: Duke University Press.

——(2011b) 'Geopolitics of sensing and knowing: on (de)coloniality, border thinking and epistemic disobedience', *Postcolonial Studies: Culture, Politics, Economy*, vol 14, no 3, pp. 273–283.

See also: **Amin, Arrighi, Brenner, Cox, Escobar, Harvey, McClintock, Santos**.

AIHWA ONG

Aihwa Ong was born in Malaysia to a Straits Chinese family and moved to the US for her studies. She completed her Ph.D. in anthropology at Columbia University in 1982. She joined the University of California at Berkeley in 1984, where she currently holds the positions of Professor of Social Cultural Anthropology and head of the Socio-Cultural House in the Department of Anthropology.

Ong's research has contributed substantively to the establishment of an anthropology of globalization. The main focal points of her research have been the global and transnational dimensions of diasporic Asian communities, whether located in Western or non-Western societies; the reconfiguration of diasporic identities; practices of citizenship and sovereignty through neoliberal capitalist processes; and the emergence of new transnational classes as a consequence of such processes. In her early work, such as *Spirits of Resistance and Capitalist Discipline* (1987) and *Ungrounded Empires* (1997, co-edited with Donald M. Nonini), she investigates how new Malaysian and Chinese identities are shaped by an intersection between nation-building processes, development practices, cultural norms and transnational capital flows. Later on, in works such as *Flexible Citizenship* (1999), *Buddha Is Hiding* (2003) and *Neoliberalism as Exception* (2006), she develops a theory of citizenship as a process inseparable from contemporary dynamics of global capitalism. These works trace the mutations in citizenship, both in its symbolic and material manifestations, to contemporary dynamics of neoliberal logic and flexible capitalist accumulation. Thus, Ong conceptualizes citizenship as *flexible* citizenship – a political and social process whereby 'the most worthy citizen is a flexible *homo economicus*' (Ong 2003: 9).

Ong has also developed (with Stephen J. Collier) the concept of 'global assemblage'. This concept refers to the intersections among various heterogeneous global forms – knowledges, techniques, populations, politics and ethics – to capture the intertwining of various forces at both large and small scales (Ong 2009: 88). Moreover, her emphasis on 'neoliberal configurations' in *Global Assemblages* (co-edited with Collier, 2005), *Neoliberalism as Exception* and *Privatizing China* (2008, co-edited with Li Zhang) contributes to a more nuanced understanding of identity formation (both individual and collective) and to further reflection on the new meanings of being human in an age of globalization and flexible capitalist accumulation.

Global capitalism and identity

Ong's early work shows a preoccupation with the impact of capitalist processes and developmental programmes on non-Western societies. Her classic text *Spirits of Resistance and Capitalist Discipline* (Ong 1987) examines the effects of capitalist discipline on Malay peasant societies as they were undergoing industrialization projects. The establishment of special economic zones in Malaysia during the 1970s and 1980s had profound implications for the reconstitution of individual and collective identities of Malay rural societies. The industrial zones set up by the Malaysian government attracted transnational corporations (TNCs), mainly Japanese, which employed large numbers of Malay rural women. In her analysis, Ong investigates the effects of the capitalist discipline enforced by TNCs on Malay factory women's subjectivities and, more broadly, on the rural communities affected by the operations of these companies. By focusing on the encounters between global and local processes, Ong provides the initial foundations of a theory of globalization that takes into consideration the multiple interactions between global capitalist processes (such as the operations of TNCs), technologies of governance (neoliberalism and the developmental state) and knowledge (science), cultural practices, and local sociocultural systems (see also **Tsing**).

Ong is thus able to illustrate that contemporary processes of identity formation are inseparable from global processes of capitalist accumulation. In the case of the Malaysian factory workers, Ong indicates that the operations of TNCs reconfigured Malay workers' identities through coercive mechanisms that served to discipline them. She also demonstrates that non-coercive processes aimed to legitimize capitalist discipline and to reshape workers' self-perceptions as disciplined and disposable bodies. This strategy emerged not only through capitalist labour relations, but also through the flexible incorporation of local norms, gender-based hierarchies and customs, all of which inadvertently collaborated to discipline Malay women as chaste and obedient daughters and workers.

The focus on the cultural transformation effected by the encounter between the local and the global reappears in her edited volume *Ungrounded Empires* (1997, with Donald Nonini). Here she argues that it is impossible to understand transnational cultural phenomena such as diasporas, newly emerging family and gender structures, and global and regional imaginaries without attending to the 'strategies of accumulation' by various transnational communities (Ong and Nonini 1997: 4) (see also **Dirlik**). Taking modern Chinese transnationalism as an illustration, Ong and Nonini's volume elaborates upon a more nuanced anthropological approach to the link between global capitalist processes and identity formation. This link highlights how the everyday lives of people are transformed by global forces, and how their agencies are always implicated in negotiating such encounters. This new anthropological approach to globalization, with a specific focus on the material dimensions of cultural processes, aims also to demonstrate that non-Western modernities are not simply reactionary manifestations of Euro-American capitalism. Rather, they are 'organically produced' through interactions with various global, transnational and local forces, thereby creating a 'multiplicity of experienced modernities' (Allan Pred and Michael Watts quoted in Ong and Peletz 1995: 2).

In *Ungrounded Empires*, Ong begins to conceptualize the differential nature of identities produced by complex interactions between global and local conditions. The emergence of this new international division of labour becomes one of her most enduring foci of research and is further explored in *Flexible Citizenship*, *Buddha Is Hiding* and *Neoliberalism as Exception*. In these works, she examines how the interaction between global capitalist processes and transnational diasporic communities leads to the emergence of new transnational classes: the 'globalized managerial elite[s]' (the new transnational class of technocrats and professionals) and the 'semi-unfree labourers' (domestic and sex workers, low-skilled migrants). Ong indicates that new subjectivities emerge within what she calls Asian modernities, such as the 'multiple-passport holder', 'the multicultural manager with "flexible capital"' (Ong 1999), as well as the migrant maid as slave (Ong 2006) and the racialized poor Asian refugee (Ong 2003).

Global Assemblages

In *Global Assemblages*, Ong and Collier (2005) propose that a sophisticated anthropology of the global needs to transcend the model of sweeping generalizations and high-minded abstractions that had characterized many of the earlier analyses of globalization. They are equally unsatisfied with those analyses of globalization that posit the local as inherently opposed to and distinct from the global (see **Appadurai**). In contrast to **Castells**, **Giddens** and **Held**, Ong and Collier claim that scholars need to be more rigorous in identifying those processes that constitute the global through multiple intersections (see also **Robertson**). Thus, they employ the analytic term '*actual* global' to illustrate that 'global' cannot designate a space or a bounded phenomenon; rather, it involves a set of *relationships* and *interactions* between technology, politics and ethics. They understand these relations as constituting various 'global assemblages', which are intersections between diverse 'global forms' conditioned by particular 'technical infrastructures, administrative apparatuses, or value regimes'.

In her chapter entitled *Ecologies of Expertise: Assembling Flows, Managing Citizenship* in Ong and Collier (2005), Ong focuses on the 'cluster-development' strategies of the governments of Singapore and Malaysia, which rely on linking the state (now as 'venture capitalist') with foreign research institutions and global companies in knowledge-producing transnational networks. These reconfigure Singapore as a 'biotech tiger' and Malaysia as 'a knowledge stepping stone' (Ong 2005: 338). In Singapore, the assemblage of science, administrative mechanisms and foreign expertise produces not only new knowledge, but also novel ethical and political configurations. In these structures, distinctions emerge between worthy citizen subjects (flexible, enterprising, knowledgeable and risk-taking) and unworthy ones (those who are deemed to lack such traits). Thus, the assemblage constituted by technology (biotech), politics (neoliberal calculations and authoritarian rule) and ethics (the formations of (un)worthy citizenship and, thus, levels of being human) encompasses both global and local forms and creates 'distinct regimes of human worth' (2005: 350).

Neoliberalism, citizenship and sovereignty

In *Neoliberalism as Exception*, arguably her most compelling analysis of capitalist processes of globalization, Ong argues that neoliberalism, as a 'new mode of political optimization' (Ong 2006: 3), is rearranging the relationships between governance processes and governed, state sovereignty and territoriality, and power and knowledge in the Asia-Pacific region. Moreover, she indicates that the process of governing populations increasingly relies on a neoliberal logic, which employs market-driven technical solutions for what used to be sociopolitical problems (healthcare, welfare, education, citizenship). Ong calls this type of strategy 'neoliberalism as exception'. This label indicates that even though Asian authoritarian governments have not adopted neoliberalism as their political ideology, they have resorted to a neoliberal logic in specific areas of governance. In these areas, they coordinate policies (related to labour, health, welfare, social security and citizenship) to respond to corporate interests in order to attract investments and to maximize their participation in global markets. Such a neoliberal logic favours individuals who are educated, mobile, enterprising and self-affirming, whether they are citizens or not. In fact, what Ong calls the 'postdevelopmental state' is willing to include non-citizens in the range of benefits reserved for citizenship to draw on the talents, expertise and flexibility of foreign technocrats (see also Ong 1999, 2007).

In contrast, 'exceptions to neoliberalism' point to how this privileging of a particular group of transnational experts entails and, indeed, relies upon the exclusion of other groups and spaces from neoliberal calculations and choices. Exceptions to neoliberalism refer to policies which strip away social and political protections previously taken for granted. These exceptions can also indicate the need for unskilled low-waged labourers who can act as disposable bodies; through their unprotected flexible labour, they can also sustain the requirements of transnational economic circuits (see also **Sassen**). Ong focuses, for example, on the plight of migrant domestic workers in the Asia-Pacific region, whom she calls the 'neoslaves' of the capitalist economies in the region, such as Singapore, Hong Kong and Malaysia. As she points out, their neoslavery – a condition where individuals are deprived of the most basic social, economic and political rights – emerges in tandem with the overvaluation of highly skilled individuals who enjoy most of the citizenship rights without actually being citizens (see also Ong 1999; Ong and Collier 2005).

The foreign experts and technocrats, however, are not the only privileged class of neoliberal subjects. In *Flexible Citizenship* (Ong 1999) and, more recently, *Privatizing China* (Zhang and Ong 2008), Ong focuses on how the infusion of neoliberal logic into authoritarian Asian societies has produced a new transnational class of Asian subjects who enjoy the benefits and privileges of 'flexible citizenship'. This concept characterizes the capitalist logic of flexible capitalist accumulation (see **Harvey**), where individuals respond opportunistically and flexibly to changing political and economic conditions (Ong 1999: 6). Thus, the multiple-passport holder shuffling between Asia and the West has become, in her estimation, an apt contemporary example of this flexible logic, according to which some individuals can afford to choose from among several citizenships based on economic calculations. As she explains, citizenship itself has been reconfigured by neoliberal calculations into flexible citizenship. This sociopolitical innovation represents the 'strategies of mobile managers, technocrats, and professionals seeking to both circumvent *and* benefit from different nation-state regimes by selecting different sites for investment, work, family life' (1999: 112, emphasis in the original).

The transformation of citizenship from a modern condition based on political rights and participation within a single sovereign state into a choice based on economic calculation involves, therefore, a mutation of sovereignty. Ong coins the term 'graduated sovereignty' to express the strategy of the postdevelopmental state that no longer treats national territory as a uniform political space (Ong 2006: 77). Rather, the state chooses to fragment its territory into 'noncontiguous zones', which are administered differently. For example, the creation of industrial zones or special economic zones in Malaysia is part of this strategy, where the state can integrate these zones within the global markets and administer the populations working in these zones according to market-driven logics, while protecting other areas from global forces. Special economic zones are not bound by national territories; they can span the borders of several countries, such as the 'growth triangles' or the 'subregional economic zones' in Asia-Pacific.

Ong remarks that the logic of globalization has thus produced neither a hardening nor a disappearance of state sovereignty, but rather a 'proliferation of differentiated sovereignty' both within and across borders (2006: 92). For example, the growth triangle between Singapore, Malaysia and Indonesia draws upon its access to cheap disposable labour and natural resources (Malaysia, Indonesia), and the advantage of Singapore as an expertise and technological hub in the region (see also Ong 2005). Graduated sovereignty thus points to a logic not so much of market versus states, but rather one of differentiated sovereignty. Under this new logic there are zones where the state's sovereignty is preserved and its protections are quite strong, and others where sovereignty is dissipated to leave room for the type of flexibility that allows certain regions to be integrated within global markets without political impediments (Ong 2006: 95–96) (see also **Sassen**).

Aihwa Ong's conceptualization of the globalization of neoliberal logic in Asia-Pacific has produced a sophisticated and nuanced understanding of how multiple transnational processes affect citizenship, identities and political sovereignty. More importantly, it has exposed a crucial perspective – namely that 'Third World' societies are not merely passive recipients of capitalist processes. Rather, they actively participate in transnational processes of capitalist accumulation *and* create their own variants of capitalist development. This emphasis on human agency within global processes of capitalism allows us to grasp that neoliberal logic does not have homogenizing effects. Rather, Ong's analyses reveal that neoliberal and capitalist processes simultaneously produce transnational classes of empowered privileged and mobile individuals *and* of 'semi-unfree' unskilled low-waged labourers employed as cheap disposable bodies.

Major globalization writings

Ong, A. (1987) *Spirits of Resistance and Capitalist Discipline: Factory Women in Malaysia*, Albany, NY: SUNY Press.

——(1999) *Flexible Citizenship: The Cultural Logics of Transnationality*, Durham, NC: Duke University Press.

——(2003) *Buddha Is Hiding: Refugees, Citizenship, the New America*, Berkeley and Los Angeles, CA: University of California Press.

——(2006) *Neoliberalism as Exception: Mutations in Citizenship and Sovereignty*, Durham, NC: Duke University Press.

——(2007) 'Please stay: pied-a-terre subjects in the megacity', *Citizenship Studies*, vol 11, no 1, pp. 83–93.

——(2009) 'Aihwa Ong: on being human and ethical living', in J. Kenway and J. Fahey (eds) *Globalizing the Research Imagination*, London and New York, NY: Routledge.

Ong, A. and Collier, S. J. (eds) (2005) *Global Assemblages: Technology, Politics, and Ethics as Anthropological Problems*, Oxford, UK: Blackwell Publishing.

Ong, A. and Nonini, D. M. (eds) (1997) *Ungrounded Empires: The Cultural Politics of Modern Chinese Transnationalism*, London: Routledge.

Ong, A. and Peletz, M. G. (eds) (1995) *Bewitching Women, Pious Men: Gender and Politics in Southeast Asia*, Berkeley and Los Angeles, CA: University of California Press.

Zhang, L. and Ong, A. (eds) (2008) *Privatizing China: Socialism from Afar*, Ithaca, NY, and London: Cornell University Press.

Further reading

Ong, A. and Chen, N. (eds) (2010) *Asian Biotech: Refiguring Nation, Security and Citizenship*, Durham, NC: Duke University Press.

See also: **Appadurai, Castells, Dirlik, Giddens, Harvey, Held, Robertson, Sassen, Tsing.**

ROLAND ROBERTSON (1938–)

Roland Robertson was trained in sociology and served as a professor in this field at the Universities of Leeds and Essex in the UK and the University of Pittsburgh in the

US. Since 1999, he has held a chair in sociology and global society at the University of Aberdeen in the UK. During the late 1960s, Robertson began to look at international relations and worldwide phenomena. As his investigations developed, he came to work most extensively on the sociology of religion. However, he did not focus on the usual sociological topic in the field (secularization), but on how religion had become a mode for ordering societies and the relations between them. As his thinking matured he came to conclude that the processes shaping these relations as well as individuals and nation-states themselves were uniquely global. With this conclusion, he introduced the concept of globalization into his work.

Accordingly, Robertson was one of the first social scientists to work with and think systematically about the concept of globalization in the contemporary period. He began to develop his understanding of the concept during the early 1980s and published one of the first full books in the field in 1992, *Globalization: Social Theory and Global Culture*. This book compiled many of his essays on the topic from the 1980s and early 1990s, while adding new essays to introduce and conclude the book.

Defining globalization

In his work, globalization refers to processes where the world is moving towards 'unicity' or 'global unicity', the growing 'oneness' of the world as a single sociocultural place. In moving towards unicity, the significance of territorial boundaries declines – a profound change because territoriality had been a basic strategy of geographic control for much of human history. Movement towards unicity involves changes to two features of the human condition: rising connectivity across the world and 'global consciousness'. He adds that the analysis of globalization has often focused on rapid growth of trans-world connections but paid less attention to the increasingly common phenomenon of people seeing the world as one place. The emergence of global unicity, however, does not mean that the world is moving towards a single culture. To the contrary, Robertson stresses that consciousness of differences among people are, if anything, sharpened with the intensification of globalization.

Robertson specifies a model termed the 'global field' for conceptualizing the history and contemporary character of globalization. This field contains four components: national societies or nation-states (he uses both terms), individual selves, a world system of societies (international relations), and a notion of a common humanity or of humankind (see also **Falk**). These components involve autonomous processes that have been going on for a long time, at least 500 years (see also **Hopkins**). Thus, national societies/nation-states refers to the processes leading to the emergence and global spread of the nation-state form of rule and the idea that societies constituted by this form of rule will develop a cohesive collective identity. Individual selves refers to processes where a sense of individuality or personal autonomy emerges, allowing people (men at the start) to be self-deciders not necessarily controlled by religious, community or other collective organizations. Over the same period, as national societies governed by nation-states becomes a dominant form, relations between these societies (inter-national) – the third component – become more institutionalized and more important. Finally, he identifies processes leading to a sense of a common humanity. Thus, becoming conscious of belonging to humankind is exemplified in one way by the emergence of notions of 'human' rights: rights that all human beings have whatever their national origin, their gender, their physical characteristics, their religion and so on (see also **Falk, Howard-Hassmann**).

Robertson frames his understanding of the history of globalization in terms of the relationships between these four component processes. He describes them as 'autonomous' from one another; the development of individual selves takes place distinctly from the emergence of national societies or of a society of states concretized through international relations, or from being part of humankind. At the same time, he argues that, over time, these components evolve to be more differentiated from one another, while becoming increasingly interdependent. And as this differentiation and interdependence intensify, the components themselves change. National societies become more ethnically and culturally diverse, international relations become more encompassing of all parts of the world, individuals assume different and multiple identities (as **Castells** observes), and understandings of humankind become the focus of debates around gender, sexual orientation, indigeneity, health and wellness, and so on. Robertson uses the concept of 'relativization' to stress the autonomy and reciprocity of these four fields. For example, one defines oneself relative to one's national society, to relations going on between societies and to humankind. All are relevant for the identities one assumes and acts upon.

Accordingly, for Robertson, globalization is not something entirely new or specifically contemporary. The four components and their growing interdependence provide a focus for historical research. And in carrying out that research, he suggests focusing not only on the increasing connectedness of the world, but also on the scope and depth of consciousness of the world as one place among individuals and communities. This latter concern about a global consciousness takes Robertson directly into cultural and subjective realms.

Unlike other sociologists, therefore, Robertson looks at the period from 1880 to 1925 as being marked by intensified globalization. He wonders why such important sociologists as Max Weber and Émile Durkheim did not theorize or even comment upon changes in this period, such as the time-zoning of the world, the establishment of the international date line, the near global adoption of the Gregorian calendar, international telegraphic and signalling codes, and international postal delivery. By focusing largely on one component – the formation of national societies – sociologists were blind to the changes in the direction of global unicity.

The global and the local

Robertson resists strongly any argument that globalization is a homogenizing force, one that will lead to a single world culture, probably from a dominant West, or to sameness or isomorphism in social institutions from one society to another, and from one local place to another. He counters by positing that contemporary globalization involves the institutionalization of a twofold process of the *universalization of particularism* and the *particularization of universalism*. Thus, the experience (indeed, the expectation) of particularity – of distinctness and differences where one lives – is increasingly the situation everywhere; it is universal. At the same time, when there are universal ideas – equality between the sexes, monotheism, free trade, human rights, 'natural' resources – they are lived out and refashioned (particularized) wherever in the world they land (see also **Sen**, **Tsing**).

Thus, for Robertson, seeing the global and the local as somehow distinct from, or opposed to, one another does not do justice to the dynamic effects of becoming more similar and more different at the same time (see **Hannerz**). To emphasize this point, Robertson introduced into the English language globalization literature the concept of 'glocalization'. By choosing to use this term (inspired by a cognate phrase in Japanese), Robertson challenges views that argue that the 'local' is the site where resistance to globalizing trends occurs, or where subaltern peoples are pitted against hegemonic societies, or where struggles against 'cosmopolitans' take place. In contrast, 'glocalization' suggests that what happens locally and what happens globally are mutually constitutive; by invoking the 'local', one is already thinking of the local as being shaped by the global and the potential for the local to change the global. For example, if a local community in France mounts stout resistance to the opening of a Wal-Mart store in its midst, its members feel themselves being shaped by the global. In resisting and fighting off that store and perhaps connecting with communities in other parts of France or the world doing the same thing, these community members also challenge a global institution and articulate an alternative view of globality (see also **Tomlinson**).

Robertson looks at the rise of fundamentalisms through these same lenses. Let us take the rise of Hindu fundamentalism as an example (see also **Sen**). On the one hand, it shares similar properties with other fundamentalisms in the world – value oriented, while seeking the reorganization of all spheres of life in terms of these particular absolute values. On the other, it focuses on differentiating itself sharply from religions such as Islam, Christianity, Sikhism and Buddhism. Followers strongly stress the culturally distinct elements of being Hindu, particularly in opposition to being Muslim. But in doing so, they change Hinduism itself by identifying core divinely inspired texts as guides, a universal characteristic of fundamentalisms elsewhere. Religious leaders employ contemporary communication media to articulate a vision of Hinduism independent of place, thus evoking a universal ambition. Fundamentalisms reflect both the particularization of universals about what a religion entails and the universalization of one notion of Hinduism that is claimed to speak to potential Hindus anywhere in the world.

Globalization and modernity

Although both Robertson and **Giddens** are sociologists, a comparison of the four processes in Robertson's 'global field' with the four dimensions of globalization identified by Giddens reveals important differences. In essence, Giddens takes his four institutional features of modernity – surveillance, military power, capitalism and industrialism – and trans-plants them from the national to the global scale: surveillance becomes the nation-state system, military power emerges as the world military order, capitalism becomes the world capitalist economy, and industrialism is cast as the international division of order. According to Robertson, Giddens simply enlarges societal modernity to the global scale, a step consistent with describing globalization as the 'radicalization' of modernity.

Robertson theorizes the four components of the global field as processes long in development with origins preceding the onset of modernity. He leaves room for the history of globalization to extend back in time, perhaps even a millennium. More importantly, Giddens' institutional approach has very little to say about culture. The tensions that Robertson sees in contemporary globalization – heterogeneity versus homogeneity, universalism versus particularism – are profoundly cultural in nature. Moreover, as we have demonstrated, Robertson puts considerable emphasis on the global spread of consciousness of the world being one place, a process he terms unicity. So a globalizing world for Robertson is one of considerable social and cultural tensions and many of these tensions are expressed through cultural activities: religious differences, varying understandings of masculinity and femininity, dietary practices, conceptions of the family, or speaking different languages. Robertson's focus on culture has been picked up by **Castells** in his reflections on the 'power of identity' and social movements.

Major globalization writings

Robertson, R. (1990) 'Mapping the global condition: globalization as the central concept', *Theory, Culture & Society*, vol 7, nos 2–3, pp. 15–30.

——(1992) *Globalization: Social Theory and Global Culture*, London: Sage.

Robertson, R. and Chirico, J. (1985) 'Humanity, globalization and worldwide religious resurgence: a theoretical exploration', *Sociological Analysis*, vol 46, no 3, pp. 219–242.

Robertson, R. and Garrett, W. R. (eds) (1991) *Religion and Global Order*, New York, NY: Paragon House.

Robertson, R. and Lechner, F. (1985) 'Modernization, globalization and the problem of culture in world-systems theory', *Theory, Culture & Society*, vol 2, no 3, pp. 103–118.

Robertson, R. and White, K. (2004) 'Globalization: sociology and cross-disciplinarity', in C. Calhoun, C. Rojek and B. Turner (eds) *The Sage Handbook of Sociology*, London: Sage.

Robertson, R., Featherstone, M. and Lash, S. (eds) (1995) *Global Modernities*, London: Sage.

See also: **Castells, Falk, Giddens, Hannerz, Hopkins, Howard-Hassmann, Sen, Tomlinson, Tsing.**

DANI RODRIK (1957–)

Dani Rodrik is a Turkish-born economist and Rafiq Hariri Professor of International Political Economy at the John F. Kennedy School of Government at Harvard University, MA. After graduating from Robert College in Istanbul, he earned an AB (*summa cum laude*) from Harvard College, followed by a Ph.D. in economics and an MPA from Princeton University, NJ. He has published widely in the areas of international economics, economic development and political economy. He is affiliated with the National Bureau of Economic Research, Centre for Economic Policy Research (London), the Center for Global Development and the Council on Foreign Relations.

In the opening pages to his book *The Globalization Paradox* (2011), Rodrik notes that in his earlier work on globalization, *Has Globalization Gone too Far?* (1997), he had concentrated on international trade and, in particular, on how the new trade regime established through the World Trade Organization placed limits on states' capacity to provide labour market and social protection policies. He did not address financial globalization at all in the book; but by the time of its publication, the East Asian financial crisis had erupted. A decade later, another financial crisis began to rock the world economy, a crisis that started in the US with sub-prime mortgage difficulties. The 2011 book analyses both trade and financial economic globalization as Rodrik works to develop what he describes as a 'new narrative' for understanding globalization and its governance. Accordingly, we concentrate on this latter publication in discussing his contribution to the study of globalization.

Levels of globalization

Rodrik distinguishes between 'hyperglobalization' and 'moderate' globalization. The key difference between the two forms relates to the degree to which they restrict the capacity of states to intervene to shape globalization's effects in their respective economies and societies. When states lose these capacities, the potential for economic and social harm rises significantly. Rodrik writes of the hyper form:

> Trade agreements now extended beyond their traditional focus on import restrictions and impinged on domestic policies; controls on international capital markets were removed; and developing nations came under severe pressure to open their markets to foreign trade and investment. In effect, economic globalization became an end in itself.
>
> (Rodrik 2011: xvii)

Accordingly, globalization is 'moderate' in Rodrik's thinking when international rules for trade and for finance leave room for states to intervene to address domestic policy objectives such as full employment, social equality and social insurance.

Like other political economy scholars (see, for example, **Amin**, **Arrighi**, **Brenner**, **Cox**, **Harvey**), Rodrik links globalization closely to capitalism. He writes that globalization is the worldwide extension of capitalism, with the two processes being so deeply intertwined that one cannot discuss the future of one without considering the future of the other (2011: 233). Accordingly, the history of economic globalization maps closely onto the history of capitalism. 'Capitalism 1.0' runs from the mid-nineteenth century to the early twentieth century, expanding on the basis of innovations in communications, travel and industrial technologies. It also thrived on the financial anchor of the gold standard and on the power of European and American imperialism. 'Capitalism 2.0' takes shape at the end of World War II with the establishment of the Bretton Woods institutions (the International Monetary Fund and the World Bank) and a modest trade regime based on the General Agreement on Tariffs and Trade. Rodrik describes this stage of capitalism as involving a 'shallow' form of economic integration with controls on international capital flows, partial trade liberalization, exceptions for socially sensitive sectors such as agriculture and textiles, and the expansion of social welfare policies (2011: 235).

Capitalism 2.0 began to fray during the 1970s and 1980s under the dual pressures of increasing financial globalization and a deepening trade regime (see also **Arrighi, Cox**). Promoters of these developments, 'hyperglobalizers' in Rodrik's terms, are seen as having two blind spots. They thought that they could push for rapid and deep integration of the world economy without worrying about social institutional underpinnings analogous to those that had been in place for the previous two versions of capitalism. Second, they believed that such hyperglobalization would have minimal, if any, effects on domestic institutions such as social welfare policies and on labour rights. Both assumptions have proven incorrect, according to Rodrik. The financial crisis beginning in late 2007 showed the necessity of institutional arrangements that can slow down globalization when needed. In addition, the pressures on social welfare policies, labour rights and other state supports such as education, which arose from such unfettered globalization, were intense and held serious social consequences. Markets, Rodrik concludes, must be deeply embedded in systems of governance. The idea that markets are self-regulating should be 'buried once and for all' (2011: 237).

Rodrik justifies this position by looking at the behaviour of East Asian states in the face of hyperglobalization. He argues that they never really signed on to this US vision of globalization. They refused to roll back social policies and they controlled how much they engaged with the global economy (see **Arrighi, Ong**). They demonstrated that the benefits of globalization come to those countries which invest in domestic social capabilities and accommodate economic globalization on their own terms (2011: 157). Countries such as China and India never gave up capital controls, for example, and were able to shelter and to grow their economies by controlling, to some degree, their engagement with globalization.

A political trilemma

In considering what the future of globalization might be, Rodrik posits that states and the world economy face a fundamental political trilemma. He argues that we cannot have hyperglobalization, democracy and national self-determination all at once. We can at best have two of these. Thus, if we want hyperglobalization and democracy, we need to forgo a significant governing role for nation-states. This choice leads towards strong global governance as the institutional answer to maintaining democracy, but building democracy at a global level. If we want to keep a governing role for states and still have hyperglobalization, then we will need to give up on democracy. States will not have the autonomy to steer globalization in ways desired by their citizens. Rodrik observes that the European Union has moved in a direction consistent with this combination. He adds that many parts of the world, particularly outside East Asia, have already begun to live under such circumstances at considerable economic and social costs. Finally, if we want to keep a significant governing role for states and to protect democracy within states, then we have to move towards a limited, moderate form of globalization. He notes that Capitalism 2.0 with the protection of the Bretton Woods institutions and capital controls illustrates the potential outcomes of this choice.

When it comes to the first option (hyperglobalization and democracy), while some globalization scholars see promise in strengthening global governance (see **Beck**, **Rosenau**, **Scholte**), Rodrik is wary of taking this path. He worries that there is 'simply too much diversity' in the world for nation-states to be 'shoehorned' into global rules (Rodrik 2011: 204). The deep differences between societies cannot be overcome with technical fixes made possible by contemporary digital technologies. Nor does he think that emerging global governance practices such as networks of regulators with particular areas of expertise, substituting markets for governance, or corporate social responsibility will work. They are simply too weak to be capable of supporting the depth of governance required. He also suggests that the kind of commitment to global citizenship necessary to support strong global governance is really found only among the wealthy or the highly educated. For most people, their attachment to nation-state governance is much deeper than it can ever be for developing global identities that might support global governance (2011: 231).

The second option, maintaining the nation-state system while supporting hyperglobalization, is also unacceptable. Rodrik argues that the world has drifted in this direction over the past 20 years with very unsatisfactory results. The differences in wealth between countries have widened considerably. The gaps in well-being and resources between the very rich and the poor have deepened. In situations such as the financial crisis that began in late 2007, democratic politics was in short supply as states moved to channel massive amounts of capital to the financial sector yet made few changes to the governance rules and regulations for global financial firms.

Based on this analysis, Rodrik argues that the only viable option would be to rein in hyperglobalization to render it more moderate and to act on a vision that would see moderate globalization in a system that recognizes the virtues of national diversity and has nation-state governance at its core (see also **Bello**). He takes as his lead the Bretton Woods compromise that was at the centre of Capitalism 2.0. But in doing so, he observes that under the existing trade regime, international trade is substantially free. He also deems it unlikely that the globalization of finance can be reversed. And he points out that the US is no longer the hegemonic power that it had been for most of the twentieth century.

With these constraints in mind, Rodrik offers seven guiding principles for a form of global economic governance that might be adopted by nation-states (2011: 237–249). First, markets are not self-regulating; they need to be deeply embedded in systems of governance. Second, democratic governance and political communities remain organized primarily within nation-states and will remain so for the immediate future. Third, there is not just one way to prosperity: 'A global economy that recognizes the need for and value of institutional diversity would foster rather than stifle such experimentation and evolution' (2011: 239). Fourth, countries have the right to protect their own social arrangements, regulations and institutions. If this means that a country has to restrict trade or capital flows, then so be it. Fifth, countries do not have the right to impose their institutions on others. Sixth, the purpose of international economic rule-making must be to provide the rules for managing the interactions between nation-states. Here Rodrik stresses the likelihood of accepting a much larger role for 'opt outs' or exit clauses in international economic rules, an argument he lays out in considerable detail in his 2007 book *One Economics, Many Recipes*. Finally, he argues that non-democratic countries cannot count on the same rights and privileges in the international economic order as democracies.

In order to accomplish these goals while following these principles, Rodrik does argue that important reforms will need to be made to existing global institutions. He lays out some suggestions for the reforms needed in the international trade regime and in the regulation of global finance. In both instances, he advocates shifting certain powers back to nation-states. Conversely, he argues for the need to open up the world's labour markets further, which he argues could lead to huge benefits for the world's poor. He also offers some ideas about how China should be accommodated in the world economy. If the seven principles are followed and these reforms are implemented, Rodrik believes that a much better world economic and political order would emerge:

> Instead of viewing [globalization] as a system that requires a single set of institutions or one principal economic superpower, we should accept it as a collection of diverse nations whose interactions are regulated by a thin layer of simple, transparent, and common sense traffic rules. This vision will not construct a path toward a 'flat' world – a borderless world economy. Nothing will. What it will do is enable a healthy, sustainable world economy that leaves room for democracies to determine their own futures.
>
> (Rodrik 2011: 280)

Major globalization writings

Rodrik, D. (1997) *Has Globalization Gone too Far?*, Washington, DC: Institute for International Economics.

——(2007) *One Economics, Many Recipes: Globalization, Institutions, and Economic Growth*, Princeton, NJ: Princeton University Press.

——(2011) *The Globalization Paradox: Democracy and the Future of the World Economy*, New York, NY: W. W. Norton & Co.

See also: **Amin, Arrighi, Beck, Bello, Brenner, Cox, Harvey, Ong, Rosenau, Scholte.**

JAMES N. ROSENAU (1924–2011)

Born in Philadelphia, PA, James Rosenau obtained his Ph.D. from Princeton University, NJ, after which he embarked on a long and distinguished career studying world politics. In the first part of his career, he was a leader among scholars who sought to bring a 'scientific' approach to the study of international relations, part of the 'behavioural revolution' that swept through US political science during the 1950s and 1960s. By the end of the 1970s, however, he became increasingly dissatisfied, if not uneasy, with the scientific approach. This approach worked well as long as one could assume that states controlled all important transactions within their own borders and could act as autonomous actors engaging with other states on matters of common concern. When those borders become more porous and when non-state actors become strong enough to become players in world politics in their own right, the assumptions underlying the behavioural approach were challenged. Rosenau found it necessary to leave the 'scientific' approach behind and dedicated the latter part of his career to studying and theorizing the increasing 'turbulence' in world politics. In carrying out this research, he engaged directly with the concept of globalization.

179

Turbulence in world politics

The growing uncertainty in world politics, Rosenau argues, arises from turbulence. Drawing from organizational theory, he describes turbulence as a situation where environments in which people live are marked by high degrees of complexity and dynamism (Rosenau 1990: 9). The number of actors involved and the extensive degrees of interdependence among them create environments dense with causal layers. Such turbulence, in turn, transforms longstanding parameters of behaviour (1990: 11). Structurally, the state-centric system in world affairs comes to coexist with an ever more dynamic, decentralized, multi-centric system. The norms, structures and processes in these two systems are mutually exclusive, adding high complexity to the world system. In relational terms, these changes in structure undermine longstanding unquestioning and compliant acceptance of authority, rendering the exercise of authority much more problematic. Finally, at the micro-level, the analytical skills of individuals are increasing to the point that they now play a different and important role in world politics. They are more involved than ever before.

According to Rosenau, the dynamics of turbulence 'penetrate to the very core of the human experience' (Rosenau 1997: 17). They give rise to the questioning of such important components of daily living as territoriality, community, productivity, commitment, work, religion and loyalty, among other factors, that have long been taken for granted. An important source of the changes leading to this questioning is the process of globalization. This concept refers to processes of a particular sort, and not to values or structures. Globalizing processes are distinguished by not 'being hindered by territorial or jurisdictional barriers. They can spread readily across national boundaries and are capable of reaching into any community everywhere in the world' (1997: 80). They can be initiated by transnational elites as much as by local groups in particular places. Accordingly, globalizing processes involve individuals, groups, societies, governments and transnational organizations engaging in similar forms of behaviour or participating in more encompassing and coherent organizations and systems. If processes have the potential of being worldwide in scale or spread in unlimited directions, while transgressing national jurisdictions, then they can be safely considered to have a global character (that is, they are globalizing ones).

Rosenau adds that the turbulence of world politics also involves localization processes: those that lead social actors to narrow their horizons and to retreat to less encompassing organizing systems or organizations. He does not link the processes of globalization and localization as intricately as **Robertson**, who speaks of 'glocalization', or as **Tomlinson**, who stresses the reshaping of local spaces by globalizing processes. For Rosenau, they are concurrent forces fostering complex responses to one another. For example, he states that globalizing processes involve the movement across boundaries of six phenomena: goods and services; people; ideas and information; money; normative orientations; and behavioural patterns and services. Thus, the movement of fruits and vegetables from across the world into particular places may trigger localizing steps in favour of nearby farmers. Or rising levels of immigration (globalization) may be combined with increasing xenophobia. Rapid changes in the values of globally traded currencies (globalization) may be accompanied by governments introducing capital controls or price controls for key commodities such as grains or vegetables.

Distant proximities and 'fragmegration'

The dialectical relationship between globalization and localization leads Rosenau to innovate conceptually in order to move beyond a singular focus on globalization. 'Distant proximities' is the first of these conceptual tools. Characteristic of the present era are situations where what seems remote also seems close at hand, 'thereby compelling individuals and collectivities alike to cope continuously with the challenge of distant proximities' (Rosenau 2003: 3). For example, when the huge earthquake and accompanying tsunami hit Japan early in March 2011, people in India, Spain, Brazil and Canada were remote from their physical effects. At the same time, in witnessing virtually the tsunami hitting the Japanese coastline at over 500km per hour with all of its destructive force, people shuddered as if they were right there on the scene. Many responded with significant financial donations to national chapters of global organizations such as the International Red Cross as if they were helping neighbours next door. Thus, Rosenau writes, 'the best way to understand world affairs today requires viewing them as an endless series of distant proximities in which the forces pressing for greater globalization and those inducing greater localization interactively play themselves out' (2003: 4). Accordingly, globalization is 'but one component of the transformative dynamics that underlie the emergence of a new epoch in the human condition' (2003: 8).

In focusing on the dynamics of the shrinking of social and geographic distances in ways that render the environments of people, organizations and communities both distant and proximate, Rosenau suggests a second new concept, 'fragmegration'. With this term, he is better able to describe the pervasive interaction between fragmenting and integrating dynamics unfolding in all aspects of contemporary living. Fragmegration captures in a single word 'the large degree to which these rhythms consist of localizing, decentralizing, or fragmenting dynamics that are interactively and causally linked to globalizing, centralizing, and integrating dynamics' (2003: 11). He adds that this concept pushes analysts away from narrow analysis of globalization, focusing on economic factors, and towards including cultural, social, political and ecological processes.

In contrast to some globalization thinkers, Rosenau devotes considerable space and energy to assessing the consequences for individuals of distant proximities and fragmegration. This emphasis is perhaps best summarized by the title of one of his last books, *People Count! Networked Individuals in Global Politics* (Rosenau 2008). He argues that the decline of fixed systems of roles and norms of behaviour and, therefore, fixed identities leads to 'the imposition of an inescapable and unrelenting autonomy on many people' (Rosenau 2003: 25) (see also **Castells**). Contemporary digital technologies enable individuals to greatly expand the range of their interpersonal relationships beyond face-to-face contacts and to participate in the formation and enlargement of groups in an ever more networked world, what **Castells** refers to as the 'network society'. Rosenau postulates that the values, identities, capacities, strategies and interests of individuals become key variables that can aggregate into substantial consequences for macro-structures, which interact with collectivities and communities. Central to these fragmegration processes is the proliferation of organizational networks, 'a trend so pervasive that many networks are linked to each other and thus add further to the density of nongovernmental collectivities' (2003: 58).

Global governance

One of the best-known applications of Rosenau's theorization of contemporary globalization is found in his discussion of global governance. He argues that an irreversible process is under way where authority is increasingly disaggregated and associated with diverse spheres of governance. Consequently, the system of global governance comprises more and more centres of authority in every corner of the world and at every level of community (Rosenau 2002: 71).

Rosenau distinguishes 'government' from 'governance'. Both phenomena consist of rule systems and steering mechanisms by which authority is exercised and desired goals are realized:

> While the rule systems of governments can be thought of as structures, those of governance are social functions or processes that can be performed or implemented in a variety of ways at different times and places (or even at the same time) by a wide variety of organizations.
>
> (Rosenau 2002: 72)

Key, then, to this distinction is the idea of spheres of authority, which can take formal or informal forms. What is characteristic of any site of authority is a capacity to generate compliance on the part of those individuals or organizations towards which objectives are being issued. As we have noted above, Rosenau sees governance as a bifurcated system. There is an interstate system of states and their national governments that has long dominated the course of events. Increasingly alongside this system is another multi-centric system comprised of diverse types of other collectivities. This multi-centric system embraces a host of new spheres of authority that sometimes cooperate with, other times compete with, but all the while endlessly interact with the state-centric system.

Similar to **Cerny**, Rosenau (2002: 80) identifies a variety of different participants in global governance:

1 subnational and national governments founded on hierarchical structures formally adopted in constitutions;
2 for-profit transnational corporations formally hierarchically structured by articles of incorporation;
3 international governmental organizations (IGOs) based on formal treaties and charters;
4 subnational and national not-for-profit non-governmental organizations (NGOs) sustained by either formal laws or informal undocumented arrangements;
5 international or transnational not-for-profit NGOs either formally structured as organizations or informally linked together as associations or social movements; and
6 markets that have both formal and informal structures that steer horizontal exchanges between buyers and sellers, producers and consumers.

He adds to this list unorganized elite groups or mass publics who informally organize around an important issue and then disband afterwards.

This mix of different actors gathering around an increasing number of spheres of authority gives rise, in turn, to six different types of governance. Rosenau develops a typology of governance by drawing on several variables: *processes*, which can be unidirectional or multidirectional and vertical or horizontal; and *structures*, which can be formal, informal, or a mix of both (2002: 81). Accordingly, the most familiar form of governance is what he calls 'top down' and refers to the familiar activities of governments, which trigger unidirectional vertical processes and draw upon formal structures. The most novel and distinctive departure from 'top-down' governance is a form identified as 'mobius-web'. This type involves multidirectional vertical and horizontal processes and draws upon a mixture of formal (governmental) and informal structures. This type constitutes 'a hybrid structure in which the dynamics of governance are so intricate and overlapping among the several levels as to form a singular, weblike process that, like a mobius, neither begins nor culminates at any level or at any point in time' (Rosenau 2003: 297). Rosenau suggests that the complex politics around the environment and climate change are suggestive of mobius governance.

Major globalization writings

Rosenau, J. (1990) *Turbulence in World Politics: A Theory of Change and Continuity*, Princeton, NJ: Princeton University Press.

——(1995) 'Governance in the twenty-first century', *Global Governance*, vol 6, no 2, pp. 13–43.

——(1997) *Along the Domestic–Foreign Frontier: Exploring Governance in a Turbulent World*, Cambridge, UK: Cambridge University Press.

——(2002) 'Governance in a new global order', in D. Held and A. McGrew (eds) *Governing Globalization: Power, Authority, and Global Governance*, Cambridge, UK: Polity Press.

——(2003) *Distant Proximities: Dynamics beyond Globalization*, Princeton, NJ: Princeton University Press.

——(2008) *People Count! Networked Individuals in Global Politics*, Boulder, CO: Paradigm Publishers.

Further reading

Held, D. and McGrew, A. (eds) (2002) *Governing Globalization: Power, Authority and Global Governance*, Cambridge, UK: Polity Press.

See also: **Castells, Cerny, Robertson, Tomlinson**.

ARUNDHATI ROY (1961–)

Arundhati Roy, an accomplished novelist and outspoken political activist, was born in Meghalaya, a province in the north-east of India, but grew up in Kerala on the south-western coast. She studied architecture in New Delhi. Roy attained international recognition through her novel *The God of Small Things*, which was awarded the prestigious Man Booker Prize in 1997. In spite of these accolades she has gathered for her literary skills, Roy's work consists primarily of political writings. She is considered one of the best-known spokespersons for the anti-globalization/alter-globalization movement, alongside other well-known public intellectuals such as Noam Chomsky, Richard **Falk**, Naomi **Klein**, Vandana **Shiva**, Joseph **Stiglitz** and others.

Roy's political essays throw light on the devastating effects of neoliberal capitalism, as championed by multinational corporations, on the livelihoods of ordinary citizens and on national politics in India. In particular, she highlights the consequences of building massive dams in India (with a specific focus on the Narmada Dam; see Roy 1999) and the plight of the local communities devastated by these projects. Roy persuasively shows how the Indian nation-state, in its uncritical adoption of developmentalism, has become a willing and eager accessory to the excesses of corporate globalization. Contrary to theorists who claim that corporate globalization is threatening national sovereignty (see **Held**), Roy draws attention to how 'it undermines democracy' (Roy 2003: 72, 106). According to Roy, democracy and the prospect of democratic processes are the first victims of neoliberal corporate globalization.

Democracy in an age of corporate globalization

Throughout her writings, Roy traces the impact upon democratic practices of corporate globalization. By focusing on India as a prime example of what she calls the fusion between free market and democracy, Roy illustrates the political and social dynamics unfolding in one of the major emergent economies 'at the forefront of the corporate globalization project' (Roy 2003: 104). She argues that such a fusion entails the adoption of a predatory model of development, which revolves almost exclusively around 'the maximization of profit' at the expense of vast numbers of citizens, usually those most vulnerable (Roy 2009: 2–5). Under such conditions, words such as 'freedom', 'market', 'development' and 'progress' change meaning under pressures from capitalist globalization (2009: 5) as the most devastating policies are adopted and implemented in the name of these 'ideals'. One of the perverse consequences of this 'theft of language', as Roy aptly calls it, is that those who oppose these policies are accused of being 'against development' and 'against progress' (2009: 6). Roy points to how decades of such policies have created 'a vast middle class punch-drunk on sudden wealth and the sudden respect that comes with it – and a much, much vaster, desperate, underclass' (2009: 6). In the context of such an enormous gap between the middle class and the underclasses, one can safely talk about two Indias. One called 'India Shining' is championed by the 'new [middle-class Indian] aristocracy' and by multinational corporations with the blessing and endorsement of the Indian government. The other is simply 'India' as experienced by the poor and by the marginalized who are uprooted, trodden upon and pushed to starvation in the name of 'development' and 'progress' (Roy 2004: 102–105). Roy notes that the increasing chasm between the two Indias bodes ill for Indian democracy. When the nation-state becomes a willing instrument in facilitating the interests of corporate actors in profit maximization, the electoral process itself becomes a market where 'voters are seen as consumers, and democracy is being welded to the free market. Ergo: those who cannot consume do not matter' (Roy 2009: 17). This prognosis means that those who are seen as not contributing to the national economy as *potential consumers* become superfluous to the economic and political system and thus easily dispensable.

In an age of globalization, 'the Free Market [...] needs the State': major corporate projects cannot happen without the active support and facilitation of the 'state machinery' (Roy 2004: 105). So, far from being a victim of corporate globalization, the state is an important instrument in facilitating its operations (see also **Brenner**, **Cerny**, **Helleiner**, **Ong**). By adopting the mantra of 'Creating a Good Investment Climate', the (developmentalist) state can even embark on projects that are against the economic interests of the nation. This paradoxical situation arises due to pressures from powerful corporate actors with the leverage of their equally strong home governments (such as the US), and the corruption of the ruling Indian class. Roy gives the example of the privatization of the energy sector in India during the 1990s, when Enron (with the blessing of and aggressive pressure from the US government) pushed a deal (the first private energy deal in India) with the government of Maharashtra for the opening of a power plant in that state. The contract was 'the largest ever signed in the history of India' (Roy 2001: 55). The power produced by the Enron plant is twice as expensive as that produced by competitors and up to seven times more expensive than the least expensive energy option available in the state (2001: 56). In fact, so exorbitant are the prices charged by Enron that the organization responsible for the regulation of energy in Maharashtra decreed that it would be cheaper simply to pay Enron the contractually agreed upon fixed fees without actually buying its power (2001: 56). Most businesses in the state prefer to rely on their own power generators rather than pay outrageous electricity bills to Enron. According to the terms of the contract, Enron stands to gain an estimated US$220 million annually from fixed fees alone (2001: 56). This situation shows the Indian state bleeding enormous amounts of money to private corporations without actually benefiting from the contracts.

Roy remarks with deep concern that in this context of aggressive liberalization, 'Democracy has become Empire's euphemism for the neo-liberal capitalism' (Roy 2004: 56). In a grim prognosis of democracy under pressure from neoliberal capitalism, Roy foresees that what she calls 'India Pvt. Ltd.' will no longer be ruled by local politicians but by a handful of corporations whose CEOs are unaccountable to the peoples of India and are far removed from their daily reality (2004: 104–105). Such concerns over the prospects of democracy and democratic processes under pressure from globalizing neoliberal capitalism echo David **Harvey**'s and Dani **Rodrik**'s warnings about the devastating impact that neoliberal capitalism has had upon democratic political processes in both the developed and the developing world during the last three decades. Quoting Milton Friedman's dictum that 'The hidden hand of the market will never work without a hidden fist', Roy indicates that the globalization of neoliberal capitalism goes hand-in-hand with state-sponsored repression of those groups or communities who are seen as impediments to this process (Roy 2003: 69) (see also **Harvey**, **Klein**, **Shiva**). 'Today corporate globalization needs an international confederation of loyal, corrupt, authoritarian governments in poorer countries to push through unpopular reforms and quell the mutinies' (2003: 72). This last concern is arguably at the core of her political activism. Unlike intellectuals who see power as faceless and diffused throughout the capitalist system (see, for example, **Hardt and Negri**), Roy's contribution to the debate on globalization is her painstaking effort to identify those actors driving the globalization of neoliberal capitalism. It is this 'international confederation' of loyal governments, powerful corporations and the US government's imperialist pursuance of its interests that Roy identifies as Empire (2003: 107), an issue to which we now turn.

Empire, imperialism and globalization

As a public intellectual and an outspoken political activist, Roy refuses to take refuge in intellectual abstractions. Both Roy and **Hardt and Negri** define Empire as a vast network of interests including corporate and governmental ones (with the US being dominant). However, the difference between the two conceptualizations of Empire is that Hardt and Negri emphasize the decentralization and de-territorialization of Empire (thus focusing on the diffuse, faceless and pervasive character of contemporary power), while Roy's analysis highlights the need to name and put a face on the manifestations of neoliberal power. Her approach to understanding the notion of Empire thus aims to indicate the clear agency of those who wield power and make decisions, and also of those who become the victims of those decisions. In several of her writings on the war in Iraq, for example, Roy points to the corporatization of war in an age of neoliberal capitalism. She attempts to expose the many faces of Empire by calling out the names of those actors involved both in the decision-making process that led to the invasion of Iraq and to the portioning of major Iraqi economic sectors (such as energy and construction) to select (American) corporate actors. Western media corporations played a decisive role in ideologically packaging and selling the conflict for the consumption of global audiences around the world. In this context, Roy remarks that an Empire needs a *Lebensraum*, a living space whose resources would sustain its ambitions and its search for profit (Roy 2009: 152, 161). In order to access this living space, Empire is willing to wage war (such as the war in Iraq), put pressure on governments in the developing world where most valuable resources lie, and eliminate those who stand in the way.

Confronting Empire

Roy considers that the best strategy for tackling the violence and injustice created by the workings of Empire is not direct confrontation, but 'isolat[ing] Empire's working parts and disabl[ing] them one by one' (Roy 2004: 66). A key initiative of this kind would be to understand the many actors involved in championing corporate globalization and its attending imperial violence. For example, she suggests imposing 'a regime of People's Sanctions on every corporate house that has been awarded a contract in post-war Iraq' (2004: 66). Identifying, naming and boycotting such actors serve to expose the workings of Empire (2004: 66). Another approach is to build alternative channels of communication and dissemination of information that do not serve the interests and propagate the ideas of corporate actors and powerful governments. To create 'a universe of alternative information' one needs to create a truly free and independent media (2004: 66). She deems this challenge to be an urgent one if the need to reclaim democracy is to be taken seriously. Roy claims that one of the most powerful challenges posed to Empire is to stop 'buy[ing] what they are selling — their ideas, their version of history, their wars, their weapons, their notion of inevitability' (Roy 2003: 112).

Ultimately, if the struggle to reclaim democracy is to succeed, the struggle needs to be global. As Roy expresses it: 'fighting isolated, single-issue battles [...] is no longer enough' (Roy 2004: 116). Activists and people around the world need to look beyond 'special interest politics' and develop a vision of politics that is both egalitarian and democratic (2004: 116). Fighting against intolerance, for example, cannot take place outside a concern with the economic injustice that perpetuates internal inequalities. Therefore, a new vision of politics must be thought up where issues and causes are linked with a view to securing 'justice and equal rights for all' (2004: 117).

Major globalization writings

Roy, A. (1997) *The God of Small Things*, New York, NY: HarperCollins.
——(1999) *The Cost of Living*, New York, NY: Modern House.
——(2001) *Power Politics*, 2nd edition, Cambridge, MA: South End Press.
——(2003) *War Talk*, Cambridge, MA: South End Press.
——(2004) *An Ordinary Person's Guide to Empire*, Cambridge, MA: South End Press.
——(2009) *Field Notes on Democracy: Listening to Grasshoppers*, Chicago, IL: Haymarket Books.

Further reading

Ghosh, R. and Navarro-Tejero, A. (eds) (2008) *Globalizing Dissent: Essays on Arundhati Roy*, London and New York, NY: Routledge.

See also: **Brenner, Falk, Hardt and Negri, Harvey, Held, Helleiner, Klein, Ong, Rodrik, Shiva, Stiglitz.**

JOHN RUGGIE (1944–)

John Ruggie was born and raised in Graz, Austria. In 1967 he obtained a BA in politics and history from McMaster University, Canada, and in 1974 he completed his Ph.D. in political science at the University of California, Berkeley. Ruggie's scholarly contributions to the discipline of international relations (IR) have earned him various international distinctions. He is considered one of the most influential contemporary IR scholars, and his research on the impact of globalization upon global rule-making has received wide recognition. Aside from his academic pursuits, Ruggie has been involved in policy and consultancy work, most notably with the United Nations and the US government. In this capacity, he served as UN Assistant Secretary-General for Strategic Planning between 1997 and 2001, overseeing the establishment of the UN Global Compact – a corporate citizenship initiative of the then UN Secretary-General Kofi Annan. Ruggie is currently the Berthold Beitz Professor in Human Rights and International Affairs at Harvard's Kennedy School of Government, and Affiliated

Professor in International Legal Studies at Harvard Law School. He also serves as the United Nations Secretary-General's Special Representative for Business and Human Rights.

'Embedded liberalism' and multilateralism

In focusing on the shape of the international order that emerged at the end of World War II, Ruggie highlights the central role played by the US in helping to create and sustain a stable international system (Ruggie 1993, 1996, 1998). Ruggie thus accepts a well-known theory in international relations, hegemonic stability, whose proponents claim that central to the emergence and maintenance of various international orders is the existence of a hegemonic power that is willing to assume the costs and responsibilities for ensuring the stability of a given order. He offers the examples of international orders established and sustained during the nineteenth century by Great Britain and in the twentieth century by the US (Ruggie 1993: 21; 1998: 63) (see also **Amin, Arrighi, Cox**). Both of these international orders, known as *Pax Britannica* and *Pax Americana*, respectively, placed free trade at the core of the system. These examples explain the prevalence, over the last two centuries, of *laissez-faire* liberalism as an economic doctrine and, hence, the priority given to liberalizing international trade.

He finds this theoretical framework incomplete, however, and contends that it does not explain the shape taken by the international order after World War II. More specifically, he argues that it is crucial to look beyond military or economic capabilities of hegemonic powers to understand well the dynamics of a given international order. Specifically, he suggests that paying closer attention to 'state–society relations' is necessary for understanding the specific characteristics, and indeed uniqueness, of the post-World War II international order (1998: 62). Recently emerged from a devastating world conflagration that led to the loss of millions of lives and the destruction of a number of national economies, European political leaders argued that reconstruction would be more effective and stable if a new international framework was put in place. This order was to be built around free trade between states coupled with governments having strong capacity to intervene through policies ensuring the equitable allocation of economic gains, particularly by providing workers and other vulnerable groups with social protection against the inequalities and excesses arising from free markets (see also Polanyi 2001).

Thus, Ruggie points to a significant social and political shift in the first half of the twentieth century. States introduce universal suffrage and there is 'the emergence of working-class political constituencies, parties, and even governments' who demand increased social protections (especially in the aftermath of the Great Depression) (1998: 69). As Ruggie notes, however, 'demands for social protection were very nearly universal, coming from all segments of the political spectrum and from all ranks of the social hierarchy (with the possible exception of orthodox financial circles)' (1998: 69). The ideas behind these changes represent a departure from the liberal economic views dominant during the late nineteenth and early twentieth centuries, which emphasized unregulated financial markets combined with minimal state intervention in social matters. After 1945, the new ideas arising from Keynesian economics supported significantly more state intervention in balancing economic liberalism with social welfare policies that gave some protection to vulnerable groups in society. Ruggie characterizes the post-World War II international order as one of 'embedded liberalism', a term which acquired wide usage in the study of international relations (see **Harvey**, **Rodrik**, **Rosenau**, **Scholte**). The concept refers to the embeddedness of the liberal compromise between labour and business, particularly finance (and, thus, between free trade and state protectionism), within an international institutional order through the establishment of the Bretton Woods system of currency exchange management, capital controls and the US dollar serving as a kind of world currency. In Ruggie's words:

> This was the essence of the embedded liberalism compromise: unlike the economic nationalism of the thirties, it would be multilateral in character; unlike the liberalism of the gold standard and free trade, its multilateralism would be predicated upon domestic interventionism.
>
> (Ruggie 1998: 73)

Ruggie credits the efforts of the US and its willingness to cover the majority of the costs associated with the erection of multilateral institutions within the Bretton Woods system. Part of the US rationale for assuming this hegemonic position was its support for building wide acceptance and adherence to the principle of multilateralism in liberalizing international trade relations (1998: 73). For example, Roosevelt 'sought a global version of the "open door" [economic policy]' that involved the freeing up of trade flows and, thus, the progressive elimination of various economic tariffs (Ruggie 1996: 19, 35). The policy involved a push for the implementation of 'uniform rules governing trade and monetary relations together with minimal state-imposed barriers to the flow of economic transactions' (1996: 22).

Ruggie calls this new international system 'a mildly communitarian world order vision' which would bring economic stability to the world after 1945. The establishment of such a multilateral order by the US reflects, in Ruggie's perspective, the US view of governance established on an 'elective community based on a universal or general foundation open in principle to everyone' (1996: 49; see also Ruggie 1993: 8). The open door policy in the economic sphere is best illustrated by the principles governing the General Agreement on Tariffs and Trade (GATT) and now the World Trade Organization (WTO), trade agreements aimed at a progressive lowering or even elimination of 'point-of-entry barriers' (1996: 137). The neoliberalism-inspired push for progressively deeper economic interdependence through trade in the 1980s and early 1990s, however, raised questions about the fate of social protections that were part of the embedded liberal thinking in the immediate post-war period (1996: 137).

This feature in itself – namely, the rise of multilateral institutions as formal international settings – is unique to the twentieth-century world order (Ruggie 1993: 22). Ruggie defines multilateralism as 'an institutional form that coordinates relations among three or more states on the basis of generalized principles of conduct' (1993: 11). The extent to which multilateralism has been formalized in international institutions and arrangements reflects the decisive role of American hegemony in bringing about this type of world order (1993: 31).

The emergence of a global public domain

In the previous section we discussed Ruggie's understanding of 'embedded liberalism', which he sees as a historical lesson for national governments that 'markets must be embedded in broader frameworks of social values and shared objectives if they are to survive and thrive' (Ruggie 2002: 29). Ruggie contends that the post-1945 bargain did not last for more than two decades because it presupposed an *international* world, where the main interactions and transactions happened between states (2002: 29). Since the early 1970s, however, we now live in a *global* world, where the dynamics and interactions of markets have spilled over territorial borders, leaving behind 'national social bargains' (2002: 29) that do not fit with the new global scale.

This shift from international to global relations has increasingly concerned Ruggie since the mid-1990s. He notes that there is a clear distinction between the international public domain which involves exclusively state-to-state interactions and intergovernmental arrangements, and the emerging global public domain. Here he points to new forms of transnational participation in spaces, including a 'massive global corporate sector', which along with states has important impacts upon global rule-making (Ruggie 2004: 500). These transnational corporate actors have come to play an increasingly important role in global governance even though they stand outside most formally institutionalized intergovernmental arrangements (2004: 501) (see also **Rosenau**).

Accordingly, the idea of a global public domain or private authority, as it is called elsewhere (see **Scholte**), refers to:

> [... the] apparent assumption by TNCs [transnational corporations] and global business associations of roles traditionally associated with public authorities [...] ranging from instituting new accounting standards to the expanding role of rating agencies and commercial arbitration as well as various 'private regimes', such as eco-labeling and other forms of certification designed to impress consumers with the social responsibility of participating firms.
>
> (Ruggie 2004: 502–503)

Ruggie adds that the space of global governance has become more fluid and open, as non-governmental actors (such as businesses, civil society actors and social movements) interact with each other and with governments, generating global norms and rules – a function traditionally associated with the public authority of states. Ruggie offers the example of the massive mobilization of civil society actors across the world during the 1990s in protest against the Multilateral Agreement on Investment (MAI), which strongly favoured the interests of TNCs and businesses. The MAI would have made it possible and lawful for TNCs to challenge environmental and labour regulations on the grounds that they adversely affected the profit-making abilities of companies (2004: 511). The massive mobilization spearheaded by civil society organizations drew the support of mass media, eventually leading to the dropping of pursuit of the agreement (2004: 511). Ruggie notes, however, that the emergence of a global public domain does not serve to replace states, but rather 'to embed systems of governance in broader global frameworks of social capacity and agency that did not previously exist' (2004: 519) (see also **Cerny, Scholte**).

Major globalization writings

Ruggie, J. (1993) 'Multilateralism: the anatomy of an institution', in J. Ruggie (ed.) *Multilateralism Matters: The Theory and Praxis of an Institutional Form*, New York, NY: Columbia University Press.

——(1996) *Winning the Peace: America and World Order in the New Era*, New York, NY: Columbia University Press.

——(1998) *Constructing the World Polity: Essays on International Institutionalization*, London: Routledge.

——(2002) 'The theory and practice of learning networks: corporate social responsibility and the global compact', *Journal of Corporate Citizenship*, vol 5, pp. 27–36.

——(2004) 'Reconstituting the global public domain: issues, actors and practices', *European Journal of International Relations*, vol 10, no 4, pp. 499–531.

Further reading

Polanyi, K. (2001 [1944]) *The Great Transformation: The Political and Economic Origins of Our Time*, Boston, MA: Beacon Press.

See also: **Amin, Arrighi, Cerny, Cox, Harvey, Rodrik, Rosenau, Scholte.**

EDWARD SAID (1935–2003)

Edward Said, a Palestinian-American literary critic, was born in 1935 in Jerusalem in the then British Mandate of Palestine. His family shifted between Cairo and Jerusalem during the first 12 years of his life. He completed his BA in 1957 at Princeton University, NJ, and his Ph.D. in English literature at Harvard, MA, in 1964. He joined the Department of English and Comparative Literature at Columbia University, NY, in 1963, where he taught until his death in 2003.

Said is best known for his theory of Orientalism, which he defines as a style of thought where the West has produced and controlled knowledge about the Orient. His book of the same name, *Orientalism*, published in 1978, is considered to be one of the founding texts of postcolonial studies, and raised the crucial issue of how knowledge is produced in Western humanities and social sciences about non-Western worlds (see Bayoumi and Rubin 2000). This preoccupation with the production of Western knowledge about non-Western societies is not limited to the examination of various Western writings about the Orient. Rather, it probes into the political, institutional and academic links forged between the production of knowledge about non-Western others at a global scale, and foreign policy practices, diplomatic considerations and the birth and development of academic disciplines, in general. Said develops this theme further in his other writings, such as *The World, the Text, and the Critic* (1983), *Culture and Imperialism* (1993), *Representations of the Intellectual* (1996) and *Humanism and Democratic Criticism* (2004; published posthumously). In these works, he examines not only the link between culture and the global spread of imperialism (see also **McClintock, Spivak, Tomlinson**), but also the duty and responsibility of what he calls the secular intellectual to oppose imperialism and unmask it in all its manifestations, whether cultural, aesthetic, social or political.

Orientalism

In *Orientalism*, Said (1979) brings together the philosophies of Michel Foucault and Antonio Gramsci in order to contest the assumed legitimacy and authority of Western knowledge about the Orient.

Foucault's theory of the link between power and the production of knowledge provides Said with the framework for examining the various writings of a large array of nineteenth-century French and British novelists, statesmen, diplomats, artists, historians and poets. By examining these writings, Said is interested in several aspects: first, how this varied spectrum of Western knowledge is able to produce and manipulate knowledge about non-Western others by positing a clear-cut opposition between 'Oriental' and 'Occidental'; second, how colonialism as a political and military global enterprise has been rendered possible by the production of knowledge about the Orient (1979: 36–37); and, third, how Orientalism as discourse persists and endures in various contemporary aspects of globalization, such as the mass media portrayal of the Oriental or of the Arab (see also Said 1981), the contemporary practices of foreign policy influenced by Orientalist ideas, and the global span of academic disciplines such as area studies. Accordingly, during the twentieth century, there are two primary methods of disseminating Orientalist ideas: through modern learning as instituted in universities and research institutions (a practice that ensures the self-perpetuating character of Orientalism) (Said 1979: 222), and through what Said terms 'manifest' Orientalism. The latter involves not merely the colonial enterprise, but the actual translation of Orientalist knowledge into policy and practice of European travellers, statesmen and colonial administrators (1979: 223).

The importance of *Orientalism* lies not only in what it unmasks about the global production of Western knowledge about non-Western others, about its dissemination, and its institutionalization into stereotypes, policies, practices and discourse. It also arises from its tremendous implications for globalization studies with regards to the global production and entrenchment of an 'imaginative geography', which places non-Western worlds on the fringes of knowledge, progress and modernity (see also **Chow, McClintock, Mignolo, Santos**). Said's argument is that this 'imaginative geography' informs, for example, current American foreign policy, the academic production of knowledge and widespread racist attitudes, among others.

Cultural imperialism

One of the most crucial contributions made by Said is the notion that culture is not politically innocent. This idea is given substance in many of his writings, but perhaps most forcefully in *Culture and*

Imperialism. Here, Said (1993) postulates that the role of culture in maintaining and legitimizing imperialism cannot be overemphasized since it is culture that provides the moral clout that sanctifies and normalizes imperialism. Thus, he pursues two major goals: mapping 'the global pattern of imperial culture' and understanding how culture can provide a moral impetus for global domination and oppression; and, second, investigating the 'historical global patterns of resistance' that emerged against Western hegemony in the poorer countries (Said 1993: xii) (see also **Escobar**, **Mignolo**, **Santos**). Although critics were quick to point out that Said does not outline a substantive and systematic theory of Western imperialism, or offer a credible and exhaustive theory of resistance, the crux of Said's *Culture and Imperialism* – as well as of his later works – is to expose the linkages between culture and imperialism and, hence, to unmask culture *as* imperialism.

Through an examination of certain texts of British and French writers, Said elaborates a method of reading imperialism against its grain, which he calls 'contrapuntal reading'. Such a message involves a 'reading back' of the history and knowledge of the West from the perspective of the colonized (see also **Mignolo**). In doing so, the reader exposes that all cultural experience and cultural forms in an age of colonial imperialism, and later of globalization, are 'radically, quintessentially hybrid' (1993: 68). Said's contrapuntal reading has significant implications for globalization studies insofar as it dislodges the notion that the world's history is synonymous with European history (see also **Hopkins**). Instead, Said posits that contrapuntal reading involves a simultaneous awareness of metropolitan history and of subjugated voices and perspectives (1993: 59). Through the exposure of concealed histories, Said engages in a rethinking of global geography and brings into productive tension hegemonic and subaltern/subjugated histories.

For example, he focuses on Rudyard Kipling's celebrated novel *Kim* and reveals how 'its picture of India exists in a deeply antithetical relationship with the development of the movement for Indian independence' (1993: 32). To read the novel or the political event independently from each other would be to '[miss] the crucial discrepancy between the two given to them by the actual existence of empire' (1993: 32). Thus, as Bill Ashcroft and Pal Ahluwalia note in their monograph on Said's work, the contrapuntal reading lays bare the global dimensions of the geographical reality of imperialism, in both its material and symbolical/ideational implications (Ashcroft and Ahluwalia 2001: 94–95).

Secular humanism and the public/global intellectual

In one of his interviews, Said noted that what he calls his paradoxical 'worldliness' – which inspired him later to conceptualize the idea of contrapuntal reading – would be unthinkable without his own personal trajectory as an exile within imperial history. As a Palestinian exile living and writing in the West, Said felt acutely conscious of his own role as a public intellectual in voicing a critique of imperialism (see Said 1983, 1996, 2000, 2004). This awareness translated into a secular humanism that aimed to speak truth to power and to be constantly vigilant to the insidious workings of imperialism through various means such as politics, culture, ideology and aesthetics. For Said, secularism – as the ethical basis of the public (and global) intellectual – entails a freedom from and opposition to particularistic biases such as nationalism, tribalism and fundamentalism.

Said's work and life not only contributed to the conceptualization of the role of the public intellectual in an age of globalization, but also accomplished a rethinking of the global geography forged by colonial and imperial ventures. His focus on the centrality of culture in legitimizing and sanctifying imperial designs remains one of his most enduring legacies to globalization studies.

Major globalization writings

Said, E. (1979 [1978]) *Orientalism*, New York, NY: Vintage Books.
——(1981) *Covering Islam: How the Media and the Experts Determine How We See the Rest of the World*, New York, NY: Vintage Books.
——(1983) *The World, the Text, and the Critic*, Cambridge, MA: Harvard University Press.
——(1993) *Culture and Imperialism*, New York, NY: Vintage Books.
——(1996 [1994]) *Representations of the Intellectual: The 1993 Reith Lectures*, New York, NY: Vintage Books.
——(2000) *Reflections on Exile and Other Essays*, Cambridge, MA: Harvard University Press.
——(2004) *Humanism and Democratic Criticism*, New York, NY: Columbia University Press.

Further reading

Ashcroft, B. and Ahluwalia, P. (2001) *Edward Said*, London and New York: Routledge.
Bayoumi, M. and Rubin, A. (eds) (2000) *The Edward Said Reader*, New York, NY: Vintage Books.

See also: **Chow, Escobar, Hopkins, McClintock, Mignolo, Santos, Spivak, Tomlinson**.

BOAVENTURA DE SOUSA SANTOS (1940–)

Boaventura de Sousa Santos is Professor Emeritus of the Faculty of Economics, University of Coimbra in Portugal, Legal Distinguished Scholar of the Institute for Legal Studies at the University of Wisconsin-Madison and Global Legal Scholar at the University of Warwick. He is also director of the Centre for Social Studies, University of Coimbra, scientific coordinator of the Permanent Observatory of Portuguese Justice and a member of Democracy, Citizenship and Law. He has published extensively on issues related to law and globalization, legal pluralism, multiculturalism and human rights.

Santos' contribution to globalization studies arises from the depth of his thinking about what he calls 'counter hegemonic globalization'. He argues that there is not just one globalization but various 'globalizations'. He sees counter hegemonic globalization to be a response to neoliberal globalization, itself a continuation of Western imperialism. Accordingly, Santos' analysis builds on his critical assessment of imperialism, where he stresses that injustices are not only social and economic but also epistemological. Imperialism leads to the disparaging of alternative knowledges and epistemologies, a potential crucial loss to the world. Hence, there can be no global social justice without global cognitive justice. For Santos, the World Social Forum (WSF), in which he participates and offers guidance and critical reflection, opens up avenues of anticipating how counter hegemonic globalization might work. And central to this work, he shows, is the importance of epistemological and cultural 'translation'.

Neoliberal globalization

A useful starting point for understanding Santos' concept of globalization is an abstract process-based definition he provides:

> [...] a set of unequal exchanges in which a certain artefact, condition, entity or local identity extends its influence beyond its local or national borders and, in so doing, develops an ability to designate as local another rival artefact, condition, entity or identity.
>
> (Santos 2006a: 396)

Accordingly, at the heart of any globalization is a particular localism (Spanish imperialism during the fifteenth century or British imperial ambitions during the eighteenth century). Built into this definition is also the thesis that globalization presupposes localization: 'the process that creates the global as the dominant position in unequal exchanges is the same one that produces the local as the dominated, and therefore hierarchically inferior, position' (2006a: 396). To continue with our example of the British Empire, the processes that permitted Britain to create a global empire are the same ones that permit it to designate India, for example, as a colony and as an inferior space with a primitive population. Santos identifies two main modes of production of globalization. The first he calls a 'globalized localism', the process by which a particular phenomenon is successfully globalized. Such a process might be one that sees a formerly national corporation becoming a transnational global one or that involves a predominantly Western notion of intellectual property ownership becoming part of global law under the World Trade Organization (WTO). What is globalized is the winner of a struggle over the appropriation of resources such as the transnational corporation or a particular conception of intellectual property. The word 'localism' in this term thus reminds us that it is a local phenomenon that becomes a tool under global control.

The second process is 'localized globalism': 'the specific impact on local conditions produced by transnational practices and imperatives that arise from globalized localisms' (2006a: 397). To continue with our examples, a newly transnational corporation specializing in the mining of minerals uproots local communities, forcing outward migration. Here the migration becomes a globalized localism. Or if the WTO notion of intellectual property is applied in India, leading to the use of genetically modified seeds for the growing of cotton, the globalized localism is the gradual end of farmers gathering and trading seeds to improve their crops.

This conceptual framework assists us in understanding Santos' views on neoliberal globalization. Central to this phenomenon, he argues, is a neoliberal consensus that originated in the US and was quickly adopted by the core capitalist states. This consensus rests on an ideology that promotes the notion of a neoliberal economy; a smaller state focused on competing in the global economy (see also **Brenner**, **Cerny**, **Harvey**); liberal (but not social) democracy; the privatization of social protection and the primacy of rule of law and, thus, the judicial system; and a diminishing of the parliamentary component. Accompanying this ideology are beliefs that the great capitalist powers are highly interdependent and no longer engage in wars with one another and that institutionalizing ways to cooperate both globally and regionally is helpful. These ideas become globalized localisms, for example in the form of Structural Adjustment Programmes in poorer countries, in policies attracting investment from transnational corporations, or in introducing school fees and privatized medicine into sub-Saharan African schools and hospitals. The resulting phenomena of poorer health and rising levels of illiteracy thus become localized globalisms.

Counter hegemonic globalization

It will be evident that any counter hegemonic globalization would be radically different from the various forms of hegemonic globalization. In short, an entirely new conceptual framework would be necessary. Accordingly, Santos borrows Antonio Gramsci's idea of counter hegemonic struggles, seeing them as efforts to erode the ideology (in this instance, neoliberalism) and coercive institutions (transnational corporations, weak states, international agreements) that sustain and naturalize the hegemony of those social classes and groups benefiting most from contemporary global capitalism (Santos 2005a: 18). At the core of any counter hegemonic globalization will be those who have been victimized most by the neoliberal forms – for example, indigenous peoples, landless peasants, impoverished women, squatters, sweatshop workers and undocumented migrants, among others. It is in these groups that Santos sees the beginnings of 'insurgent' or 'subaltern' cosmopolitanism. In contrast to the use of the term 'cosmopolitanism' by **Beck** and **Held**, Santos employs it to describe resistance against the exchanges arising from globalized localisms and localized globalisms. The word 'cosmopolitan' is used to suggest that such resistance will be organized on a global scale. Unlike traditional left thinking, which focuses on the working class, Santos stresses that social groups will be organized on a non-class basis to include 'the victims of exploitation as well as the victims of social exclusion, of sexual, ethnic, racist and religious discrimination' (Santos 2006a: 397).

Santos' argument about how the form of such resistance might develop is influenced deeply by his participation in, and reflections on, the WSF. He sees its novelty arising from its high degree of inclusiveness both in scalar terms – local, national, regional, global – and in its thematics. It is not focused on specific themes but is trans-thematic, a 'movement of movements' (Santos 2008: 250). There are no leaders in the normal sense, nor are there any hierarchies. WSF participants take advantage of contemporary communications technologies to speak to and build small networks with one another as needs arise. It works on the basis of participatory democracy. In short, the WSF has 'created a meeting ground for the most diverse movements and organizations, coming from the most disparate locations in the planet, involved in the most diverse struggles, and speaking a Babel Tower of languages' (2008: 252).

As a scholar of globalization studies, Santos differs from others such as **Bello** on the role of the WSF in the future. Whereas **Bello** finds the WSF too diffuse and too decentralized for challenging neoliberal globalization, Santos argues that the very organizational characteristics of the WSF can be built upon to advance counter hegemonic globalization. Like **Escobar**, he notes the importance of local struggles as the basic actions of counter hegemonic globalization. He also agrees with **Escobar** that the networking between local groups fighting particular localisms of neoliberal globalization enriches these local struggles. Although the issues and specifics of the local struggles differ, they have in common the same opposing forces.

Perhaps more than any other globalization scholar, Santos has thought through the difficulties and challenges facing the many groups working towards a counter hegemonic globalization. He suggests that the ways in which the WSF has provided space for the aggregation and articulation of movements from across the world may no longer be sufficient if neoliberal globalization is to be successfully challenged. If the goal is to build and support counter hegemonic struggles, ones that might include ecological, indigenous, pacifist, feminist and workers' movements, among others, then an enormous effort to build mutual recognition, dialogue and debate will be required (Santos 2005c: 17). And for these processes to take place, a systematic and intensive exercise of 'translation' will be necessary.

Santos uses the concept of translation in a broad sense, describing it as a process that permits the development of mutual intelligibility between highly diverse groups with different experiences of the world, and without jeopardizing their respective identities and autonomies and without reducing them to homogeneous entities (Santos 2008: 261). Translation will be most relevant when diverse actors or movements have similar problems and aspirations. Such translation will be needed in two different but highly interlinked dimensions of life: knowledge and culture.

Although many have commented on the tremendous injustices that have occurred in the relations between cultures as a result of Western imperialism, few have deepened this critique to include knowledge. Santos writes that:

> the epistemological privilege granted to modern science from the 17th century onwards [...] was also instrumental in suppressing other, non-scientific forms of knowledges and, at the same time, the subaltern social groups whose social practices were informed by such knowledges. There is an epistemological foundation to the capitalist imperial order that the global North has been imposing on the global South.
>
> (Santos *et al.* 2007: xix)

Or put more bluntly: 'In short, in the name of modern science, epistemicide has been committed, and the imperial powers have resorted to it to disarm any resistance of the conquered peoples and social groups' (Santos 2005b: xviii). Accordingly, Santos argues that in addition to the familiar cultural differences that exist among groups, there are epistemological ones, often concretized in practices used to counter imperialism in local struggles.

In his thinking about how translation in these ways might take place, Santos identifies two necessary activities. First, he suggests that building inter-knowledge and inter-cultural coalitions will require the creation of 'contact zones': social fields where different movements will meet and interact to learn about and evaluate respective normative aspirations, cultures, practices and knowledges. Each group will decide what aspects of its culture, knowledge and practices it will share and what it will keep to itself. In this way, they can identify and reinforce what they have in common. Second, each group has to accept that its culture, its ways of knowing and its resulting practices are limited; they have their strengths and their weaknesses. The process of dialogue should lead to the creation of a self-reflective consciousness of cultural and epistemological incompleteness (Santos 2007: 27). Accordingly, the building of contact zones and the acceptance of incompleteness will make possible the creation of collaborations and alliances to permit the fight against neoliberal globalization across the world in pursuit of a counter hegemonic globalization.

Major globalization writings

Santos, B. de S. (2002) *Toward a New Legal Common Sense: Law, Globalization and Emancipation*, 2nd edition, London: Butterworths LexisNexis.

——(2005a) 'The future of the World Social Forum: the work of translation', *Development*, vol 48, no 2, pp. 15–22.

——(2005b) 'General introduction: reinventing social emancipation: toward new manifestos', in B. de S. Santos (ed.) *Democratizing Democracy: Beyond the Liberal Democratic Canon*, London: Verso.

——(2005c) 'Law, politics and the subaltern in counter-hegemonic globalization', in C. A. Rodríguez Garavito and B. de S. Santos (eds) *Law and Globalization from Below: Towards a Cosmopolitan Legality*, Cambridge, UK: Cambridge University Press.

——(2006a) 'Globalizations', *Theory, Culture & Society*, vol 23, nos 2–3, pp. 393–399.

——(2006b) *The Rise of the Global Left: The World Social Forum and Beyond*, London: Zed Books.

——(2007) 'Human rights as an emancipatory script? Cultural and political conditions', in B. de S. Santos (ed.) *Another Knowledge Is Possible: Beyond Northern Epistemologies*, London: Verso.

——(2008) 'The World Social Forum and the global left', *Politics and Society*, vol 36, no 2, pp. 247–270.

Santos, B. de S., Nunes, J. A. and Meneses, M. P. (2007) 'Opening up the canon of knowledge and recognition of difference', in B. de S. Santos (ed.) *Another Knowledge Is Possible: Beyond Northern Epistemologies*, London: Verso.

See also: **Beck, Bello, Brenner, Cerny, Escobar, Harvey, Held.**

SASKIA SASSEN (1949–)

Saskia Sassen grew up in Buenos Aires where her parents moved from the Netherlands soon after her birth. She did her undergraduate studies in Europe and then her graduate studies in the US. She received a Master's degree in sociology at the University of Notre Dame in 1971, focusing on blacks and Chicanos and their contributions to the US political economy as 'non-dominant ethnic populations'. Her doctoral dissertation continued to look at social stratification involving Anglos and Chicanos in the US. These early topics of enquiry signalled her interest in urban and economic sociology. As she moved forward as a researcher and a scholar, she studied patterns of immigration in cities and the role that immigrants played in urban economies. By the mid-1980s, she had identified 'global' cities as opposed to 'world' cities as a particular focus of study (see also **Abu-Lughod, Brenner, Taylor**). In 1988, she published *The Mobility of Labor and Capital: A Study in International Investment and Labour Flow*, which followed a number of important articles in this area. From there, she went on to publish her path-breaking study entitled *The Global City* in 1991. She updated this work, publishing a second edition in 2001.

These two early books demonstrated her ability to use careful empirical sociological and economic analysis at more micro-levels to raise important questions about the increasingly global political economy. In the first, she argued that, contrary to mainstream thinking, foreign investment in less developed countries can actually raise the likelihood of emigration. In the second, she noted how the global economy was not 'placeless' but required the concentration of particular economic, financial and technological services in large cities to function. She thus countered the idea that emerged in **Castells**' work around the concept of 'spaces of flows'. Throughout the 1990s, she continued to work on issues of labour and immigration, on the one hand, and added a focus on highly paid professionals, particularly in financial markets, on the other. This research was published in several important books: *Losing Control? Sovereignty in an Age of Globalization* (1996); *Globalization and Its Discontents: Essays on the Mobility of People and Money* (1999a); and *Guests and Aliens* (1999b).

By the end of the decade, she had begun to integrate systematically into her work the role of the rapidly emerging innovations in communication and information technologies. These technologies were important not only for the functioning of global finance, but also for enabling the direct passage from local to global scales of social movements and other groups who were challenging dominant forces in the global economy. Throughout the 1990s and early 2000s, she refined her understanding of globalization and presents it in fully developed theoretical form in her exceptional 2006 book *Territory, Authority and Rights* (*TAR*). Some of her analysis of globalization was then carried over to permit some methodological reflections on the discipline of sociology in *A Sociology of Globalization* (2007).

Globalization

Sassen's most important contribution to globalization studies is to argue that globalization processes include not only the development of institutions working on a global scale, such as the World Trade Organization (WTO) or transnational corporations, but also the transformation of particular institutions and practices of the nation-state or national societies. In these transformations, nation-state components or national organizations are reoriented from serving a national logic to a global one. All the while, these institutions and practices remain formally part of nation-states or national societies. She employs the term *denationalization* to describe these shifts from national to global logics. Such shifts also have the consequence of increasing the importance of other scales, including subnational ones, particularly cities.

This crucial argument is most fully developed in *TAR* (Sassen 2006). This ambitious and comprehensive work provides a set of key concepts – capabilities, tipping points, organizing logics – which Sassen uses to mine and reflect upon historical analysis of evolutions in territory, authority and rights. She argues that these three components became subject to the monopoly control of nation-states in the transition from medieval arrangements. These transformations permitted the rise of the nation-state and the constitution of a 'world' scale of capitalism through the extraterritorial projection of several major 'national capitalisms' such as the British and later the American empires. She distinguishes a world scale from a global one in that the former was built to serve the development of the imperial nation-states and their societies. In contrast, the constitution of a global scale supports the development of a global economic capitalist system (see also **Abu-Lughod, Braudel**).

This analysis leads Sassen to be more specific than many globalization scholars about when the contemporary form of globalization took off. She notes that the setting up of the Bretton Woods institutions (for example, the International Monetary Fund and the International Bank for Reconstruction and Development) marked a resurgence in the building of a *world* scale. They permitted *some* states to enter into a far broader range of international transactions, while protecting national economies from external forces, particularly foreign capital movements. She argues that the tipping point for the global era arose out of the Third World debt crisis of the early 1980s. The resolution of this crisis led to new institutions of global capitalism, the constitution of fully global financial markets, and the 'financializing' of other parts of the economy (see also **Cox, Helleiner**).

It is with these moves towards the construction of a global capitalist economy, Sassen argues, that we see the denationalization of certain key state bodies. Take, for example, central banks. They had become important tools in the nineteenth and especially twentieth centuries in protecting currencies and supporting Keynesian macroeconomic policies, particularly after the Great Depression. They were tools used by states in pursuit of their own interests in the world economy. Increasingly, after the debt crisis, these institutions became more oriented towards supporting the operations of a global-scale economy. For example, they developed agreements for supervision of global banks and worked more closely to stabilize the global economy (see also **Helleiner**). Their heads met ten times a year at the Bank for International Settlements in Basel, Switzerland. They reached unprecedented levels of cooperation in supporting the global economy in the financial crises of 1997 to 1998 and then 2007 to 2010. All the while, they occupied the same buildings and operated under the same national legislation, but they became increasingly 'independent' of their national finance ministries. Their 'governors' came to work and cooperate more with each other than with other parts of their given nation-states. In short, Sassen's analysis suggests that scholars need to look closely at different parts of the state. One can no longer assume that they are functioning only on a national or a world scale.

Sassen outlines other indicators of the onset of globalization. There is a reversal of centuries-old trends that saw the growth and strengthening of a formalized public domain. In its place, we see the formation of new public–private arrangements (see also **Cerny**, **Ruggie**). She adds that this change is accompanied by a new formalization of a private sphere, including the emergence of sites of 'private authority' beyond the nation-state scale. The outcome is the emergence of a new 'spatio-temporal order' that has both considerable governance capabilities and structural power. This order has invited the emergence of civil society networks operating at the same global scale. Consequently, she adds, the distance between the citizen and the state lengthens under contemporary globalization.

Global cities

Growing out of and also motivating Sassen's approach to globalization is her resistance to conceptions of the global that emphasize 'spaces', 'flows' and the 'declines' of states. She argues that globalization is only possible because of activities, practices and material forms existing in 'places'. This argument emerges most strongly in her extensive research on the global city. The emerging importance of global cities is an aspect of denationalization: urban places that once served a key role in constituting the national scale and in supporting the projection of that scale through imperialist ties are now harnessed to creating a global scale. They provide the material components needed for corporations to operate and build a global economy (see also **Taylor**).

For corporations to operate on a global scale, they need to centralize more complex and strategic operations. And given the complexity of these operations, they outsource them to highly specialized services firms in areas such as accounting, legal services and telecommunications. This outsourcing, in turn, gives rise to agglomeration dynamics: firms offering these services to global corporations tend to cluster in the same places (see also **Taylor**). And like the corporations they serve, these service firms need to be networked with counterparts across the world. This dynamic leads to the concentration of highly paid professionals in these cities, on the one hand, and of lowly paid service labour, often moving in transnational migration circuits, on the other. For their part, the relative importance of the middle classes declines. There is no such thing for Sassen, however, as a single global city. Such a city is constituted by its functions in a cross-border network of strategic places. It is distinguished from other cities by the wide scope of functions it provides. Some cities might participate in these networks by providing special services but without being global cities. For example, Singapore plays such an accessory role through its specialization in currency trading.

For Sassen, then, the 'placeness' of global cities is a key theoretical contribution to understanding globalization. It is also an important methodological contribution: the global needs to be studied by focusing not only on global institutions, but also on particular places such as cities and the movements of workers, whether professional or low-skilled. In addition, these places become sites not only for the concentrations of immense economic power, but also for the making of claims for entitlements to place and citizenship. New forms of transnational politics take place in global cities, often supported by the same information and communication technologies so crucial to the functioning of the global cities networks. Finally, the formation of global cities and the changes in other cities to enable them to contribute to the network require the active support of states. Sassen resists arguments about the decline of states and counters with urging the study of how states change roles to support the development of the global economy, including enabling cities to draw the highly skilled professionals and low-paid workers they need to fulfil their material contributions (see also **Brenner, Taylor**).

Digital technologies

Contemporary globalization intensified during the 1990s with the rapid developments in digital technologies. As these technologies became facilitators for the linking of financial centres, the deepening of financial markets, and social and political activism often in the same urban sites, Sassen expanded her research agenda to look at them more closely. This research is extensive and we comment here only on how it adds to her analysis of globalization *per se*.

As in all of her research, she pays attention to the social embedding of the technologies, as well as their contributions to the building of networks of various forms that challenge the longstanding dominance of the national scale. She identifies four different network types that provide these challenges. First, there is the formation of global domains that function in a self-evident way on a global scale. Transnational or global corporations and organizations such as the WTO are examples here. Second, electronic financial markets illustrate a formation where local practices and conditions become directly articulated with global dynamics, not having to move through the traditional hierarchy of scales. Currency markets and rapid changes in the values of currencies illustrate this category. Third, global formations can be embedded in subnational sites, notably global cities, and move horizontally and vertically across subnational and global scales. The financial centres in New York, London and Tokyo are examples of this network type.

Fourth, Sassen spends some time looking at cross-border political activism. She notes that place-centred activist groups focusing on local issues connect with other such groups around the world. Some of this activism might be built on the fact that specific types of local issues recur in different localities around the world (see **Escobar**). In building networks of these localities, activists pool resources and draw upon political support and ideas from other localities in a way that adds to their political clout at home. Other forms of such activism do most of their work in the digital network itself, which may result in a concentration of activism in a particular site (the 1999 Seattle anti-WTO events) or in organizing against proposals such as the Multilateral Agreement on Investment or the US's plans to invade Iraq. In this context, Sassen offers a useful concept for understanding the nodes in these networks: *microenvironments with a global span*. These networks challenge long-dominant conceptions of the 'local' in the social sciences which assume physical or geographic proximity and clear territorial boundaries. They also assume that the local is part of a fixed hierarchy of scales – local, subnational, national, regional, global.

Similarly, living in a microenvironment with a global span loosens identities from traditional sources, sometimes engendering new identities, new transnational forms of community membership and even new understandings of entitlement. Sassen illustrates such developments with some case studies of women's activism at local scales and with some of the patterns of organization among immigrants and migrants in global cities. Clearly, the latter three forms of digital formations she identifies are examples of 'denationalization': common and familiar institutions and groupings become tuned to a global logic and move away from their previously firm moorings to the nation-state and the national logic.

Major globalization writings

Sassen, S. (1996) *Losing Control? Sovereignty in an Age of Globalization*, New York, NY: Columbia University Press.

——(1999a) *Globalization and Its Discontents: Essays on the Mobility of People and Money*, New York, NY: New Press.

——(1999b) *Guests and Aliens*, New York, NY: New Press.

——(2006) *Territory, Authority and Rights: From Medieval to Global Assemblages*, Princeton, NJ: Princeton University Press.

——(2007) *A Sociology of Globalization*, New York, NY: W. W. Norton.

Further reading

Sassen, S. (1988) *The Mobility of Labor and Capital: A Study in International Investment and Labour Flow*, Cambridge, UK, and New York, NY: Cambridge University Press.

——(1991; 2001) *The Global City: New York, London, Tokyo*, Princeton, NJ: Princeton University Press.

See also: **Abu-Lughod, Braudel, Brenner, Castells, Cerny, Cox, Escobar, Helleiner, Ruggie, Taylor**.

JAN AART SCHOLTE (1959–)

Jan Aart Scholte is a professor in the Department of Political Science and International Studies and professorial research fellow in the Centre for the Study of Globalisation and Regionalisation (CSGR) at the University of Warwick, UK. He received his BA from Pomona College in California and a MA and a D.Phil. in international relations from the University of Sussex. Before moving to Warwick in 1999, he worked at the University of Sussex, Brighton, and the Institute of Social Studies, The Hague. Professor Scholte has also held visiting positions at Cornell University, the London

School of Economics, the International Monetary Fund, Moscow State University, Gothenburg University and Jawaharlal Nehru University, New Delhi. He has worked with many academic, civil society, public official, business and mass media actors on questions of democracy in global affairs.

Defining globalization

Before providing his definition of globalization, Scholte carefully underlines the premises he follows in articulating a definition. First, a definition should advance knowledge and lead to new insights. It should not be simply a matter of restating what is already understood with different terminology. Second, because no definition will be normatively and politically neutral, it is important to think through such implications before finalizing a proposal. Third, every definition is tied to a particular time and context. It cannot be universal and ever useful. Furthermore, as time goes on, social conditions change, and as knowledge is deepened, the relevance of a definition may decline. Finally, each definition should be as 'clear, precise, concise, explicit, and cogent as possible' (Scholte 2005: 53). Following these premises, Scholte explains why terms such as 'internationalization', 'universalization', 'liberalization' and 'Westernization' are redundant if they are supposed to mean 'globalization'. If these processes are all that globalization entails, then it is better to use one of the prior terms itself.

Scholte defines globalization as the 'spread of transplanetary – and in recent time also more particularly supraterritorial – connections between people' (2005: 59). In proceeding, Scholte treats the terms 'transplanetary', 'transworld' and 'global' interchangeably. His definition of globalization alerts us to a shift in social space: the planet, the world as a whole, becomes a field of social relations in its own right (see also **Robertson**). Scholte uses the word 'globality' to indicate living in a global social space. The definition highlights two characteristics of that social space: trans-planetary connectivity and supra-territoriality. He adds that trans-planetary connections between people are not necessarily new; they have been developing over a number of centuries. What is novel about the contemporary period is that these connections involve more people than at any time before and they are more prominent factors in people's lives than at any other time in human history.

Even more important in distinguishing the contemporary situation from earlier times is the fact that many of these trans-planetary connections are supra-territorial; they substantially transcend territorial geography. 'They are relatively delinked from territory, that is, spatial domains that are mapped on the land surface of the earth, plus any adjoining waters and spheres' (2005: 61). Thanks to contemporary communication and information technologies, global connections often have qualities of trans-world simultaneity (they extend across the world at the same time) and trans-world instantaneity (they move anywhere in the world in no time) (see also **Castells, Tomlinson**). An example of the former would be people in different parts of the world watching the final game of the Football World Cup at the same time. An example of the latter, instantaneity, is found in financial markets when a change in the value of the US dollar vis-à-vis the euro takes place in Shanghai, New York, London, Tokyo and Mumbai at the same time. In short, when it comes to supra-territorial global connections, 'place is not territorially fixed, territorial distance is covered in no time, and territorial boundaries present no particular impediment' (2005: 62).

Drawing on this definition, the distinction between 'international' and 'global' becomes clearer. 'International' relations take place between country units while 'global' relations occur within a planetary-wide unit. Whereas international relations are 'inter-territorial' relations, global relations are trans-territorial and sometimes supra-territorial. For Scholte, then, international economics is different from global economics, global politics from international politics, and global corporations from multinational companies. It follows that Scholte's definition has implications for the methodologies used by social scientists in their research. In their work, they often refer to 'society' or to the 'economy' or to 'culture' or to the 'polity'; these concepts all reflect a territorialist methodology in that they point to the economy of a particular country, the society or the culture of that country, and so on. In fact, most of our social statistics are collected by countries and are explicitly territorial. The logic of Scholte's argument is that research and understanding of globality and globalization will need to break free of this territoriality-based thinking if they are to succeed. More importantly, social scientists will need to approach the world differently using a new paradigm (see also **Appadurai, Beck, Dirlik, Robertson**).

Explaining globalization

With this definition in hand, Scholte is well placed to comment on two important questions in globalization studies. Does globalization have a history? And what are the forces behind globalization that drive these global processes (see also **Hopkins**)? Scholte enters the debate about the history of globalization using his two key categories: trans-planetary connections and supra-territoriality. He observes that trans-planetary connections developed gradually in human history. However, if one looks back 200 to 500 years ago, these connections were few in number. Compared to other connections at the village, city and eventually country level, they were much less important and touched far fewer people than today. Moreover, none of these connections could be described as supra-territorial. He adds that this situation began to change in the middle of the nineteenth century, when the number of global connections grew considerably. Some of the technological innovations in this period (telephone, telegraph) permitted a limited amount of supra-territorial connections to develop. After a systematic review of changes in communication, travel, markets, money and finance, institutions, military activity, consciousness, and the development of law, he concludes, however, that the importance and the number of trans-world connections and of supra-territoriality were relatively limited when compared to the present day.

Upon completing a similar review of changes in the same phenomena but in the contemporary period (after World War II), Scholte concludes that globalization is mainly new to contemporary history (see also **Sassen**):

> Only since the middle of the twentieth century has globality figured continually, comprehensively and centrally in the lives of a large proportion of humanity. Hundreds of millions of people now experience direct and often instantaneous written, auditory and/or visual contact with previously distant others several times a day.
>
> (Scholte 2005: 118)

He departs from those who argue, for example, that the period between 1870 and 1914 was just as intensive a period of globalization as the late twentieth and early twenty-first centuries (see **Hirst**, **Thompson and Bromley**). He concludes: 'It makes ample sense that the vocabulary of "globality" and "globalization" was absent in the nineteenth century and has only surfaced in recent times' (2005: 119).

Scholte concludes his discussion of globalization and its origins by reviewing different explanations for the rapid growth of contemporary globalization: a market-led extension of modernization; the exercise of power by a hegemon (the US) or by several powerful states; the impulses of capitalist development, particularly the extension of surplus accumulation to a global scale; 'Western rationalism' imposing itself across the world on indigenous cultures and other non-modern life worlds; or the product of masculinist behaviours and patriarchal subordinations. Scholte sees value in each of these approaches to explaining the emergence of contemporary globalization. Rather than privileging one of these approaches, however, he suggests a kind of synthesis of them. Thus, he sees the growth of trans-planetary connections and supra-territorial connectivity to be linked to four other developments: shifts from capitalism to 'hypercapitalism'; statist governance to polycentric governance; nationalist to pluralist and hybrid identities; and rationalist knowledge giving way to reflexive rationality (2005: 136). After looking carefully at these forces behind globalization, he concludes that the growth of trans-planetary connections between people is unlikely to reverse itself in the near future.

Impacts of globalization

Scholte is also interested in the impacts that globalization is having upon the world. His discussion of impacts is detailed and comprehensive. We choose to focus on his discussions of capitalism, governance and identities.

Scholte argues that globalization has changed capitalism, leading to the emergence of 'hypercapitalism'. Some of the most important effects of globalizing processes are the expansion of commodification and the greater efficiency of accumulation. Changes in commodification are exemplified by more global production of primary and industrial goods; by the globalization of consumerism, which has expanded the range of industrialization; and by the vast growth of financial markets for banking, securities, derivatives and insurance. Scholte adds that commodification has spread into new areas, including communication and information, and 'services' such as healthcare, care of the elderly and childcare. These changes in commodification have been accompanied by new institutions such as the proliferation of trans-world or global corporations and the growth of offshore centres. In short, with the emergence of 'hypercapitalism', globalization has led to the deepening of the hold of capitalism on all parts of contemporary societies across the world (see also **Brenner**, **Castells**, **Harvey**).

Scholte summarizes the changes in governance by pointing to the replacement of 'statism' by 'polycentrism'. Statism refers to a 'condition where societal governance is more or less equivalent to the regulatory operations of territorial bureaucratic national governments [...] all formulation, implementation, monitoring and enforcement of societal rules occur more or less directly through the state and inter-state relations' (Scholte 2005: 186). In contrast, 'polycentrism' refers to a situation where governance has become more multi-layered and transscalar. No single level (municipal, provincial, national, macro-regional, global) reigns over the other as in statism (see also **Cerny**, **Rosenau**, **Ruggie**). 'Instead, governance tends to be diffuse, emanating from multiple locales at once, with points and lines of authority that are not always clear' (2005: 186). Scholte proceeds to review the various novel forms of governance: multi-scalar public governance (trans-border sub-state, macro-regional and trans-world), privatized governance and (global) civil society. He concludes by noting that such a dispersion of governance forms leads to major challenges when it comes to producing coherent and effective policy. This conclusion seems particularly apt when one views the difficulties global authorities had in responding to the economic and financial crisis that began in late 2007.

In extending his analysis of the effects of globalization into the cultural realm, Scholte focuses on identities and hypothesizes that the de-territorialization of social space will occur hand-in-hand with the relative de-territorialization of social identity (see **Castells, Hannerz**). The general rise of supra-territorial connections should be reflected in, and encouraged by, the growth of non-territorial identities and solidarities. He adds that globalization has tended to generate hybridity, 'where persons have complex multifaceted identities and face challenges of negotiating a blend of sometimes conflicting modes of being and belonging within the same self' (2005: 226). A subset of these changes arises from the loosening of the connections between states and nations under globalization, resulting in what he calls the 'pluralization' of national identities (micro-nations, macro-regional nations, trans-world nations (for example, diasporas)) (see also **Appadurai**). He also comments on non-territorial identities (cosmopolitanism, religion, class, gender, social orientation and so on). When surveyed as a whole, Scholte concludes that globalization has led to the construction of collective identities that are more multi-dimensional, fluid and uncertain (hybridization) (see also **Appadurai, Castells, Hannerz**).

Democracy

Throughout his career, Scholte has been concerned about the impacts of globalization upon democracy. In his analysis of these impacts, he sees democracy involving three facets: education (citizen awareness and mobilization), effective institutions (public participation and accountability) and equality (equal opportunity for involvement for all concerned). After examining these three aspects of democracy under conditions of contemporary globalization, Scholte concludes that democracy stands in a rather weak position. Polycentric governance of global affairs has had low citizen participation and mobilization; in fact, citizen knowledge and understanding of the objects of governance are remarkably poor. Institutions involved in global governance are not usually open to public participation and are scarcely accountable to the people around the world whose lives they are shaping and often destabilizing. The degree of equality of participation, already poor and worsening at the country level in most states, poses much more profound problems in polycentric governance. Democratic legitimacy is poor if not completely absent.

Scholte does not necessarily despair at this situation. He is encouraged by the emergence of civil society organizations that are demanding more democracy at regional and global scales. He acknowledges that new concepts and practices might be necessary if democracy is to become a feature of globalized polycentric governance. During recent years, he acted directly on these conclusions by securing funding for, and then initiating, a major worldwide research project on Building Global Democracy (www.buildingglobaldemocracy.org). The project brought together interested academic researchers, civil society activists, entrepreneurs, journalists and officials from all world regions. Participants examined issues such as rethinking democracy for a global age; citizen learning for global democracy; the inclusion of the excluded in global policy-making; resource redistribution for global equity; and intercultural constructions of legitimate global governance.

Major globalization writings

Scholte, J. A. (1996) 'The geography of collective identities in a globalizing world', *Review of International Political Economy*, vol 3, no 4, pp. 565–607.

——(1997) 'Global capitalism and the state', *International Affairs*, vol 73, no 3, pp. 427–452.

——(2004) 'Civil society and democratically accountable global governance', *Government and Opposition*, vol 39, no 2, pp. 211–233.

——(2005) *Globalization: A Critical Introduction*, 2nd edition, London: Palgrave Macmillan.

——(2007) 'Civil society and the legitimation of global governance', *Journal of Civil Society*, vol 3, no 3, pp. 305–326.

——(2008) 'Defining globalisation', *The World Economy*, vol 31, no 11, pp. 1471–1502.

——(2011) *Building Global Democracy? Civil Society and Accountable Global Governance*, Cambridge, UK: Cambridge University Press.

See also: **Appadurai, Beck, Brenner, Castells, Cerny, Dirlik, Hannerz, Harvey, Hirst, Thompson and Bromley, Robertson, Rosenau, Ruggie, Sassen, Tomlinson.**

AMARTYA SEN (1933–)

Amartya Sen is an Indian economist who was awarded the 1998 Nobel Prize in Economic Sciences for his contributions to welfare economics and social choice theory, and for his interest in the problems of society's poorest members. Sen is best known for his work on the causes of famine, which led to the development of practical solutions for preventing or limiting the effects of real or perceived shortages of food. Sen was educated at Presidency College in Calcutta (now Kolkata). He went on to study at Trinity College, Cambridge, where he received a BA (1955), an MA (1959) and a Ph.D. (1959). He taught economics at a number of universities in India and England, including the Universities of Jadavpur (1956–1958) and Delhi (1963–1971), the London School of Economics, the University of London (1971–1977) and the University of Oxford (1977–1988), before moving to Harvard University, MA (1988–1998), where he was Professor of Economics and Philosophy. In 1998 he was appointed master of Trinity College, Cambridge – a position he held until 2004, when he returned to Harvard as Lamont University Professor.

Sen's contribution to globalization studies comprises a small part of his academic corpus. This contribution arises out of his scholarship relating to the deepening of globalization, on the one hand, and the intensification of sectarian violence, on the other. He argues that the connection between violence and globalization is, at best, indirect. Violence does not arise directly out of globalizing processes but from new forms of identity that have gained increased prominence with globalization. He joins **Castells** in posing questions about changes in identities arising from religion and other cultural forms. He is reluctant to condemn economic globalization for increasing violence. In fact, he sees globalization as part of a solution, providing that some dimensions of economic globalization are reformed.

Identity

Sen distinguishes between a 'solitarist' and a 'non-solitarist' identity. The former refers to a sense of identity that involves the primordial attachment to one group only. In contrast, a person with a non-solitarist identity has a host of attachments or affiliations, which leads to a plurality of relationships with other human beings. He writes:

> In our normal lives, we see ourselves as members of a variety of groups – we belong to all of them. A person's citizenship, residence, geographic origin, gender, class, politics, profession, employment, food habits, sports interests, taste in music, social commitments, etc., make us members of a variety of groups. Each of these collectivities, to all of which this person simultaneously belongs, gives her a particular identity. None of them can be taken to be the person's only identity or singular membership category.
>
> (Sen 2006: 5)

People can choose which of these identities they are emphasizing at a given moment.

In the contemporary period of globalization, Sen notes several situations where this plurality of identities is being strongly challenged, with serious consequences for violence. For example, he comments on the increasing focus by some public intellectuals and groups on the idea that there are various competing civilizations in the world. Perhaps the most notable example of this tendency comes in the writings of Samuel Huntington, who partitions the world into competing civilizations ('Western', 'Islamic', 'Hindu', 'Buddhist') and foretells a coming 'clash of civilizations' in the world.

Sen identifies two problems with this way of thinking. First it lays the foundations for 'misunderstanding nearly everyone in the world' (2006: 42). He adds: 'The conceptual weakness of the attempt to achieve a singular understanding of the people of the world through civilizational partitioning not only works against our shared humanity, but also undermines the diverse identities we all have which do not place us against each other along one uniquely rigid line of segregation' (2006: 46). Second, in classifying people this way, one ignores the immense diversity that exists within a given civilizational category and the often longstanding productive relationships between individuals from two civilizational groups.

Second, he sees these civilizational categories as being remarkably crude. For example, Huntington describes India as a 'Hindu civilization'. This position conveniently overlooks the fact that India has the third largest number of Muslims in the world after Indonesia and Pakistan, and that both Hindus and Muslims have contributed to the wide range of Indian art, literature, music and films. Moreover, India also contains other non-Hindu groups: Sikhs, Jains, Buddhists, Christians and so on. Sen notes the harmful consequences of overlooking this cultural pluralism. Radical movements such as the Hindutva, which have adopted a singular Hindu identity of a particular form, have engaged in massive killing of non-Hindu groups, particularly Muslims, in sectarian conflicts.

Sen extends this analysis to religious affiliations, focusing, in particular, on fundamentalism, which again stresses the dominance of one identity. He argues that these fundamentalisms have become more common among Christians, Muslims, Jews, Hindus and Sikhs, and others. He adds that if one looks at Muslims, their cultures vary widely from Indonesia to Pakistan to Saudi Arabia to Tunisia to Nigeria to Guyana. To subtract all the cultural differences that come from living in these highly different places and focus only on religion is again a recipe for violence. People who would have seen many commonalities between themselves and with other religious groups within their countries are constrained to move away from such pluralism. Often, Sen observes, solitary religious identity leads to serious sectarian violence (see also **Appadurai**). He also points out that a focus on a singular religious identity gives religious leaders tremendous authority, and thus ends up pushing out other, more pluralistic, leaders. These religious leaders can then play a key role in classifying all other groups as the 'other', and in fomenting sectarian violence.

Global ethics and justice

Having argued that the search for global equity cannot be successful through singular identity-based conflicts between the West and 'the rest', or between civilizations or religions, Sen considers other approaches. He believes that the anti-globalization movement raises important questions about how economic globalization is undermining social equality. He suggests that these expressions of global discontent are evidence in themselves of a sense of a global identity and a search for global ethics (Sen 2006: 123).

In considering some of the social and economic problems facing the contemporary world, he sees the development of such global ethics and identities as powerful supports for societal change. He comments on global economic connections, the technological progress in communication and information technologies, and greater political interchanges on a global scale as enablers of change. The task at hand is to find avenues for addressing the challenges facing the poor without destroying the benefits of a global market economy (see also **Rodrik, Stiglitz**). Sen argues that states themselves have key contributions to make. The economic outcomes 'are massively influenced by public policies in education and literacy, epidemiology, land reform, microcredit facilities, and appropriate legal protection' (2006: 136). But the application of such policies cannot produce general economic prosperity without using 'the opportunities of exchange and specialization that market relations offer' (2006: 37). Contrary to neoliberal thinking, he stresses that the mere globalization of market relations cannot on its own bring about world prosperity.

In addition to policy initiatives that could be taken by states, he laments the extensive involvement of the strongest world powers in the globalized trade of arms. He notes that 85 per cent of this trade comes from the Group of 8 countries. Like **Rodrik**, he believes that the current international trade regime that began with the creation of the World Trade Organization in 1995 protects severely restrictive and inefficient trade barriers erected by the wealthiest countries in such areas as agriculture. Along with other critics of the trade regime, he observes how the international patent regime is highly inequitable, providing distinct advantages to transnational corporations headquartered in these same wealthy countries.

In closing his argument, Sen points out that the critiques raised by the anti-globalization movement which focus on inequities foisted upon the poorer countries of the world by the wealthier ones 'cannot sensibly be seen as being really anti-globalization. The motivating ideas suggest the need for seeking a fairer deal for the deprived and the miserable, and for a more just distribution of opportunities in a suitably modified global order' (2006: 147). The voices of this movement are articulating a new global ethics for the world at large. There is a compelling need, he adds, to ask questions not only about the economics and politics of globalization, but also about the values, ethics and sense of belonging that shape our conception of the global world (2006: 185). But he concludes that entering into these kinds of discussions will only succeed when it involves individuals with a 'non-solitarist' understanding of human identities.

Major globalization writings

Sen, A. (1999) *Development as Freedom*, Oxford, UK: Oxford University Press.
——(2006) *Identity and Violence: The Illusion of Destiny*, New York, NY: W. W. Norton.

See also: **Appadurai**, **Castells**, **Rodrik**, **Stiglitz**.

VANDANA SHIVA (1952–)

Vandana Shiva is an Indian scientist, an internationally known environmental activist and a prominent advocate of ecofeminism. Trained as a physicist in Canada, she obtained her Ph.D. in quantum physics from the University of Western Ontario. She is a renowned figure in the alter-globalization movement (which includes public intellectuals such as Richard **Falk**, Arundhati **Roy** and Joseph **Stiglitz**) and is a member of the International Forum on Globalization. She is the founder of Navdanya International, an organization that aims to '[promote] local and ecological food models'. It acts as a 'network of seed keepers and organic producers spread across 16 states in India' (see www.vandanashiva.org).

Shiva's foremost contribution to debates on globalization lies in her efforts to expose the devastating global effects of the Green Revolution, 'the name given to [the] science-based transformation of Third World agriculture' (Shiva 1991: 19). She traces the roots of the Green Revolution to the development of Western modern science, which perceives nature as something disconnected from human beings to be studied, conquered and exploited 'in accordance with a "scientific" method which generates claims of being "objective", "neutral" and "universal"' (1991: 22; see also Shiva 1988; Shiva and Mies 1993). The Green Revolution relies on the premise that 'technology is a superior substitute to nature, and hence a means of producing limitless growth' (Shiva 1991: 24). By implementing the introduction of intensive agricultural methods and the development of genetically modified seeds, Shiva contends that the Green Revolution has led to widespread ecological destruction in the poorer countries outside the OECD (and beyond) by reducing the availability of fertile land, through an increase of soil erosion and degradation, and by diminishing the genetic diversity of various crops (1991: 24). These negative consequences created the conditions for scarcity in the agricultural yields of crops grown in poorer countries instead of the much-promised abundance (see Shiva 1988, 1991, 2000a, 2000b, 2002). Moreover, Shiva suggests, current political conflicts in various places have their origins in the distortion of local agricultural knowledge by corporatized agriculture and in the scarcity and food insecurity this distortion has brought about (see Shiva 1991, 2002, 2008).

Ecofeminism

In 1993 Shiva collaborated with German sociologist Maria Mies in writing a book on ecofeminism. Mies and Shiva suggest that much of the environmental destruction we witness today has its roots in the 'capitalist patriarchal world system' (Shiva and Mies 1993: 2). By defining the current world system as both capitalist and patriarchal, Mies and Shiva indicate two major and interrelated sources of oppression: the reckless exploitation of nature in the name of development, progress and capital accumulation, and the exploitation of women and their subordination to men and to the principle of masculinity. The capitalist patriarchal world system is thus steeped in a view of the world that privileges a hierarchy where 'nature is subordinated to man; woman to man; consumption to production; and the local to the global' (1993: 5). In an earlier work, Shiva had noted that the practice of development, as an ideology of Western patriarchy, entailed the removal of women from adequate participation in development projects, producing a situation where they 'bore the costs but were excluded from the benefits' (Shiva 1988: 2). For example, the privatization of land led to the displacement and impoverishment of women by 'eroding their traditional land rights' (1988: 3). Moreover, the top-down practice of development implemented by poorer countries' governments at the behest of international institutions ultimately 'destroyed women's productivity by removing land, water and forests from their management and control' (1988: 3). Shiva draws attention to the fact that women have been, in many cultures, 'the custodians of biodiversity' since they possess invaluable knowledge and expertise in agriculture and forestry. They are the ones responsible for the preparation of seeds for new harvests, a process requiring complex skills and knowledge of 'germination requirements and soil choice' (Shiva and Mies 1993: 167). They are also responsible for the nurturing of the plants and for harvesting. Shiva notes that increasing reliance at a global level on 'large-scale monoculture-based agricultural production' has resulted in the erosion of biodiversity and has increased the workload of rural women by taking away their 'control over seeds and genetic resources' (1993: 168). Shiva's ecofeminism thus draws the connection between the global adoption of corporate agricultural practices (based on monocultures and on high-yield varieties from genetically modified seeds) and the degradation of women's livelihoods in poorer countries, and thus their impoverishment and disempowerment (for a feminist critique of ecofeminism, see Agarwal 2001). Therefore, 'the devastation of the earth and her beings by the corporate warriors' (1993: 14) is not simply an environmental concern, but also a feminist concern.

The global politics of food production

While Shiva does not specifically define the notion of 'globalization', she does provide an understanding of the 'global' as 'the global domination of local and particular interests' by multinational corporations (MNCs) (Shiva and Mies 1993: 9) (see also **Amin, Bello**). These corporate actors seek to appropriate the cultural and natural diversity existing in various societies around the world and harness it for their benefit as they search for capital accumulation at a global scale (1993: 9). Shiva's central concern with the consequences of the global corporatization of agricultural production should be seen, then, within this context of global domination by MNCs. In that sense, she makes the claim that the global 'erosion of biodiversity and the erosion of cultural diversity are related' (Shiva 2000b: 8). As economic globalization is premised on the dissemination of 'biological and social monocultures', it pushes out both biodiversity and the 'diversity of livelihoods of the large majority of Third World people who make their living as farmers, fishermen, craftspeople and healers' (2000b: 9). What Shiva calls 'the dominant paradigm of [agricultural] production' relies on a skewed understanding of productivity as the removal of nature's limits (through technological substitution) for the purpose of creating abundance (Shiva and Mies 1993: 28). It is on the basis of this type of productivity that the Green Revolution was implemented in poorer countries' agricultures starting in the 1970s. The brainchild of Norman Borlaug, an American agronomist who was awarded a Nobel Peace Prize for his work on agronomy, the Green Revolution was based on the claim that the development of 'miracle' seeds would spearhead the end of hunger in the poorer countries and bring about food abundance. These 'miracle' seeds were genetically modified to overcome natural limits of various crops, such as resistance to diseases and pests, and thus offer higher yields. This American-style agriculture was soon adopted by various national governments in poorer countries outside the OECD under pressure from international institutions with long-term devastating consequences, both ecological and sociopolitical. As Shiva remarks: 'The crop and varietal diversity of indigenous agriculture was replaced by a narrow genetic base and monocultures [...] While the new varieties reduced diversity, they increased resource use of water, and of chemical inputs such as pesticides and fertilizers' (Shiva 1991: 45–46).

The Green Revolution led to the formation of huge corporate agribusiness monopolies, which concentrated ownership of seeds and agricultural technologies in the hands of a few global corporations, such as Monsanto. Shiva gives the example of the detrimental impact of introducing soybean monocultures upon Indian farmers and agriculture. As she remarks, since 'every fourth farmer in the world is an Indian, the impact of globalization on Indian agriculture is of global significance' (Shiva 2000a: 7). In August 1998, a tragedy hit New Delhi when massive supplies of mustard oil (one of the preferred seeds in India for oil extraction) became contaminated with dangerous chemicals, killing scores and making thousands of people ill. Soon after this incident the Indian government banned the selling of mustard oil throughout the country and announced the free importation of soybeans for the purpose of substituting mustard with soybean oil. The impact was soon felt by thousands of farmers across India who were no longer able to sell their mustard seeds. As Shiva explains, the soybean monocultures are genetically 'engineered by Monsanto to contain a bacterial gene that confers tolerance to the herbicide Roundup, also manufactured by Monsanto' (2000a: 26). Since European markets have expressed serious concerns about the food safety of genetically modified organisms, US companies are, in the words of Shiva, 'desperate to dump their genetically engineered soybeans on countries such as India' (2000a: 27).

It is noteworthy that the global politics of food production play out in international institutions such as the World Trade Organization (WTO), which negotiated in 1994 the Agreement on Trade-Related Aspects of Intellectual Property Rights (TRIPS) that criminalized, among other things, 'seed-saving and seed-sharing', thus effectively shifting the ownership and revenues from seed owners and cultivators such as small farmers to corporate seed patent holders (2000a: 2). The consequences are clearly spelled out by Shiva:

> As the food industry becomes more concentrated and integrated, uniformity is the result, and the globalization of consumption patterns, by creating monocultures and destroying diversity, has a devastating effect on the poorest of the planet. First, they are pushed into deeper poverty by being forced to 'compete' with globally powerful forces to gain access to the local biological resources. Secondly, their economic alternatives outside the global market are destroyed.
>
> (Shiva 2000b: 17)

The emergence of 'global wars' over natural resources

Shiva traces global trends in the way in which new conflicts have arisen whose roots lie in the centralization of control over food production and natural resources by national governments and international institutions such as the World Bank. This is a theme she started exploring in *The Violence of the Green Revolution* (Shiva 1991), and which she further develops in her more recent works such as *Water Wars* (Shiva 2002) and *Soil not Oil* (Shiva 2008). By taking control over the management of natural resources away from local communities, what she calls 'eco-imperialism' has had overwhelming consequences for millions of people around the world. The dynamic of eco-imperialism 'includes the control over the economies of the world through corporate globalization and transforms the resources and eco-systems of the world into feedstock for an industrialized globalized economy' (2008: 16). Its paradigm of limitless growth is responsible for the current global food crisis, with food prices rising worldwide due to the takeover of local agricultures by corporate agribusinesses (2008: 1–2). Such a crisis converges with the on-going climate crisis and 'peak oil' crisis. The erratic climatic changes experienced recently in various regions around the world have had profound negative impacts upon agricultural production. Moreover, the market solutions proposed to meet the challenge of climate change (such as reliance on industrial biofuels) have not only failed to solve the problem of climate change but have exacerbated the food crisis by pushing peasants and farmers off their lands to make room for the cultivation of plants for biofuels to meet the non-sustainable energy needs of rich countries (2008: 3). The erosion of food security thus becomes the fuel for emerging social unrest and conflict.

In *The Violence of the Green Revolution*, Shiva examines the ecological causes of the violence that engulfed Punjab during the 1980s. She contends that much contemporary political violence, whether in Punjab or Palestine, stems from 'conflicts over scarce vital water resources' (Shiva 2002: x). She predicts the emergence of water wars on a global scale since the former involve two opposing water paradigms: one, embraced by diverse cultures, sees water as a universal right to which all beings should have access; the other, championed by corporate globalization advocates, makes water into a commodity that can be purchased and owned by those who have the means (2002: x). In that sense, globalization produces two fundamentalisms: the fundamentalism of the market where every resource can become a commodity to be traded and profited from by corporate actors; and the fundamentalism of terrorism that 'feeds on people's displacement, dispossession, economic insecurities, and fears' (2002: xii). From Shiva's perspective, the latter has its roots in the former. For example, she claims that the Israeli–Palestinian conflict is, to a certain extent, a conflict over the control of the water resources provided by the Jordan River (2002: 72–73). She argues that if oil wars were the dominant conflict paradigm of the twentieth century, water wars will be the one of the twenty-first. In her view: 'The water crisis is the most pervasive, most severe, and most invisible dimension of the ecological devastation of the earth' (2002: 1). Owing to decades of industrialized monoculture agriculture and intensive deforestation, many of the world's ecosystems have experienced severe droughts. Therefore, the control of water sources has become, according to Shiva, a matter of national security for many governments and, thus, a prominent trigger of conflict and war.

In meeting the challenges of these current crises over food and natural resources, Shiva advocates for 'ecological democracy'. What this notion entails is a paradigm shift from a reductionist worldview to a holistic one that recognizes multiple interconnections within and among ecosystems; from a 'mechanistic, industrial paradigm to an ecological one'; and from a consumerist perception of ourselves to a recognition of ourselves as embedded in nature (Shiva 2008: 43).

Major globalization writings

Shiva, V. (1988) *Staying Alive: Women, Ecology and Survival in India*, New Delhi: Kali For Women.

——(1991) *The Violence of the Green Revolution: Third World Agriculture, Ecology and Politics*, London and New Jersey: Zed Books; Penang, Malaysia: Third World Network.

——(2000a) *Stolen Harvest: The Hijacking of the Global Food Supply*, Cambridge, MA: South End Press.

——(2000b) *Tomorrow's Biodiversity*, London: Thames & Hudson.

——(2002) *Water Wars: Privatization, Pollution and Profit*, Cambridge, MA: South End Press.

——(2008) *Soil not Oil: Environmental Justice in an Age of Climate Crisis*, Cambridge, MA: South End Press.

Shiva, V. and Mies, M. (1993) *Ecofeminism*, Halifax, Nova Scotia: Fernwood Publications; London and New Jersey: Zed Books.

Further reading

Agarwal, B. (2001) 'Environmental management, equity and ecofeminism: debating India's experience', in K.-K. Bhavnani (ed.) *Feminism and 'Race'*, Oxford, UK: Oxford University Press.

See also: **Falk, Roy, Stiglitz.**

GAYATRI CHAKRAVORTY SPIVAK (1942–)

Gayatri Chakravorty Spivak, a Calcutta-born literary critic and a professor of comparative literature at Columbia University, is one of the foremost names associated with post-colonial theory. In 1959 she obtained a first-class honours BA in English and Bengali Literatures from the University of Calcutta. She then went on to pursue graduate studies in the US where she earned an MA and a Ph.D. in comparative literature at Cornell University. Spivak gained international fame for her translation of, and introduction to, Jacques Derrida's *Of Grammatology*, published in 1976 by Johns Hopkins University Press. Throughout her published work, she has blended feminist, Marxist and deconstructionist theoretical perspectives that engage an eclectic range of issues related to the Global South, such as women's voices in non-Western societies, Western imperialism, tribal societies (Spivak 1999, 2008), transnational capital and the complicity of academia in the transnationalization of capital (see **Dirlik**). Since the 1980s she has been a member of the Subaltern Studies Group – South Asian scholars whose intellectual mission has been to build an alternative historiography that accounts for the voices of those most marginalized by official history (Spivak 1988: 197–221) (see also **Chakrabarty**). Spivak has also been involved in rural education activism and social movements related to feminist and ecological issues.

Spivak's contribution to globalization studies lies in her rich reflections on the dynamics of transnational capital and on the cultural transformations that it has engendered. Her approach to cultural analysis is a unique one, paying close attention to material structures as they interact with cultural effects. She develops such an approach in *In Other Worlds* (1988), where she examines the 'micro-politics of the academy and its relation to the macro-narrative of imperialism' (MacCabe 1988: x). In her subsequent works, *A Critique of Postcolonial Reason* (1999) and *Death of a Discipline* (2003), Spivak attempts to offer an answer to the question of the academy's (and of the disciplines within the humanities, more specifically) inability to meaningfully address the most pressing global issues.

From 'transnational literacy' to 'planetarity': a postcolonial perspective on globalization

In *A Critique of Postcolonial Reason*, Spivak develops a framework for understanding how the economic logic of 'micro-electronic capitalism' engenders its own cultural logic (Spivak 1999: 334). Spivak sees the global present as the product of the intersection between processes of decolonization and imperialism, on the one hand, and 'the march of world capitalism', on the other (1999: 340) (see also **Mignolo, Santos**). With the onset of decolonization, the path was open to the transnationalization of capitalism, a process that has implied the alignment of the interests of the elites in the Global South with those of transnational capital (see also **Dirlik**). In this sense, globalization is, in Spivak's perspective, 'a new attempt to impose unification on the world by and through the market' (1999: 357) (see also Spivak 2003: 72). Here, she introduces the concept of 'transnational literacy', an elusive concept for which she does not provide a clear definition. However, she employs this idea of 'transnational literacy' in the context of the rise of 'Eurocentric migration' – the flows of migrants from the Global South to the North (Spivak 1999: 357). Spivak assigns this transnational group a crucial role in the 'unification of the world by and through the market' by making possible the transfer of aid from the nation-state 'they now call home [...] to the nation-state they still call culture' (1999: 357). In short, what Spivak calls 'transnational literacy' entails an awareness of the various complicities that constitute the transnational, such as that between 'the bourgeoisie of the Third World and migrants in the First', and how such complicities serve the interests of transnational capital (1999: 381). To put it differently, Spivak calls for a recognition of uncomfortable global complicities that point to ethical dilemmas. While attention must be paid to the racism and discrimination that Third World migrants face in Western societies, it is also an unmistakable reality that 'the interest of the migrant [...] is in dominant global capital' (1999: 382).

Accordingly, Spivak identifies liberal multiculturalism as the cultural logic of economic globalization, 'determined by the demands of contemporary transnational capitalisms' (1999: 397) (see also **Dirlik**). This cultural logic is deployed as a strategy to win 'the consent from developing countries in the dominant project of the financialization of the globe' (1999: 397) (see **Arrighi, Cox**). This strategy, pioneered by transnational corporations, entails learning the idiom of specific cultures and incorporating certain cultural elements within the economic logic of capitalism in order to make global capitalism more compatible with, and more legitimate in, local contexts. In this sense, academia (especially modern languages departments and cultural studies) is complicit with this cultural logic by attracting and training 'new immigrant students from the former colonies' who are acculturated into the dominant cultural logic (1999: 397). Spivak notes here a gap between the shrewd use of multiculturalism as a strategy by transnational capital (with its distorting effects) and the general ignorance of such a strategy (for a similar argument although conceptualized somewhat differently, see **Appadurai**).

From Spivak's perspective, until such awareness ('transnational literacy') is brought to bear on the field of cultural studies and on the work of radical scholars, radical critiques in the North will continue to remain trapped within the dominant cultural logic of transnational capital. To illustrate her argument, Spivak cites the adoption of the Child Labor Deterrent Act of 1993 by the US Senate against the importing into the US of textiles manufactured in the South (1999: 415). She notes how nationalism and racism had been hoisted in the interest of protectionism with the blessing of self-righteous anti-child labour activists in the North (1999: 415–416). She does not question the exploitative nature of child labour as a phenomenon endemic to the Global South. Instead, she takes issue with the ignorance of many activists and academics based in the North regarding the insertion of child labour within a larger transnational logic of capital. To put it differently, it is this transnational logic of capital that sustains the phenomenon of child labour in the South. Thus, Spivak decries the 'transnational illiteracy' of many 'benevolent liberals' in the North that makes them complicit with the abuses and exploitation of transnational capital (1999: 416).

In *Death of a Discipline*, Spivak (2003) reflects on the possibility of rethinking the academic field of comparative literature as a global field of studies that draws on transnational literacy and thus builds an alternative to the cultural logic of transnational capital. Here she introduces the concept of 'planetarity' to refer to an awareness of the globe that transcends the vision of globalization. As mentioned earlier,

Spivak sees globalization as the unification of the globe through the market. She also associates globalization or the 'globe' with a political cartography of 'bounded nations' and 'located cities' and thus with a limiting and limited understanding of culture (2003: 81, 93). As Spivak remarks: 'Comparative Literature remains trapped within the limiting logic of this political cartography and thus is bound to conceive of cultural difference as nothing more than cultural relativism.' She thus posits 'planetarity' as an alternative logic to that of globalization, which takes the 'Earth as a paranational image that can substitute for [the] international' (2003: 73, 95).

The politics of feminism in an age of globalization

Throughout her work, Spivak expresses concern with the consequences of 'First World'/Northern feminists' 'transnational illiteracy'. Such illiteracy is visible in the Northern feminists' vision of 'Third World'/Southern women as a homogeneous collective waiting to be rescued (Spivak 1988: 136) (see also **Chow, Ong**). Moreover, as discussed earlier, it is this same illiteracy that prompts the benevolent Northern feminist to be complicit with the workings of transnational capital. She calls this type of feminism 'dominant', 'international' or 'universalist' feminism (Spivak 2008) to indicate its collusion with the institutions of global governance, such as the World Bank and development agencies, which trap Southern women into neocolonial development projects, ignorant of their specific needs and particular cultural contexts. Thus, Spivak advocates for a responsible feminism ('feminists with a transnational consciousness'), which would help feminists to be more aware of their own neocolonial complicity and the transnational connections that implicate it in the exploitation and marginalization of Southern women (2008: 126; see also Spivak 1999: 399).

Major globalization writings

Spivak, G. C. (1988) *In Other Worlds: Essays in Cultural Politics*, New York, NY, and London: Routledge.

——(1999) *A Critique of Postcolonial Reason: Toward a History of the Vanishing Present*, Cambridge, MA: Harvard University Press.

——(2003) *Death of a Discipline*, New York, NY: Columbia University Press.

——(2008) *Other Asias*, Malden, MA: Blackwell Publishing.

——(2012) *An Aesthetic Education in the Era of Globalization*, Cambridge, MA: Harvard University Press.

Further reading

MacCabe, C. (1988) 'Foreword', in G. C. Spivak, *In Other Worlds: Essays in Cultural Politics*, New York, NY, and London: Routledge.

See also: **Appadurai, Arrighi, Chakrabarty, Chow, Cox, Dirlik, Mignolo, Ong, Santos**.

JOSEPH STIGLITZ (1943–)

A graduate of Amherst College, Joseph Stiglitz received his Ph.D. from the Massachusetts Institute of Technology (MIT) in 1967, became a full professor at Yale in 1970 and in 1979 was awarded the John Bates Clark Award, given biennially by the American Economic Association to the economist under 40 who has made the most significant contribution to the field. He has taught at Princeton, NJ, Stanford, CA, and MIT, and was the Drummond Professor and a fellow of All Souls College, Oxford. He is now University Professor at Columbia University in New York. In 2001, he was awarded the Nobel Prize in Economics, primarily for helping to create a new branch of economics, 'the economics of information'. He was a member of the Council of Economic Advisors from 1993 to 1995 and then the council's chairman from 1995 to 1997 under President Bill Clinton in the US. He took up a position as senior vice-president and chief economist at the World Bank from 1997 to 2000. It was during this period of government service that he became more and more concerned about economic globalization.

Stiglitz argues that there is nothing inherently bad or good about globalization. Its potential for lifting people up from poverty or for compounding economic problems depends upon the ideology and politics of powerful 'advanced industrial' states. To date, these states, particularly the US, have promoted a globalization that serves their interests above all, along with those of transnational corporations based in their territory. Consequently, many people in poorer countries, and even some in the advanced industrial ones, have been pushed further into poverty, with all of its consequences, such as poor health, inadequate nutrition and mentally and physically harmful workplaces. Stiglitz adds that these outcomes of economic globalization are by no means inevitable. Economic and political changes can be made that will 'make globalization work' for a larger part of the world's population.

Harmful globalization

Stiglitz defines globalization as 'the closer integration of the countries and peoples of the world which has been brought about by the enormous reduction of costs of transportation and communication, and the breaking down of artificial barriers to the flows of goods, services, capital, knowledge, and (to a lesser extent) people across borders. Globalization has been accompanied by the creation of new institutions that have joined with existing ones to work across borders' (Stiglitz 2002: 9). He sees globalization thus defined as 'neither good nor bad' but as having the 'potential to do enormous good' (2002: 20). His first preoccupation is why this potential has not been realized.

Drawing on his scholarly work as well as his experience in the US government and the World Bank, he answers this question by arguing that this failure arises from the promotion of a particular ideological approach to the economy – 'market fundamentalism' – by the US and other advanced industrial states. These steps have led to changes in their domestic policy arrangements as well as to international economic institutions such as the International Monetary Fund (IMF), the World Bank and the World Trade Organization (WTO) that have enriched economic elites and transnational corporations based in those countries. At the same time, economic options for poorer states have narrowed and living conditions for the citizens in those states have worsened (see also **Amin, Harvey**).

Stiglitz defines three components of market fundamentalism (sometimes referred to as the Washington Consensus): fiscal austerity, privatization and market liberalization. Fiscal austerity refers to governments reducing their expenditures and lowering taxes to shrink their treasuries. The thinking here was that government had become a hindrance to economic growth and prosperity, getting in the way of the private sector. Leading proponents of this ideology such as President Ronald Reagan in the US and Prime Minister Margaret Thatcher in the UK took these ideas further. They argued that many of the public goods related to social welfare and protection could be delivered more efficiently by private businesses. Pursuit of this thinking led to attempts to reduce publicly provided social services and to promote private schooling of children. Finally, proponents of market fundamentalism argued that if governments stopped regulating economic markets and institutions, particularly those providing capital and financial services, privatization of social welfare programmes would be even more successful. Proponents also argued that world prosperity would be greatly enhanced if international trade between countries was liberalized by reducing tariffs and ending other trade barriers.

Stiglitz writes passionately and in considerable detail about the immense harm done to poorer countries and their populations when these ideas were adopted by leading international economic institutions. In particular, he argues, the US, supported by other wealthy countries, imposed this ideology on the IMF and applied it unfairly in the international trade agreements that led to the creation of the WTO in 1995 (see **Rodrik**). Initially set up to help countries deal with the failures of markets, the IMF adopted with fervour the new ideas and came to tie the lending of money to poorer countries in the world to their taking drastic steps to reduce spending, privatize education and social services, and open their markets to the powerful transnational corporations of the advanced industrial countries (see **Bello**). Following hard on the Structural Adjustment Programmes of the IMF, the WTO agreement worsened the situation of poorer countries (see **Bello**, **Rodrik**): 'The Western countries pushed trade liberalization for the products that they exported, but at the same time continued to protect those sectors in which competition from developing countries might have threatened their economies' (2002: 60). Nowhere was this hypocrisy more evident than in agriculture, where poorer countries were forced to open their markets while the wealthier countries in the Organization for Economic Cooperation and Development (OECD) were permitted by the WTO Agreement on Agriculture to subsidize and keep closed many of their own agricultural markets (see also **Shiva**).

Stiglitz does not blame these failures on the international institutions themselves. Rather, he criticizes the advanced industrial countries, particularly the US:

> The end of the Cold War gave the United States, the one remaining superpower, the opportunity to reshape the global economic and political system based on principles of fairness and concern for the poor; but the absence of competition from communist ideology also gave the United States the opportunity to reshape the global system based on its own self-interest and that of its multinational corporations. Regrettably, in the economic sphere, it chose the latter course.
>
> (Stiglitz 2006: 277)

Making globalization work

Stiglitz focuses on global governance in reflecting upon how globalization should be reformed: '*The most fundamental change that is required to make globalization work in the way that it should is a change in governance*' (Stiglitz 2006: 226; emphasis in the original). In reflecting on the governance problems associated with the IMF in particular, two aspects are particularly salient for Stiglitz. First, he notes that in the IMF, the persons who speak for countries are their finance ministers and central bank governors; in the WTO, they are ministers of trade. Within their countries, finance ministers and central bank governors have close relationships with the dominant corporations and their interest groups in financial markets; similarly, trade ministers cooperate regularly with the large transnational corporations. The result is that the politics of these two key international institutions are skewed to favour the commercial and financial interests of advanced industrial countries.

Second, while working at the World Bank as chief economist during the late 1990s, Stiglitz had an opportunity to observe closely the strategic decisions taken by governments in East Asia in response to the financial crisis of 1997 to 1998. He notes that they did not follow market fundamentalism in dealing with the crisis and in developing economic policy more generally. East Asian governments liberalized markets in a carefully planned way (see **Arrighi, Ong**); they did not embark on massive privatization, nor did they embark on policies of austerity. The two largest countries, China and India, restricted flows of capital when they deemed it necessary (2006: 34). Stiglitz summarizes: 'East Asia demonstrated the success of a course markedly different from the Washington Consensus, with a role for government far larger than the minimalist role allowed by market fundamentalism' (2006: 35).

Accordingly, Stiglitz proposes that changes are needed that introduce more democracy into the system and preserve responsibilities for nation-states. All countries and their leaders will need to change their mindset to think and act more globally. Along with this change, the most important reforms to governance are ones to reduce the democratic deficits so common in international economic institutions. The voting structure at the IMF and World Bank needs to give more weight to developing countries. Countries should be represented at these institutions and at the WTO by all relevant ministries, not just trade and finance ones.

The institutions themselves need to become more transparent; they should adopt conflict of interest rules and develop procedures that make it possible for all voices to be heard. Such goals would lead to poorer countries being able to participate in meaningful ways in decision-making. Where necessary, poorer countries should be provided with technical assistance so that they can fully understand the impact of proposed changes in policy upon their citizens. More generally, Stiglitz calls for a new 'global social contract' where the well-being of developed and developing countries is better balanced. Reforms might include a fairer trade regime, a new approach to intellectual property and the promoting of research, and agreement whereby developed countries compensate developing ones for their environmental services. The social contract would thus build in the idea that all states share one planet when it comes to global warming (see also **Rodrik**).

With institutions reformed in this way, nation-states working with international institutions will be better placed to address problems that have intensified with market fundamentalist-driven globalization: the pervasiveness of poverty, the need for financial assistance and debt relief, the unfairness of trade, the inordinate emphasis on liberalization and privatization, the protection of the environment, and US dominance of global governance institutions.

In short, Stiglitz believes that globalization can be reformed from within, thus departing from authors such as **Escobar**, **Mignolo** and **Santos**: 'Globalization can be reshaped, and when it is, when it is properly, fairly run, with all countries having a voice in policies affecting them, there is a possibility that it will help create a new global economy in which growth is not only more sustainable and less volatile but the fruits of the growth are more equitably shared' (Stiglitz 2002: 21).

Major globalization writings

Stiglitz, J. (2002) *Globalization and Its Discontents*, New York, NY: W. W. Norton.
——(2006) *Making Globalization Work*, New York, NY: W. W. Norton.

See also: **Amin**, **Arrighi**, **Bello**, **Escobar**, **Harvey**, **Mignolo**, **Ong**, **Rodrik**, **Santos**, **Shiva**.

SUSAN STRANGE (1923–1998)

Susan Strange was born in the UK and educated at the Royal School, Bath, the Université de Caen and the London School of Economics, where she graduated in 1943 with a first-class degree in economics. Her first career was in journalism, working for many years as an economic correspondent for the *Observer*. She served as its correspondent at the White House and then at the United Nations for many years. In 1965 she was appointed to a research fellowship at the Royal Institute of International Affairs at Chatham House, where she later became director of the transnational relations project. She published her first important book on international finance, *Sterling and British Policy*, in 1971, in which she investigated the implications of the introduction of flexible exchange rates. In 1974 she co-founded the British International Studies Association.

Her most important contribution to the field of international relations lies in her promotion of international political economy (IPE) – which looks at the influence of the activities of states on markets – as an academic discipline. Strange's final academic post, which she held from 1993 until her death in 1998, was as Chair of International Relations at the University of Warwick, where she built up the graduate programme in IPE. Her election in 1995 as president of the International Studies Association, only the second non-American to hold the position, was an indication of the high regard in which she was held worldwide. As one of the leading scholars in the group from Warwick, she helped to secure a large grant from the Economic and Social Research Council to fund an international centre for the study of globalization.

Strange contributes to our understanding of globalization through her innovative and prescient analysis of the changing relations between states and markets, particularly as evidenced in the area of finance. She drew on these analyses to challenge globalization sceptics (see **Hirst, Thompson and Bromley**), who argued that the changes occuring in the economy were better understood as an intensification of relations between states (internationalization) (Strange 1998a).

Theoretical tools

Throughout her academic career, Susan Strange was highly critical of international relations as a field of study and was a pioneer in defining a new area of research called international political economy. Of the many contributions she made to IPE, her thinking about power has been one of the most important, and this theorizing informs her approach to globalization. She argues that there are two kinds of power in a political economy: relational and structural. Relational refers to the commonsense understanding of power: the power of A to get B to do something that the latter would not otherwise do (Strange 1994: 24). In contrast, structural power refers to the 'power to shape frameworks within which states relate to each other, relate to people or relate to corporate enterprises. The relative power of each party in a relationship is more, or less, if one party is also determining the surrounding structure of the relationship' (1994: 25). Of these two forms, she argues that structural power is the more significant for studying global political economy and society. She develops this argument by looking at four major structures within which power is exercised: security, finance, production and knowledge. Of these four structures, finance, production and knowledge are the most important for her thinking about globalization.

In the *financial structure*, power is exercised by whoever can determine how credit is to be created, in what forms and qualities, and who is to have access to it on what terms (1994: 23). The importance of financial structural power is enhanced because of its effects on the *production structure*: what determines what goods and services will be produced for the satisfaction of material needs and how these goods and services will be produced. The power of *knowledge structure* lies in how ideas, knowledge and information are valued, accumulated, stored and communicated.

Globalization

Strange's understanding of globalization relates to changes in these structures. For the production structure, she observes that instead of goods and services being predominantly produced by and for the people living in the territory of a state, they are increasingly produced by people in a number of states for a world market, not a national one (Strange 1997: 365). Similarly, the creation and use of credit now takes place across territorial boundaries in global markets linked to a single financial system. Local banks and financial markets are no longer autonomous but are part of the global system and subject to its ups and downs as the financial crises of 1997 to 1998 and 2008 to 2010 have demonstrated. These changes in production and finance structures, in turn, affect what she calls the 'levels of perceptions, beliefs, ideas and tastes': a certain amount of homogenization is taking place in these perceptions. The individuals affected perceive themselves as living and working in a worldwide context, instead of a local or national one (Strange 1995: 292).

The knowledge structure enters this picture through its contribution to the accelerating rate of technological change. When it comes to production, Strange argues that the more technology contributes to the production of goods and services, the more markets need to expand to pay for the technology. The changes in finance arising from technological innovations are just as pronounced. Computers have permitted money to take on a digital form, permitting, in turn, payment systems to operate instantly and on a worldwide scale. Innovations in computer chips make it possible for credit cards to be used globally, while satellite technologies have led to banks synthesizing their global operations (Strange 1998a: 24–25). More generally, Strange observes that technological innovation has led to both new financial products (derivatives) and new processes for doing business (computer banking). Particularly novel consequences are the global scale on which financial transactions take place and the rapid pace at which they have proliferated (see also **Helleiner**). She notes that these innovations, in turn, have taken place with the tacit or explicit permission of political authorities and regulators, a degree of political involvement not found in industrial production (Strange 1998b: 26).

Globalization's effects

Strange outlines three important political consequences of globalization. First, there is a shift in power from states to markets. The rapid growth of transnational corporations (TNCs) operating more and more on a global scale in world markets is central to this shift (see **Amin**, **Arrighi**). These corporations become key political actors in their own right because of their structural power. Accordingly,

Strange argues, diplomacy under globalization becomes triangular. Although governments continue to negotiate with one another, they also have to negotiate more and more with TNCs. In effect, these corporations play a significant role in who gets what in the world system. She points to several pieces of evidence to support this position. States have retreated from their former participation in the ownership of and control over industry, services, trade, and the direction of research and development in technology. Markets have been doing more than states in redistributing wealth from the developed industrialized countries to less developed ones. TNCs have taken away from governments the major role in resolving or managing conflicts of interest in labour–management relations. Finally, corporations have increasingly escaped the taxation of corporate profits by governments (see Strange 1996: chapter 4). In addition, governments have had to adjust to the diplomacy between firms: 'Taking a variety of forms, from franchising, licensing and sub-contracting to strategic alliances in research and development, this new diplomacy is probably the fastest expanding and in the long term the most instrumental of the three' (Strange 1995: 298). Consequently, TNCs have become less and less beholden to or constrained by so-called home governments (Strange 1998b: 181).

Second, Strange argues, there has been growing asymmetry between states. The differences in power and autonomy between states have widened considerably in the post-war period. In particular, Strange points to the US, which has expanded its influence and structural power in a variety of different ways. She discusses in some detail the advantages that accrue to the US through the rapid growth of the information and communication industries, which have tended to be led by US corporations. She describes this development as the emergence of a 'non-territorial empire' where authority is exercised directly on people, not on land as in earlier empires (Strange 1989: 170). At the same time, Strange also observes that with the growing importance of TNCs and their increasing autonomy from states, the US position could be undermined as business shifts to other parts of the world, including East Asia (see also **Amin**, **Arrighi**, **Cox**).

Finally, Strange observes that these two sets of changes lead to a third problem: an increasing number of gaps between what people need and what states can do. She notes that state authority has declined in providing citizens with security from violence. The globalization of finance means that increasingly the reliability of money, as a means of exchange, unit of account and a store of value, has fallen. The provision of social welfare policies, developed over the course of the first 70 years of the twentieth century, is falling off (Strange 1997:

368) (see **Cerny**). In several of her writings, she explores the growth of the global criminal economy, including money laundering, tax evasion, private fraud and public embezzlement, as an illustration of the shift in power from states to markets (see also **Castells, Cox**). The same technological advances that have prompted the globalization of finance are being used by mafias across the world to expand their activities. As with TNCs, territorial borders no longer confine their enterprises.

Susan Strange passed away before being able to participate in discussions on alternative globalizations that emerged early in the twenty-first century. In her final writings, she emphasized two serious threats to humankind: the progressive destruction of the environment as TNCs expand their power with no countering global authority on the horizon (see also **Cox**); and the more immediate threat of a collapse of the financial system, causing credit to shrink and world economic growth to slow to zero (Strange 1998b: 2) (for the latter, see also **Helleiner**). Both of these worries appear prescient as environmental degradation continues apace and the financial crisis of 2008 has brought the world closer to the Armageddon she anticipated. As she noted: 'we do not have a system of global governance right now by any stretch of the imagination, but rather a ramshackle assembly of conflicting sources of authority' (Strange 1996: 199) (see also **Cerny, Scholte**).

Major globalization writings

Strange, S. (1989) 'Toward a theory of transnational empire', in E. O. Czempiel and J. N. Rosenau (eds) *Global Changes and Theoretical Challenges: Approaches to World Politics for the 1990s*, Lexington, MA: Lexington Books.
——(1994) *States and Markets*, 2nd edition, London: Pinter Publishers.
——(1995) 'The limits of politics', *Government and Opposition*, vol 30, no 3, pp. 291–311.
——(1996) *The Retreat of the State: The Diffusion of Power in the World Economy*, Cambridge, UK: Cambridge University Press.
——(1997) 'The erosion of the state', *Current History*, vol 96, no 610, pp. 365–369.
——(1998a) 'Globaloney?', *Review of International Political Economy*, vol 5, no 4, pp. 704–710.
——(1998b) *Mad Money: When Markets Outgrow Governments*, Ann Arbor, MI: University of Michigan Press.

See also: **Amin, Arrighi, Castells, Cerny, Cox, Helleiner, Hirst, Thompson and Bromley, Scholte**.

PETER J. TAYLOR (1944–)

Peter James Taylor is a UK geographer. Born in Tring in Hertfordshire, he was Professor of Political Geography at the University of Newcastle upon Tyne between

1970 and 1996. He was then appointed Professor of Geography at Loughborough University. He is the founder and director of the Globalization and World Cities Research Network (www.lboro.ac.uk/gawc) and is the author of over 300 publications, of which over 60 have been translated into other languages. He was elected a fellow of the British Academy in 2004 and designated Distinguished Scholarship Honors for 2003 by the Association of American Geographers. He was a founding editor of *Political Geography* in 1982 and of the *Review of International Political Economy* in 1992. In September 2010 he became Professor of Geography at Northumbria University.

Drawing on creative methodologies that he developed for analysing world city networks and on findings gathered from their extensive application to the study of such networks, Taylor demonstrates that profoundly new metageographies have been emerging in the world since the early 1970s. Driven by the information and communication technologies that began to appear at that time, varying globalizations, he argues, are taking place, with the most significant of these involving the networking of cities worldwide. These networks represent a significant departure from the nation-state-based geography of the world that had characterized the previous two centuries. In his view, it is possible that they represent the most profound structural change to date, resulting from globalization, on the one hand, while accelerating it, on the other.

Metageographies and networks

Taylor uses the term 'metageography' to describe the geographical structures through which people order their knowledge of the world (Taylor 2004: 180). These structures are sufficiently entrenched that they are taken for granted. Speaking of the onset of modernity in Europe, the beginning of the scientific revolution, and the gradual secularization of the state, he identifies several metageographies where the balance between the physical or material and the metaphysical changes. In modernity, it is the material and physical aspects that are in constant change, outweighing more and more the metaphysical aspects, leading to new metageographies that provide anchors to societies in the face of such instability.

Similar to **Amin**, **Arrighi**, **Braudel** and **Cox**, he argues that each metageography is associated with a hegemon (2004: 181–182). The first one is the United Provinces in Europe, which created a new mercantile modernity during the seventeenth century, with navigation being the key practical knowledge. The second hegemon, the UK, led the development of an industrial modernity in the late eighteenth and nineteenth centuries, drawing upon engineering as the key practical knowledge. Following the UK, the US was a third hegemon in leading the creation of consumer modernity, with media/advertising being the key practical knowledge. He describes this last modernity as having a 'mosaic metageography of nation-states', with national markets for the buying and selling of consumer goods. In this instance, over time, every person, through her or his nationality, is placed in a spatial framework where humanity is segmented into 'nationalities' based on the boundaries of states.

The transition from one metageography to another is a gradual process; as one disintegrates, a new one replaces it, providing new ways in which the world is viewed and interpreted. Taylor argues that the world currently is in a phase of such transition, with contemporary globalization being the engine of the change. He adds that what one would expect to find in such a period is a decline in the acceptance of states as the natural locus of power and with it a shift in the orientation of human activities to new power formations. He argues that changes in the material basis of cities and in the ways in which they link to one another are central components driving this fundamental change.

In framing these changes analytically, he borrows insights into globalization from two other globalization scholars: **Castells** and **Sassen**. From Castells, Taylor expands upon the concept of 'space of flows'. These spaces are ones where information, money and communications flow quickly in networks linking cities to one another in varying ways across the world. The network concept and its emphasis on facilitating these flows through space differs from the metaphor of a 'mosaic', which Taylor uses to characterize the control of territory and borders by states in consumer modernity. In Castells' terminology, the mosaic is consistent with his concept of 'spaces of places'.

From Sassen, Taylor borrows the idea that 'global cities' are distinguished by the presence of advanced producer services companies which provide advice and support to capitalist enterprises operating on regional and global scales. These firms play key roles in the networks (another concept borrowed from Castells) that link global cities. In assessing these networks, Taylor expands upon Castells' theorization to emphasize that the network structure linking cities consists of three, not the usual two, levels:

> In most network analysis, there are nodes [...] whose interactions generate a network [...] In such cases the nodes are the agents in the process of network formation: their inter-relations define the network. In an interlocking model the network-making agents are not the nodes but are to be found within the nodes, thus producing three levels of operation: sub-nodal, nodal and net.
>
> (Taylor *et al.* 2011: 3–4)

In Taylor's three-level model, advanced service producer firms constitute the sub-nodal. He adds that flows of information, knowledge, direction and advice from service firms to other corporations create the worldwide linkages between cities. In short, cities are the service centres (nodes) and the agents are the service firms in those cities (sub-nodes).

Accordingly, Taylor understands the current situation of globalization to be a transition period to a new metageography where the material base is shifting from nation-states to globally linked cities. Rather than the vertical top-down structures of states, the world is moving to a horizontal set of networks built upon cities. Taylor departs from **Sassen**, who reserves the term 'global cities' for a select few key nodes such as Tokyo, New York and London. Instead, he argues that under contemporary globalization, all cities are globalizing: 'The experience of cyberspace is not essentially hierarchical; it operates as innumerable networks, albeit across an uneven globalization. In this sense, then, all cities are global: they operate in a contemporary space of flows that enables them to have a global reach when circumstances require such connections' (Taylor 2004: 43). In moving away from an emphasis on a few nodes as 'global cities', Taylor focuses upon 'the network of relations of many more cities in the servicing of global capital' (Taylor *et al.* 2011: 3). He specifies the situation as one of a 'world city network' that takes the form of an 'interlocking network model'.

World city networks

Taylor identifies four key agencies that provide the infrastructure of world city networks. The first component includes business service firms that export services beyond the local city market. Trading in services usually requires directly attending to the needs of the buyer or client, which means that exporting a service normally requires expanding office networks to many places (Taylor 2004: 58). Second, cities are the sites where local economic and political networks are constituted and concentrated. Third, with a network, there develops 'a multiplicity of supervisory institutions that oversee the practice of individuals and firms within particular service sectors' (2004: 59). These actors furnish the regulatory frameworks and professional codes of conduct that govern the practices of the business service firms. The fourth key agency concerns nation-states themselves. What is important for the constitution of networks is the state apparatus, particularly those offices forming and implementing economic policy and the general national culture of carrying out business and business's place in the respective national society (2004: 59). Taylor describes this infrastructure as a 'political economy world': 'an economic space of flows, notably city networks, coexisting with a political space of places, notably the mosaic of states' (2004: 49).

Taylor's analysis goes beyond the work of other scholars of world cities by emphasizing the global extensity of these networks. While core-located cities such as London, New York and Tokyo are universally regarded as world cities, he stresses that 'Mexico City, São Paulo, Istanbul, Johannesburg, Bangkok, Mumbai, Singapore, Shanghai, Taipei, Seoul and Hong Kong also have world city status' (2004: 198). These former 'Third World' cities have become central nodes for the office location strategies of global business service firms as they seek to provide services on a global scale. In this respect, his empirical analysis reveals new locales of power as the networks form. These 'non-core cities' have become integral and central to the servicing of global capital (2004: 199).

Taylor is wary about seeing this structure as a new global hierarchy, adding that 'cities do not operate by command: inter-city relations are not primarily about cities directly controlling, or being controlled by, other cities' (2004: 52). What is most crucial for the cities in the networks is cooperation when it comes to their relations with one another. The mutuality in the system comes from the service firms and their global location strategies. Such a development thus departs from earlier thinking about 'Third World' cities as '*entrepôts*'. Taylor describes the outcome as a 'world city conundrum': there is a 'dispersion of economic power in a polarizing world of increasing concentration of power' (2004: 198).

Taylor's methodology permits him to analyse networks that involve both inter-state and supra-state activities. He notes that world cities are more than global service centres; many of them are capital cities and thus play key political roles. In addition, many are also cultural centres and sites where global social practices are emerging. In these respects, cities can be nodes for global governance and for global civil society, as well as for the global economy. He analyses three additional, more political, networks. First, the 'inter-state' network privileges capital cities. These are the political command-and-control centres, the headquarters of the network-making institutions and the foreign affairs government departments (Taylor 2005: 707). Second, a 'supra-state' global governance network is studied by focusing on the cities in which the vast family of institutions associated with the United Nations are located. In this network, leading nodes include some cities not prominent in the global services ones, notably Geneva and Washington, DC. Third, a 'trans-state' global civil society network is found by looking at the locations of offices of non-governmental actors whose range of activities is worldwide in scope.

In examining the results from this analysis, Taylor reaches four main conclusions (2005: 720–721). First, supra-state and trans-state networks are creating more structured political geographies than are found in looking at inter-state networks. Second, the political geographies of supra-state and inter-state processes are significantly different from one another, with capital cities being less important for the former. Third, surprisingly perhaps, supra-state processes especially, but also trans-state ones, are creating a more hierarchical political structure than is apparent in Westphalian inter-state ones. Finally, trans-state processes (NGO networks), but also supra-state ones, are creating political structures that clearly transcend the longstanding North–South divide. In Taylor's eyes, these conclusions point to 'the emergence of new "deep" political geographies, spatialities of power not subject to rapid change like the inter-state alliances that create new spatial dispositions of power in geopolitical transitions' (Taylor 2004: 721).

Major globalization writings

Taylor, P. J. (2004) *World City Network: A Global Urban Analysis*, London: Routledge.

——(2005) 'New political geographies: global civil society and global governance through world city networks', *Political Geography*, vol 24, no 4, pp. 703–730.

Taylor, P. J., Derudder, B., Hoyler, M. and Ni, P. (2011) 'New regional geographies of the world as practised by leading advanced producer service firms in 2010', *GaWC Research Bulletin*, vol 392, 21 December.

See also: **Amin**, **Arrighi**, **Braudel**, **Castells**, **Cox**, **Sassen**.

JOHN TOMLINSON

John Tomlinson is Professor of Cultural Sociology, head of research in communications, Cultural and Media Studies, and director of the Institute for Cultural Analysis, University of Nottingham Trent, UK. He has published on themes such as cultural globalization, cosmopolitanism, cultural modernity and mediated cultural experience. His books have been translated into 12 languages. He has lectured at many distinguished universities and research institutions across Europe, the US and East Asia, as well as at artistic institutions such as the Bauhaus Institute, Dessau. Tomlinson has also made presentations and acted as a consultant on issues of culture and globalization to several international public-sector organizations, including the United Nations Educational, Scientific and Cultural Organization (UNESCO), the Council of Europe and the Commonwealth Secretariat.

Complex connectivity, proximity

Tomlinson is concerned principally with the relationship between globalization and culture. He defines a series of concepts and elaborates upon them in ways that not only help us to understand this relationship but also deepen our knowledge of globalization itself. He describes globalization as an 'empirical condition' of the modern world that is best captured by the term 'complex connectivity': 'the rapidly developing and ever-densening network of interconnections and interdependences that characterize modern social life' (Tomlinson 1999: 2). These connections are economic, political, cultural, environmental, social, interpersonal and technological. To focus on only one of these dimensions, according to Tomlinson, would be to miss the complex and multidimensional character of globalizing processes. If we try to separate these into the usual categories and study them in the usual disciplinary ways, we will lose the complexity and, thus, the understanding needed of globalization.

Defined in this way, globalization makes more complex our notions of proximity – what we understand by 'closeness' (see **Rosenau**). He begins this discussion by speaking of 'functional proximity'. With the significant changes in technologies permitting physical movement, it is much easier for business people, for example, to fly to one place or another for important strategic meetings focused on building global markets; for young people to explore the Buddhist temples of South-East Asia, the beaches of Bali and the wild game reserves of Eastern Africa; and for tourists more generally to travel in short periods of time to visit more places in the world than at any other period in human history. Such proximity, however, is functional or manufactured in that it does not permit those individuals to fully experience the challenging reality of cultural difference.

Tomlinson argues that the more important changes coming from globalization are experienced locally. Globalization is transforming the nature of localities themselves (see also **Appadurai**, **Escobar**, **Tsing**). In fact, for Tomlinson, the paradigmatic experience of people in the contemporary era is that of staying in one place while living the displacement that globalization brings to them (cf. **Escobar**, **Santos**). In exploring these transformations, Tomlinson invokes **Robertson**'s concept of global unicity, the idea of the world being compressed into one place. Thus, a person living in Toronto, Canada, will have experienced over the past 25 years the increased presence of immigrants from over 100 countries in the world, vast changes in the kinds of restaurants available, the displacement of ice hockey by soccer as the most popular game of young people, and the politics of Sri Lanka or Jamaica or Mexico or Somalia or India and Pakistan in the city's streets.

Within localities, closeness or proximity takes on various forms. In addition to physical proximity for face-to-face interactions, Tomlinson stresses 'mediated proximity': closeness that is achieved through the mediation of contemporary technologies. These technologies may involve dialogical or person-to-person closeness through telephone, email, webcams and internet telephony. Or they may be monological in the sense of bringing celebrities, physical disasters such as hurricanes or mining explosions, sporting events, food and other cultural imports, or unusual living creatures to televisions or computers or local markets. In doing so, individuals in localities may feel just as 'close' to those celebrities or the victims of those disasters or the social lives of chimpanzees or relatives back in the 'home' country as they do to the people with whom they share the same locality.

De-territorialization

This discussion of complex connectivity and proximity leads to perhaps Tomlinson's most important concept for the study of globalization and culture: de-territorialization. He draws upon **Giddens'** concept of dis-embedding for framing this definition. Giddens' concept refers to the 'lifting out' of social relations from local places and restructuring them across indefinite spans of time and space. Building on this idea, Tomlinson sees de-territorialization as the weakening or the dissolution of the connection between everyday lived culture and territorial location (see also **Scholte**). He emphasizes that this experience is not simply one of estrangement from, or loss of, an everyday lived culture in a particular locality. It is more complex and ambiguous than that. For example, for an elderly woman who has lived her whole adult life in Toronto, a trip on the subway 'downtown' today would reveal what is familiar – other women who look and dress like her – and what is different – newspapers in many different languages not found in her younger days scattered on the floor. Her cultural horizons would be expanded as well, while also feeling vulnerable in not knowing how to relate to or understand the different lifestyles around her. She would have unparalleled access to the world 'out there' when compared to her youth, all the while finding that her private world has also drastically changed.

Borrowing from the work of Garcia Canclini, Tomlinson proffers the concept of hybridization to describe the substantive aspects of the process of de-territorialization. Hybridity captures well the general phenomenon of cultural mixing that emerges with the intensification of globalization. He adds that the notion of hybrid cultures may be particularly useful for understanding contemporary youth culture in wealthier countries. Tomlinson stresses that de-territorialization occurs not only for the elites in these countries, but also for the middle and lower classes. He suggests that the phenomenon may be less prevalent in poorer countries, but is present nonetheless.

He concludes this discussion by recognizing the process of re-territorialization as a countervailing force. People may respond to the vulnerabilities associated with the condition of de-territorialization by trying to re-establish cultural stability or a cultural home. These steps might involve diaspora communities in large cities conceiving imaginative projects that make the spaces in which they live more like 'home'; or citizens' groups running festivals for local films when larger 'international' film festivals come to their locality. Tomlinson adds that re-territorialization in some aspects will come from the fact that we remain embodied and physically located in a given place (see also **Brenner**).

Modernity, cosmopolitanism

In reflecting upon the implications of this definition of globalization, Tomlinson joins **Giddens** and **Beck** in linking the phenomenon to the extension of modernity across the world. His definition of globalization departs from that of Giddens; but he argues at the same time that Giddens' concepts of time, space, place, distance and proximity are key tools for understanding complex connectivity when linked to processes of disembedding and time–space distanciation. Tomlinson thus shares with Giddens and Beck the position that globalization does not have deep roots in the pre-modern world (see also **Scholte**); the break from pre-modernity to modernity sets the stage for globalization and, thus, de-territorialization and the overcoming of cultural distance through information and communication technologies.

Tomlinson's position that globalization's most important effect is the transformation of localities leads him to consider favourably **Robertson**'s concept of glocalization: the idea that the local and the global are mutually penetrating (see also **Chow, Escobar**). In this view, then, what happens locally can have implications for the world as a whole, what Robertson refers to as the universalization of the particular. This implication, in turn, leads Tomlinson to pose the question: what does it mean to have a global identity, to think of oneself as a 'citizen of the world'? In reply, he suggests that a cosmopolitan orientation becomes a critical resource, a position that he shares with **Beck**. Such an orientation includes an active sense of belonging to the wider world, the possession of a 'distanciated identity': embracing a sense of what unites everyone as human beings (see also **Falk, Held**). The cosmopolitan is also someone who understands the world to be one of many 'cultural others', who is open to cultural difference, and who sees a plurality of cultures to be legitimate, if not highly welcome. Coining a phrase from **Robertson**, he sees the cosmopolitan as practising 'ethical glocalism'. In this respect, the cultural condition of de-territorialization can develop in tandem with this cosmopolitan ethic, favouring the emergence of mutuality, if not solidarity, between individuals physically distant and culturally distinct from one another.

Major globalization writings

Tomlinson, J. (1991) *Cultural Imperialism: A Critical Introduction*, Baltimore, MD: Johns Hopkins University Press.

——(1999) *Globalization and Culture*, Chicago, IL: University of Chicago Press.

——(2007) *The Culture of Speed: The Coming of Immediacy*, London: Sage.

Further reading

Canclini, N. G. (2005) *Hybrid Cultures: Strategies for Entering and Leaving Modernity*, Minneapolis, MN: University of Minnesota Press.

See also: **Appadurai, Beck, Brenner, Chow, Escobar, Falk, Giddens, Robertson, Rosenau, Santos, Scholte, Tsing**.

ANNA LOWENHAUPT TSING

Anna Lowenhaupt Tsing is a professor of anthropology at the University of California, Santa Cruz. She is a specialist in the fields of feminist anthropology, South-East Asia, ethnography and social theory. She received her BA from Yale University, CT, in 1973 and her MA and Ph.D. from Stanford University, CA, in 1976 and 1984, respectively. On completing her doctoral degree she served as a visiting assistant professor at the University of Colorado, Boulder (1984–1986) and as an assistant professor at the University of Massachusetts, Amherst (1986–1989), before joining the faculty at the University of California, Santa Cruz. She has also been a visiting professor at the University of Chicago, IL, Harvard University, MA, and Aarhus University in Denmark. During 1994 to 1995, she was a member of the Institute for Advanced Study at Princeton, NJ. Her work focuses on politics and culture in Indonesia, rainforest ecology, globalization and gender.

Tsing's contributions to understanding globalization arise out of her research in the Meratus Mountains and rainforests of Indonesia, her interests in environmentalism and her thinking about indigeneity (see also **Chakrabarty, Dirlik, Mignolo**). She argues that we gain a deeper understanding of globalization by studying how global connections are made. She suggests that universals such as 'nature', 'development' and 'capitalism' are often the focus of these connections. But these connections do not take place easily; they involve *friction*. In laying out a set of methodological constructs for studying globalization, she challenges the type of thinking that focuses on large global processes flowing and sweeping across the world. In fact, global connections are difficult to make, have immense consequences for all concerned, and are not fixed and stable for all time.

Global connections, friction, engagement

Tsing's early writings on globalization challenge the thinking of many scholars in the 1990s who emphasized the power of flows that swept capitalism, Western cultural forms and science across the world, bringing homogenization and rapid change in their wake (for example, **Castells, Giddens**). The danger of this thinking, Tsing argues, is that it 'takes us inside its rhetoric until we take its claims for true descriptions' (Tsing 2000a: 330). 'We lose sight', she adds, 'of who is defining the landscape, of the coalitions of claimants, and of the material and institutional components through which powerful and central sites are constructed, from which convincing claims about units and scales can be made' (2000a: 330). She underlines that this rhetoric is often futurist in assuming newness of social relationships, which then distorts our understandings of the past. She also finds that alliances, collaborations and complicities in different places are conflated and linked to the development of a single world system.

The consequences of this thinking lead to a blurring of differences among places and perspectives, blinding us to the diversity of struggles in different parts of the world. In this regard, she questions models of globalization that emphasize circulation – that is, the movement of people, things, ideas and institutions, such as the healthy flow of blood in the body. She counters that channel-making involves contestation and place-making and, thus, that there are always obstacles to flows and free movements (2000a: 333). Hence, we need to stop making distinctions between 'global' forces and 'local' places (see also **Appadurai, Dirlik, Escobar**). Such distinctions draw us into 'globalist fantasies' that obscure the fact that cultural processes of 'place'-making and 'force'-making are both local and global simultaneously (2000a: 352).

To avoid these kinds of problems, Tsing focuses on the study of how global connections are made. By looking at such interactions in shared spaces, the unexpected and unstable aspects of global connections are revealed. Thus, she writes, 'Cultures are continually co-produced in the interactions I call "friction": the awkward, unequal, unstable, and creative qualities of interconnection across difference' (Tsing 2005: 3). By invoking this concept, she challenges globalization definitions that see flows of goods, ideas, capital and people as being pervasive and unimpeded (2005: 5): 'Friction refuses the lie that global power operates as a well-oiled machine. Furthermore, difference sometimes inspires insurrection. Friction can be the fly in the elephant's nose' (2005: 6).

At the heart of these connections are universals. In Tsing's area of research, for example, one such universal is 'science'. This universal is invoked by environmentalists, conservationists, corporations, governments and local actors. Friction emerges in the engagement over such universals in the building of global connections:

> To turn to universals is to identify knowledge that moves – mobile and mobilizing – across localities and cultures. Whether it is seen as underlying or transcending cultural difference, the mission of the universal is to form bridges, roads, and channels of circulation.
>
> (Tsing 2005: 7)

Thus, to study engagement in global connections is to see how a universal such as 'science' is used. It can be used by conservation NGOs seeking to preserve rainforests as pristine sites of nature, by environmentalists to challenge forestry companies eyeing these forests, and by local residents seeking to maintain a way of life and culture. Tsing notes that universals travel because they 'beckon to elite and excluded alike' (2005: 9). And in the process, such engagements involve friction.

Methodological suggestions

We illustrate how Tsing proceeds in the study of global connections by looking at several of her methodological constructs: scale-making, collaborations and generalizations, and translations.

Scale-making. Globalization literature is replete with mentions of scales: global scale, supra-regional scale, regional scale, national scale and local scale are those most commonly mentioned. These different scales are important in constructing viewpoints from which to observe global connections. What Tsing stresses, however, is that scales must be made. 'Scale must be brought into being: proposed, practiced, and evaded. A "globalism" is a commitment to the global and there are multiple, overlapping and somewhat contradictory "globalisms"; a "localism" is a commitment to the locality and so on' (Tsing 2005: 58). She suggests that scales such as the global or the local are created or 'conjured' often in relation to one another.

Her analysis of the Bre-X mining fraud in Indonesia illustrates these points well. For mining development to take place in remote mountainous regions of the country, the terrain had to be re-imagined through the conjuring of three different scales: regional, national and global. The global scale was constructed through building relations between finance capital in other parts of the world (Canada, in particular), the Indonesian government and foreign transnational mining companies. At the same time, nation-making as a project in Indonesia had to include the idea of supporting foreign investment to exploit 'natural resources'. The Indonesian government had to add such investments to its own 'nation-making' agenda, creating a 'national' scale. In doing so, however, the government needed to view its mountainous areas differently. Rather than seeing them as a wilderness sparsely populated by small groups of people, they were constructed as 'regions' for resource development. In creating this regional scale, it recast these territories as being empty of inhabitants and ripe for development. In other words, the Indonesian government had to create a 'frontier' where the rights of rural residents 'would be wiped out entirely to create a Wild West scene of rapid and lawless resource extraction' (2005: 59).

Collaborations and generalizations. We can illustrate this aspect of Tsing's analysis by our own example of the United Nations Convention Concerning the Protection of the World Cultural and Natural Heritage. Part of this convention refers to a universal: 'nature' or 'natural'. One way in which the convention casts this universal is *'geological and physiographical formations and precisely delineated areas* which constitute the habitat of threatened species of animals and plants of outstanding universal value from the point of view of science or conservation' (emphasis added). If a particular place in the rainforests of Indonesia with such formations were to be designated by the World Heritage Committee as a World Heritage Site, considerable collaborations would be needed. One can imagine that scientists, local residents, conservation NGOs, environmental NGOs, national government representatives, corporations and UN staff, among others, would be involved. Each group would view the area differently. For local residents and politicians, the very idea of something called 'nature' being separate from living beings, including humans, may be difficult to comprehend. Conservationists might see such a site as one requiring no human occupancy and, thus, the displacement of some people. Environmentalists might have different interests not involving such displacements. Transnational corporations in the mining or forestry sectors might speak of conserving nature by replanting trees or cleaning up mines after resources are extracted.

Tsing refers to 'generalization' as a process where 'small details support great visions and the universal is discovered in particularities' (2005: 89). To get to the point of seeing a given area in the rainforests as 'natural heritage', collaboration between such disparate groups is necessary if they are ever to agree upon what they observe. They have to reach an understanding of what being 'natural' means and, thus, a view of this particular place as fitting this understanding. They must agree upon how they know that something is natural and what particularities they need to overlook in reaching such an agreement. Collaborations often fail: 'Negotiators must agree upon common objects. As long as they refuse all compatibility, generalization is impossible' (2005: 106). Tsing adds: 'Making the globe our frame of reference is hard work [...] Global Nature can inspire moral views and actions. In nature appreciation and the parks model, localities are charged with global insight; they are microcosms of universal knowledge' (2005: 111–112).

Translations. In her subsequent research, Tsing has collaborated with other scholars in looking at 'words in motion' (Tsing 2009a, 2009b). By looking at words and their movement, Tsing is able to show how 'words' and 'worlds' are made in power-laden encounters at varying scales. As scholars follow the movement of words across the world, new meanings are invented. She introduces Lydia Liu's (1995) concept of 'translingual practice' as informing her thinking: 'the process by which new words, meanings, discourses, and modes of representation arise, circulate, and acquire legitimacy within the host language due to, or in spite of, the latter's contact/collision with the guest language' (Liu 1995: 26). In these processes, some words become universal, again in processes of forging global connections where the words are engaged, giving rise to friction.

Tsing expands on this thinking in light of her research related to indigenous peoples. The words 'indigenous' and 'indigeneity' have emerged as universal terms, particularly through engaged global connections made by different peoples at the United Nations, culminating in a Declaration of the Rights of Indigenous Peoples in 2007. She examines how and why the word '*adat*' in Indonesian has come to be equivalent to the English word 'indigenous.' Both words have 'moved' some distance from their original meanings. '*Adat*' comes from the Arabic *ada*, meaning that which cannot be codified into universal law. 'Indigenous' derives from the Spanish '*Indigenas*', meaning those who stand outside civilization. The histories of *adat* and indigenous rights cross in the contact zone of global mobilization of peoples sharing similar local concerns. Again, through collaborations between the *adat* peoples and others interested in indigenous rights, the generalization to the universal 'indigenous' takes place. Both words no longer have the same meaning: 'Through these connections words may shift and turn back against the purposes of the original users. Coalitions form, offering unexpected opportunities' (Tsing 2009a: 60).

Major globalization writings

Tsing, A. L. (1993) *In the Realm of the Diamond Queen: Marginality in an Out-of-the-Way Place*, Princeton, NJ: Princeton University Press.

——(2000a) 'The global situation', *Cultural Anthropology*, vol 15, no 3, pp. 327–360.

——(2000b) 'Inside the economy of appearances', *Public Culture*, vol 12, no 1, pp. 115–144.

——(2005) *Friction: An Ethnography of Global Connection*, Princeton, NJ: Princeton University Press.

——(2009a) '*Adat*/indigenous: indigeneity in motion', in C. Gluck and A. L. Tsing (eds) *Words in Motion: Toward a Global Lexicon*, Durham, NC: Duke University Press.

——(2009b) 'Worlds in motion', in C. Gluck and A. L. Tsing (eds) *Words in Motion: Toward a Global Lexicon*, Durham, NC: Duke University Press.

Tsing, A. L. and Greenough, P. R. (eds) (2003) *Nature in the Global South: Environmental Projects in South and Southeast Asia*, Durham, NC: Duke University Press.

Further reading

Liu, L. (1995) *Translingual Practice: Literature, National Culture, and Translated Modernity – China, 1900–1937*, Stanford, CA: Stanford University Press.

United Nations Convention concerning the Protection of the World Cultural and Natural Heritage. Available at: http://whc.unesco.org/en/conventiontext.

See also: **Appadurai, Castells, Chakrabarty, Dirlik, Escobar, Giddens, Mignolo**.

LINDA WEISS (1952–)

Linda Weiss received her Ph.D. from the London School of Economics (LSE) and is a fellow of the Academy of the Social Sciences in Australia. She has held concurrent positions as Professor in Government and International Relations at the University of Sydney, and Honorary Professor of Political Science at Aarhus University. She has lectured widely in North America, Europe and East Asia and has held visiting research appointments at the University of California, Los Angeles (UCLA), Cornell, NY, the LSE, the European University Institute, University of Rome, Seoul National University and the Academia Sinica. In her research, she has focused on the comparative and international politics of economic development, with a focus on state capacity, public–private sector relations and globalization. Weiss has contributed to the study of globalization by questioning assumptions made about the role of the state in globalization.

Defining globalization

Weiss' first foray into globalization studies came in her widely read book *The Myth of the Powerless State*, published in 1998. She sought to contest the views of hyper-globalists such as Kenichi Ohmae (1990, 1995). These scholars postulated that a new global economy dominated by transnational 'stateless' corporations where capital, finance and technology flowed easily across borders was rapidly eroding the powers of nation-states. She quotes Ohmae as saying that states have become 'unnatural – even dysfunctional – as actors in a global economy [... They] are no longer meaningful units in which to think about economic activity' (Weiss 1998: 1). Her first response to this argument was to question whether globalization was a useful analytical concept at all, siding with **Hirst**, **Thompson and Bromley**, who argue that the world is not globalizing but returning to the high levels of internationalization that had occurred between 1870 and 1914.

As she deepened her research, she moved away from this position, ultimately agreeing that globalizing processes were distinct from internationalizing ones. She refers to globalization as a 'trend towards the increasing interconnectedness of social relations across the globe. As a worldwide process it embraces both the structural economic linkages associated with rising levels of trade, finance and investment, the political and cultural influences of transnational actors and international institutions, and the impact of their ideas on domestic policy' (Weiss 2008a: 1). In framing her definition this way, she is careful not to say that globalization places 'constraints' on states. She contrasts her thinking with 'moderate globalists' such as **Cerny**, **Held**, **Rosenau** and **Scholte**. These thinkers assume, in her view, that the growing interconnectedness is increasing the power of global economic and political networks at the expense of national networks (Weiss 2003a, 2003b). In this respect, she sees such theories as emphasizing too strongly 'constraints' being placed upon states, thereby ignoring how states can exploit globalizing processes (see also **Brenner**). Drawing on Michael Mann's work, she argues that the growth of national and supranational networks cannot be reduced to a zero-sum game as they can complement and reinforce one another. Globalization and state growth 'have gone hand in hand because economic interdependence [...] increases, not decreases, the social utility of the state' (Weiss 2006: 170). (**Cerny** makes a similar argument in some respects, but sees changes in states to be more profound.)

Globalization and the state

In constructing her argument that globalization can 'enable' states' roles in policy-making, Weiss questions a common assumption made by some globalization scholars such as **Held** and **Rosenau**, who argue that the system of authority becomes bifurcated under globalization: states come to share governance responsibilities with a multiplicity of public and private institutions at local, regional, national, transnational and global levels (Weiss 2003a: 9). **Scholte** captures this argument in his reference to 'polycentric' governance. With authority now being 'divided' between the state and a host of other actors, states' capacities for governance are in decline, relatively speaking.

Drawing on her own empirical research, Weiss responds by suggesting that the state cannot be seen as a single coherent unit. Rather, it should be disaggregated into different policy areas and varying institutions central to these areas (a position similar to that taken by **Ong** and **Sassen**). Once disaggregated, it becomes more evident that some sectors, such as finance, conform well to the 'divided authority' model, while others do not. In fact, if anything, some sectors seem to have enhanced powers, or to use Weiss' term, they are 'enabled' by globalization.

Based on these observations, Weiss proposes that 'globalization and state growth have gone hand-in-hand precisely because economic interdependence – or the exposure of social relations to international pressures – increases, not decreases, the authority of the state' (Weiss 2006: 170). Such an increase in authority arises from two sources: the insecurity felt by citizens in the face of global competition, and the desire by states to take advantage of increased global competition. With respect to the first of these sources, Weiss observes that citizens will demand increased social protection as they become more exposed to globalizing processes. Weiss pursues this idea by examining two policy areas: taxation and social welfare. She shows that despite the rhetoric of neoliberalism, there is no evidence of states shrinking because they take in less money through the tax system (contrary to arguments advanced by scholars such as **Cerny, Harvey, Scholte** and **Rodrik**). In fact, between the 1990s and the first part of the 2000s, state levels of taxation increased in all countries examined.

Weiss also carefully assessed social welfare spending and policies in a number of countries. She found that spending on social welfare programmes had not withered as globalizing processes intensified. She also noted that even though states were exposed to similar globalizing pressures, they diverged with respect to reforms of social welfare programmes. And perhaps most surprisingly, those states most integrated within the global economy and most intensely subjected to globalizing pressures had maintained higher levels of social welfare support than those less exposed to globalization.

Contrary to claims that the role of the state in supporting domestic economic development is declining, Weiss argues that the political logic of increased global competition draws states into intervening to support domestic businesses. She notes that they target and support new growth sectors in the economy, subsidize technological innovation, upgrade infrastructure, increase their financing of education and training, and put in place active labour market policies (2006: 178) (see also **Cerny**).

In examining numerous examples of globalization's enabling of state actions, Weiss also discovers that not all states are equally successful in these endeavours. She puts forward the concept of transformative capacity for analysing why some states are more enabled than others by globalizing processes. She observes that states are not unitary and monolithic structures, but 'organizational complexes whose various "parts" represent different ages, functions and (at times) orientations' (Weiss 1998: 15–16). Strategies for adjusting to and taking advantage of globalization are formulated not by the state alone, but through policy linkages between politicians, state bureaucracies and organized business. She characterizes these partnerships between the state and business as 'governed interdependence'. She hypothesizes that the more globalized the market and the greater the systemic risk or perceived risk to national economic security, the greater the incentives for governed interdependence.

In examining this hypothesis empirically, she finds that the more effective states are in generating governed interdependence with relevant sectors of their domestic economies, the more enabled they become from globalization. She writes:

> Even the so-called liberal states at the technological frontier are deeply, if not widely engaged in governing the market for high technology, targeting knowledge-intensive sectors for special promotion as the global technology race intensifies. Climbing the ladder of technology development is a continuous enterprise and where the stakes are high, states rarely leave things to the market.
> (Weiss 2008b: 203–204)

In summary, Weiss outlines a more complex understanding of the role of the state in a globalizing world. She argues against those who see states' roles to be on a sharp decline or to be significantly constrained. She counters by showing that globalization also stimulates the expansion of governing capacities through both the transformation of public–private sector relations and of 'governed interdependence', and through the growth of new policy networks. As the title of her 1998 book suggests, globalization does not leave states powerless; in fact, it enables many states to strengthen their economies, all the while providing social protection to their citizens.

Major globalization writings

Weiss, L. (1998) *The Myth of the Powerless State: Governing the Economy in a Global Era*, Cambridge, UK: Polity Press.

——(2003a) 'Introduction: bringing domestic institutions back in', in L. Weiss (ed.) *States in the Global Economy: Bringing Domestic Institutions Back In*, Cambridge, UK: Cambridge University Press.

——(2003b) 'Is the state being "transformed" by globalization?', in L. Weiss (ed.) *States in the Global Economy: Bringing Domestic Institutions Back In*, Cambridge, UK: Cambridge University Press.

——(2005) 'The state-augmenting effects of globalization', *New Political Economy*, vol 10, no 3, pp. 345–353.

——(2006) 'Infrastructural power, economic transformation and globalization', in J. A. Hall and R. Schroeder (eds) *An Anatomy of Power: The Social Theory of Michael Mann*, Cambridge, UK: Cambridge University Press.

——(2008a) 'Globalisation', in B. Galligan and W. Roberts (eds) *The Oxford Companion to Australian Politics*, Oxford: Oxford University Press; available online at: www.oxfordreference.com/views/ENTRY.html?subview=Main& entry=t250.e149 (accessed 11 April 2011).

——(2008b) 'The state in the economy: neoliberal or neoactivist?', in G. Morgan, J. L. Campbell, C. Crouch, O. K. Pedersen and R. Whitley (eds) *The Oxford Handbook of Comparative Institutional Analysis*, Oxford, UK: Oxford University Press.

Further reading

Ohmae, K. (1990) *The Borderless World*, New York, NY: Collins.

——(1995) 'Putting global logic first', *Harvard Business Review*, vol 73, no 1, pp. 19–25.

See also: **Brenner, Cerny, Harvey, Held, Hirst, Thompson and Bromley, Ong, Rodrik, Rosenau, Sassen, Scholte.**

INDEX

http://www.routledge.com/books/series/RKG/

Globalization in *The Key Guides*

Globalization: The Key Concepts

Annabelle Mooney, Roehampton University and **Betsy Evans,** Cardiff University

Viewed as a destructive force or an inevitability of modern society, globalization is the focus of a multitude of disciplines. A clear understanding of its processes and terminology is imperative for anyone engaging with this ubiquitous topic. *Globalization: the Key Concepts* offers a comprehensive guide to this cross-disciplinary subject and covers concepts such as:

- homogenization
- neo-Liberalism
- risk
- knowledge society
- time-space compression
- reflexivity.

With extensive cross-referencing and suggestions for further reading, this book is an essential resource for students and interested readers alike as they navigate the literature on globalization studies.

February 2007 – 304 pages
Pb: 978-0-415-36860-5 | Hb: 978-0-415-36859-9

For more information and to order a copy visit
http://www.routledge.com/books/details/9780415368605/

Available from all good bookshops

International Relations in *The Basics*

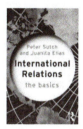

International Relations: The Basics

Peter Sutch, Cardiff University
and **Juanita Elias** University of
Adelaide

International Relations is a concise and accessible introduction for
students new to international relations and for the general reader.
It offers the most up-to-date guide to the major issues and areas of
debate and:

- explains key issues including humanitarian intervention
  and economic justice
- features illustrative and familiar case studies from around
  the world
- examines topical debates on globalization and terrorism
- provides an overview of the discipline to situate the new
  reader at the heart of the study of global politics

Covering all the basics and more, this is the ideal book for anyone
who wants to understand contemporary international relations.

May 2007 – 214 pages
Pb: 978-0-415-31185-4 | Hb: 978-0-415-31184-7

For more information and to order a copy visit
http://www.routledge.com/books/details/9780415311854/

Available from all good bookshops

http://www.routledge.com/books/series/RKG/

International Relations in *The Key Guides*

International Relations: The Key Concepts 2nd Edition

Martin Griffiths, Griffith University, **Terry O'Callaghan,** University of South Australia and **Steven C. Roach,** University of South Florida

Featuring over twenty new entries, *International Relations: The Key Concepts*, now in its second edition, is the essential guide for anyone interested in international affairs. Comprehensive and up-to-date, it introduces the most important themes in international relations in the post 9/11 era.

Key areas cover international criminal law, human rights, the developing world (the Arab League, African Union), globalization and strategic studies. New entries include:

- the English School
- the Digital Divide
- the War on Terror
- the Bush Doctrine
- the International Criminal Court
- legitimacy
- global warming
- unilateralism
- the Organization of Petroleum-Exporting Countries (OPEC).

Featuring suggestions for further reading as well as a unique guide to web sites on international relations, this accessible guide is an invaluable aid to an understanding of this expanding field and is ideal for the student and non-specialist alike.

October 2007 – 424 pages
Pb: 978-0-415-77437-6 | Hb: 978-0-415-77436-9

For more information and to order a copy visit
http://www.routledge.com/books/details/9780415774376/

Available from all good bookshops

CPSIA information can be obtained
at www.ICGtesting.com
Printed in the USA
LVHW010212040519
616663LV00018B/108/P